PILGRIMS
OF THE
STARS

PILGRIMS
OF THE
STARS

Autobiography of two yogis

Garuda Flies through the Night Sky with Lakshmi and Vishnu: Rajput miniature
c. 1760 from the collection of Edwin Binney, 3rd

Dilip Kumar Roy and Indira Devi

Timeless Books

ISBN 0-931454-10-7
Library of Congress Cataloging in Publication Data
    Roy, Dilip Kumar, 1897-
       Pilgrims of the stars.
       Includes bibliographical references and index.
       1. Hindus—India—Biography. 2. Roy, Dilip
       Kumar, 1897- . 3. Indira Devi, 1920- . 4. Sri
       Aurobindo Ashram. I. Indira Devi, 1920- . II. Title.
       BL1273.89.R69 1985 294.5'56 [B] 84-16377
       ISBN 0-931454-10-7 (pbk.)
First edition published by Macmillan Publishing Co., Inc. 1973
Published in paperback by Dell Publishing Co., Inc. 1974
This new edition published by Timeless Books, 1985
First Printing 1985

Published by

Timeless Books

Box 160
Porthill, ID 83853
Printed and Bound in U.S.A.

DEDICATION

To

MIRA, KRISHNA'S MESSENGER,
When in the dark and pathless ocean, at night,
I cried: "The helmsman is nowhere to be seen!
Who'll lead my bark in the storm to His Harbor of
    Light?"
Answered His Flute: "Take heart: His song-serene
Maid Mira, His Minstrel, through Her music of Grace
Will steer your boat to His Haven of Blessedness."

Hari Krishna Mandir
Poona, India
April 17, 1972

                    In deep gratefulness,
                    Dilip and Indira

CONTENTS

PART THREE—by Dilip Kumar Roy

FOREWORD

to

PILGRIMS OF THE STARS

by

D. K. Roy and Indira Devi

Whoever picks up this book is bound for a big surprise. For Dilip does not write his autobiography, he sings it. And that is as it should be. An artist who lives his life as a symphony ought to sing every bit of it as an enchanting melody.

Actually, this is the autobiography of a remarkable couple of artists: Dilip, the musician and philosopher, and Indira, the dancer and visionary poetess. What a combination! One would have to search a long way to find again such an account of a combined life of inspiration.

Dilip is a man of the highest aristocracy who attracts practically all the leading philosophers and statesmen of India as his friends and companions and manages to get in touch with leading spirits of Europe. Few are left out. That alone would make this book valuable as a source of personal information about so many great men. But beyond these exciting contacts there is always the voice of Dilip to be heard in its immense capacity of reverberation.

Naturally in a time like ours, when the so-called mysterious East is investigated and admired by millions of young people eagerly searching for an answer to their never ending quest, the appeal of such a highly personalized account of spiritual adventure by a leading Indian would be great.

But beyond that, it is the altogether human feeling, far beyond any racial or geographical specialty, that sounds through all these chapters. Here a man and a woman are talking to us beyond the difference of centuries or continents. Whoever has read Dr. C. G. Jung's autobiography will agree that today no one ought to write such a book without having been stimulated by this unusual approach into the depths of the soul. And nobody will be bored by meaningless accounts of outer events, to which very few pages in Dilip's book are devoted. As Sri Aurobindo wrote in one of his personal letters to Dilip (talking about the life of Krishna):

What matters is the spiritual Reality, the Power, the influence that came with him or that he brought down by his action and his existence. First of all, what matters in a spiritual man's life is not what he did or what he was outside to the view of the men of his time (that is what historicity or biography comes to, does it not?) but what he was and did within: it is only that that gives any value to his outer life at all.

Aurobindo is Dilip's guru. I hope he will not consider it too presumptious when accordingly I call myself his gurubhai; *i.e.,* the follower of the same teacher, inwardly and deeply connected by a mysterious bond. Presumption it certainly is, for while Dilip had constant contact with that greatest of Indian minds through several decades, I had but the privilege of facing him eye to eye for five seconds. But quantity vanishes into nothing when quality is so overwhelming. When in 1949 I was in eager search of the message of India, I contacted and even lived with most of the Masters and Yogis in their ashrams. Naturally I was aware of Dilip and his enormous reputation as an artist and made an effort in Calcutta to meet him. He was singing upstairs in a private mansion in a huge old park and my taxi driver had, as often, the hardest time finding that place. When I arrived, the performance was in full swing and I, being too shy to open the door to the room, sat down in the hallway just to be enchanted for a long time by the sounds of Dilip's voice, muffled by thick wooden doors. He never knew I was there.

A month later Dilip, Indira and I met person to person, or rather soul to soul, in Pondicherry. It was the great day of Sri Aurobindo's Darshan, when the great man, living mostly in complete solitude, came out of hiding to thus "become visible" to his many devotees. More than two thousand of them had come to the ashram in Pondicherry. I was appalled at seeing that huge crowd, the way a traveler feels when he reaches his destination only to find that it is overcrowded by swarms of tourists. But I was a spiritual sightseer, eager to have a good long look at what I was after. I indicated this desire to the secretary of the ashram, pointing out that I had come to this place from farther away than anyone else and that I most certainly would take my time. "Oh," he replied, "but you must not do that; how long would Sri Aurobindo have to sit there if everybody would linger longer than five seconds? That will be your appointed time. And, incidentally," he added; "when your doctor in America sends you a bill for ten dollars for X-Ray treatment received, do you then reply to him saying that the treatment lasted only five seconds and you would not pay his bill unless he would give you a much longer one? No, you will not," he said, "for more of this treatment will burn you severely." So I was squatting there in the garden with thousands of others waiting patiently, till the voluntary "policemen" of the ashram directed my group closer and even closer to the entrance of the building, where Sri Aurobindo was sitting upstairs.

Then it was that the thought came to me; here I sit waiting to look at a very old man for a few seconds—this may easily turn out to be the greatest disappointment of my life. Sure, I have read a shelfful of the philosophical books of this genius, but looking at him, what will it amount to?

Finally the great moment came. Events like that can be described only by circumscribing the circumstances under which they occur. The event itself is, as it were, the blind spot around which everything happens and arranges itself, but which remains the invisible focus of all. Thus, I will only tell that, walking downstairs, the thought came to me: gee, that was much more than I had expected! For it dawned upon me that instead of only looking at him, as I had expected, he had looked at me! Oh!

As I left the ashram gate a young devotee sold to me a photograph of Sri Aurobindo and said the unforgettable words: "Sir, you will please remember that this photograph shows you only the body of Sri Aurobindo." Well, that would be true of any photograph, but, I had to admit, it was particularly true of this one.

If the experience of the Darshan could be summed up in a few words, I would have to say it was an amazing and everlasting shock to behold to what extreme height of perfection the human face can be developed. Sri Aurobindo certainly became my guru during these five seconds, though I do not follow the monotheistic rule of India, which allows only one guru to you and one only. I have had other gurus like Rudolf Otto, Paul Tillich, Martin Heidegger, C. G. Jung, and their part is not to be belittled.

These and other things were discussed at breakfast two days later with Dilip and Indira, and again when he was singing at the ashram in his magnificant gown and cap—a most handsome fellow indeed! Dear Dilip, I have gone astray with my tale. It remains for me to wonder, when five seconds could mean so much to your gurubhai, how huge must have been the transforming power of that Spirit to a man who, like you, was privileged to be in such close contact for almost a lifetime! Are you still just yourself or have you become a reflection of something towering over all human possibilities?

Singing and dancing are in many parts of India considered to be the highest forms of Yoga. The Bhagavadgita says that Yoga is skill in action. We know that to be accomplished in one field means often to be able to attain mastery in other fields, too. Thus Dilip and Indira, singing and dancing their way through life, have also been able to project themselves into our hearts by writing a fascinating autobiography. Not they, but we, the readers, ought to be congratulated.

—Frederic Spiegelberg

Stanford University
California

"Sri Aurobindo, my guru and the one fixed point in my otherwise kaleidoscopic life."

INTRODUCTION

by Dilip Kumar Roy

IT WAS under the illumined aegis of my guru Sri Aurobindo that I first blossomed into a writer of novels, plays, poems and biographies, impelled through it all by my inveterate urge to limn the human greatness that seemed to accost me at every turn. I have never considered this inclination of mine to be mere hero worship, especially as Krishna Himself declares in the Gita:

> *yad-yad vibhutimat sattvam shrimad-urjitam eva vā*
> *tat-tat evāgaccha tvam mama tejomsha-sambhavam*
> (10:41)

which means:

> Wherever thou findest a flowering of grace,
> Glory or opulence that thrills the eye,
> Know: they all stem from a gleam of My sun-splendor.

So it was with a certain joy that Indira Devi and I received an invitation from our dear disciple Prashanta, on behalf of The Macmillan Company, to write a book about our lives as spiritual seekers. In my own case, I was spurred on by a letter Aldous Huxley had written to me some years ago in which he complained about the vast pseudo-literature that had been pullulating on the subject, inspired by ends very different from those of true spirituality.

Some of our readers will be familiar with my older work *Among the Great* where I have written at length about the great personalities whose ideas and friendship have had a significant impact on my life. For reasons of space as well as to avoid needless repetition, I have here greatly curtailed such biographical material, except, of course, in the case of Sri Aurobindo, my guru and the one fixed point in my otherwise kaleidoscopic life.

I must pause briefly to say a word about Sri Aurobindo, whose birth centenary is being celebrated this year all over the world. I have quoted liberally from his works only to testify that it was he who, in his infinite compassion, molded me into whatever I may amount to now.

From my boyhood days I had heard of him as the great revolutionary who sacrificed everything for the cause of the Motherland, as he called India. When I finally came to know him, however, it was in a different light, for by then he had retired from politics, declining the leadership of his country to pursue a greater vision that progressively revealed itself to him through the practice of yoga. I lived under his beneficent aegis from November, 1928, to his passing in December, 1950, and went through the trials that befall every aspirant who seeks "to make his life a bridge twixt earth and heaven," as we are exhorted in his immortal *Savitri*. To be with him was to enjoy a foretaste of heaven, and his sudden passing would have left me derelict with grief but for the consolation of my daughter disciple, Indira Devi, who had come to me the previous year. She was a highly gifted mystic and never failed to sustain me with her luminous experiences which Sri Aurobindo fully endorsed, acclaiming her *Samadhi,* or superconscious trance, as "authentic" and her visions as "beautiful."

It was at this time also that the famous Saint Mira of hallowed memory began to manifest her lead of light through Indira's visions, giving her song after ecstatic song in flawless Hindi verse which I then set to tune and sang athrill. To date Indira has dictated more than eight hundred such songs, sometimes, alas, while literally gasping for breath due to her cardiac asthma. As to the historicity of Mira, the queen turned mendicant in the Lord's name, the reader is referred to the appendixes of this work. I need here mention only that from the time of her earthly embodiment in the sixteenth century up to the present day, her life and songs have electrified countless admirers and devotees drawn by the dateless message of Krishna and God-love.

Since Indira is contributing a preface of her own, I will not further extend my own remarks except for the brief but pleasant task of acknowledgments. To Sri Prashanta, Sri H. V. Kamath, Sri Aina, Sri Mohanta and Sri Rasiklal Desai go our sincere thanks for their varied and loving help. And to the Jaico Publishing Company of Bombay, I want to extend my special appreciation for allowing me the many lengthy quotations I have made from my works *Among the Great* and *Sri Aurobindo Came to Me*.

Sri Dilip Kumar Roy. "I love my guru and call him Dada. His guru, Sri Aurobindo, called him 'a friend and a son, a part of my existence.'"

INTRODUCTION

by Indira Devi

W<small>HAT IS</small> yoga? Is it a series of exercises in the Indian way, practiced to improve the body, to cure diseases, to get a certain tranquility so necessary in this rushing world? Is it thought control, silencing the mind, attaining certain powers by manipulation? Is yoga confined to the Hindus?

No. Yoga is a junction, a meeting with the Lord, with the Universal Consciousness, with the Supreme Self or one's own highest self. Any effort or method that brings about this union, this inner harmony, knowledge, love or understanding is yoga. To aspire for perfection, as Christ said, is yoga.

Who was a greater teacher of yoga than Christ? Did he not want a transformation of nature? Did he not preach love, tolerance, humility? After all, did he not teach by example rather than precept?

Yoga is not an oriental art of making money or making faces and practicing postures. There is no shortcut in yoga. Yoga is a lifelong discipline. Yoga is a *way* of life. Yoga is the highest life possible for mankind.

In the Gita, Sri Krishna says:

> The virtuous men who worship me on earth
> Are of four kinds: He who's a derelict;
> He who prays for a boon; He who is a seeker
> Of the mystic lore and, lastly, the man of wisdom."*

* Translated by Dilip Kumar Roy.

5

In the modern world a fifth approach has come into existence. It seems to be a very popular approach too—not to bother about the Master at all but simply to forge one's own letters of recommendation. This is the approach of the professional yogis, the fortune hunters, the quacks. But then there are quacks in every walk of life, so why should one be surprised to find them in the field of spirituality? One thing which we often miss or ignore is that the very presence of quacks, imitations, frauds, only points up the existence of true yogis and saints. There would be no quack physicians if there had never been any authentic doctors. These men do debase the currency, but then that is what the majority of people want and so are attracted to them. The few who want the Truth get the Truth. "Ask and it shall be given to you, seek and you shall find, knock and the door will open"—as Christ said so beautifully.

The fundamental requirement of yoga is the same in all religions, that is, the transformation of our lower nature. If you have read all the scriptures in the world, mastered all *asanas* and postures, learned to sit still for hours, fasted for days, lived in sackcloth and ashes and suppressed all normal desires for joy—and yet your bigotry is intact, your personal ego has only bloated as part of a collective ego, you feel other religions, other prophets, other modes of worship are wrong and only your way is right, then you may be anything but you are not a yogi. A yogi is above religious chauvinism, narrowness and pettiness.

I love my guru and call him Dada. His elders in the family call him by his pet name and look upon him as their child. His friends call him Dilip. His guru, Sri Aurobindo, called him "a friend and a son, a part of my existence." Have I any right to object because others don't worship and adore him in exactly the same way as I do?

A yogi must be free from the shackles of pride, of false humility. It is more important to be than to seem.

The Gita speaks of three paths of yoga: *jnan* (knowledge), *bhakti* (love) and *karma* (works). The true yogi must follow the triune path, as Sri Aurobindo calls it. How can one love unless one knows, and how can one truly know unless one has the insight that only love can give? And, lastly, how can one express love except through service? A love that is content with only sentimentality and acrobatics may be self-love but it is certainly not God-love.

"Work is worship," Sri Aurobindo says. "Work is love made visible," Kahlil Gibran adds. An ordinary man works for his family and his own personal prosperity. A yogi performs all his works as a part of his worship. An ordinary artist says: "Art for art's sake"; a yogi artist: "Art for the Divine's sake."

When I say "Art for the Divine's sake," I speak from personal experience. For years I had learned Indian classical dancing, Manipuri, Bharat Natyam and Kathakali. Dancing gripped me as few things did. It brought a feeling of great harmony into my life. My body, my vital emotions, my surface mind expressed themselves through dancing. Yet, something was lacking. It was only after I came to Dadaji that he taught me to look upon dancing as worship by the body. I learned to offer my heart, my love and my entire being at His altar through dance, and the great Peace descended. Through dancing I became a part of that One Great Harmony. My anklets quivered in joy dancing to His melody. Some of my most beautiful experiences of Harmony, Bliss, Power and Sweetness came through dancing. That is why I say that music, art and poetry are so helpful to a yogi when he turns his genius to the service of the Divine.

How can one transform others if one has not substantially transformed oneself? One may become a good speaker and be able to hold a large audience, but if not even a few of those who listen find that they are better men as a result, what is the use? Except for the money one gets and the acclamation of the papers the next day, one only ends up collecting a number of mediocre people who are not much good to the world or the Divine. If the leaders of our nations did practice a little bit of yoga, what a wonderful place this world would be. They would have the humility that comes from inner strength. They would have the tolerance and understanding that are the result of discrimination born of knowledge. They would know that the strongest of us are mere puppets either in the Divine's hands or in the grip of the anti-Divine forces. Finally, they would realize that it is not by criticism, still less by coercion, but only by love that one can change others.

A world of true yogis, led by yogis, leading to the one Supreme Yogi. What a dream!

"I learned to offer my heart, my love and my entire being at His altar through dance, and the great Peace descended."

PART ONE

by

Dilip Kumar Roy

1

APOLOGIA

W<small>E OFTEN</small> hear a rather cheap admonition that the cult of personality leads one astray. But my own experience has been the polar opposite: namely, that in this unstable world of ours only the light from an evolved personality is dependable in that it never goes out all of a sudden. For it can be proved by instances galore that a personality one has really loved goes on shedding its light posthumously: in other words, what one has imbibed from the sayings and life of a lovable personality sustains one at every step even when its light is no more. When I look back at what I was in the past and try to trace and assay all that I have learned through the years, I find that it is the memory of personalities I have cherished that has contributed most to the total wisdom—such as it is—that accrued to me and made me grow into what I amount to. Not that I have always been able to analyze or weigh the indefinable forces that have shaped me into what I became as I journeyed on. But even when I did not see clearly how I was being molded, I felt deep in my heart that I was being led by an unseen hand through the impact of events and personalities. Sri Aurobindo has expressed this beautifully in his *Savitri* (Book II, V):

> The conscious doll is pushed a hundred ways
> And feels the push but not the hands that drive.

Let this much serve as my apology for what, in effect, can only be described by the word "Reminiscences." More explicitly, I will try to delineate how I was pushed at every turn by those visible and invisible thrusts that have made my checkered life so interesting to me and how I dreamed and essayed to make my dream come true little by little, aspiring to the feet of the Ever-receding Elusive Godhead whom I equated above all with Sri Krishna.

2

MY FATHER

I CAME FROM a highly cultured Brahmin family: one of my ancestors was the famous saint Advaita Goswami, a staunch follower of the Messiah Sri Chaitanya. My father, Dwijendralal Roy, was wont to say to me with a proud-ironical smile: "Do you know, my son, I am a noble scion —in my veins flows the blue blood of a mighty saint!" I was at a loss at first, for I was then a boy of ten and could not believe that blood could ever be blue. He smiled and explained that it was an English phrase which connotes aristocracy of birth and breeding. He used to treat me as a friend, often actually sparring or cracking jokes with me freely like a comrade or a playmate. A few words about his high attainments will not be irrelevant, the less so as he was the first radiant personality who not only shed light on my way but also helped me materially with his beneficent influence and robust intellect. But it was his deep sincerity and integrity of character which taught and exhilarated me most in my quest for Truth.

Son of a great father himself, my father learned early to emulate my grandfather in truthfulness, sincerity, courage and honesty. He won a state scholarship at the age of twenty-one and proceeded to England where he got a degree in agriculture. But his heart was given to music and poetry. He could sing remarkably well even when he was a child, and at

15

Sri Dwijendralal Roy, the author's father. "He was the first radiant
personality who not only shed light on my way but also helped me
materially with his beneficent influence and robust intellect."

only twelve years composed a lovely song on the moon which I still sing, delighting many a music lover. My grandfather, Sri K. C. Roy, who was a famous classical singer, was startled by his beloved son's genius and prophesied that the little prodigy would flower into a great singer. My father, however, only half fulfilled his parent's prophecy because he become eminent primarily as a great dramatist and composer whose numerous patriotic songs made him, at the turn of the century, an idol of the young freedom fighters of Bengal. His love songs and poetry had to wait longer for their due recognition.

The firstborn of an eminent father, I imbibed early his love for music and could sing in perfect tune at the age of five. A few years later I learned from him more than a hundred songs, mostly his own but also a number written by other composers. My father was wont to say that he was proud of his son and encouraged me to read our ancient epics, the *Ramayana* and *Mahabharata*, which even then thrilled me to the core. Thereafter my enthusiasm carried me away and I turned to our rich mythological storehouse, the *Puranas*, the tales of heroes and devotees, with the result that my precocious mind became almost adult while I was still in my early adolescence. In this way, incidentally, I grew to love our great Sanskrit language, the veritable custodian of our noble deeds and rich romance.

But my *Grande Passion* was music and literature, even though I graduated in science, winning first-class honors in mathematics. It is not on my academic achievements, however, that I want to enlarge while reminiscing. I have taken up my pen to trace, by and large, my spiritual evolution in the course of my quest for Truth, which called to me in two forms—the Lord first as the Mother (Kali or Durga) and then as Krishna, the world's Beloved Swain, the Evergreen. My father's beautiful songs on the Mother had made the deepest impression on my juvenile mind. But later Krishna, too, came to be installed in my heart—though not to supplant the Mother. For I was told that Krishna accepted cheerfully all homage to the Mother, and so I learned joyously to equate Her with Him, praying to them alternately, as my mood prompted me. This dual aspect of the Divine is welcome to many an aspirant, even though the Mother aspect is assuredly more popular in Bengal.

But it was my father's magnetic personality and genius that drew my heart to his devotional songs on Shiva, Kali, Krishna Gouranga and Mother Ganga, the holy river which redeems sinners and enraptures saints. These songs made my adolescent heart thrill to the call of the Lord from on high in His various moods of manifestation. As Krishna He leads us through Beauty to Love, culminating in Bliss. As Kali, the Mother, He inspires us to see the Divine even in the Terrible; as Shiva He blesses us with His ineffable peace; and as the Ganga He comes to absolve us from our sins so we may sleep in her bosom of mystic beatitude. In the West they call Hinduism polytheistic, looking askance at our idolatrous penchant for multiple gods. It would be going beyond the purview of my reminiscences to want to confute scholastically this misconception. So I will only quote a few lines of a famous poem of Sri Aurobindo to illustrate how the different aspects of the Lord can make the illumined heart respond rapturously to His call in different tunes and rhythms:

> In the blue of the sky, in the green of the forest,
>   Whose is the hand that has painted the glow?
> When the winds were asleep in the womb of the ether,
>   Who was it roused them and bade them to blow?
>
> He is lost in the heart, in the cavern of Nature,
>   He is found in the brain where He builds up the thought;
> In the pattern and bloom of the flowers He is woven,
>   In the luminous net of the stars He is caught.
>
> In the strength of a man, in the beauty of woman,
>   In the laugh of a boy, in the blush of a girl;

The hand that sent Jupiter spinning through heaven,
Spends all its cunning to fashion a curl.

These are His works and His veils and His shadows;
But where is He then? by what name is He known?
Is He Brahma or Vishnu, a man or a woman?
Bodied or bodiless? twin or alone?

We have love for a boy who is dark and resplendent,
A woman is Lord of us, naked and fierce;
We have seen Him a-muse on the snow of the mountains,
We have watched Him at work in the heart of the spheres.

This is not just a fancy-free worship of the gods, but a soulful paean to the One-in-All's various bounteous moods, duly answered by the corresponding receptive moods of the devotee who feels His touch even in the deepest anguish and so chants in ecstasy:

We will tell the whole world of His ways and His cunning:
He has rapture of torture and passion and pain,
He delights in our sorrow and drives us to weeping,
Then lures with His joy and His beauty again!

How could it be otherwise since He is all and ensouls all?

All music is only the sound of His laughter,
All beauty the smile of His passionate bliss;
Our lives are His heart-beats, our rapture the bridal
Of Radha and Krishna, our love is their kiss.

Hence, He is not merely our Best-Beloved, inspiring us to laugh and sing, love and kiss; He is also Shiva who, paradoxically, chastises—prompted by compassion:

He is strength that is loud in the blare of the trumpets
And He rides in the car and He strikes in the spears;
He slays without stint and is full of compassion,
He wars for the world and its ultimate years.

Tennyson was not wrong when he sang:

Closer is He than breathing and nearer than hands and feet.

Sri Aurobindo sings of Him more vibrantly:

> The Master of man and His infinite Lover,
> He is close to our hearts had we vision to see.

But alas!

> We are blind with our pride and the pomp of our passions,
> We are bound in our thoughts where we hold ourselves free.

But once the devotee opens his heart he cannot help but envision these diverse aspects of His divinity—this is what we, His worshippers, learned at our mothers' knees. My father did open his heart now and again, and so the inspiration came to him, impelling him to limn in his songs the different aspects of the Divine—of love and beauty, fear and war, bliss and music.

I was initiated first into the Mother's Grace when I sang to and of her—mostly through my father's beautiful songs; thereafter I learned to offer my love lyrics to Krishna of Brindaban who comes still to play at hide and seek with His devotees, performing miracles, fanning our human joy into divine ecstasy.

But my father being a brilliant intellectual, the elite of Bengal, the intelligentsia, used to come to him, not only to sing with him, often dissolving in tears, but also to laugh with him when he in his popular comic songs pilloried the hypocrites or lashed out at the sanctimonious (for he was a brilliant satirist as well), after which—as often as not—debates rang out on various questions of the hour. So, little wonder that I came to give in to my doubts and misgivings, too, although my malaise alternated with delectable upsurges of religious fervor buttressed by faith.

Needless to say, I did not know in my adolescence that a man could be a skeptic and believer at the same time, or alternately, if you will. Years later I was told by my guru, Sri Aurobindo, that a man is the sum total of many personalities so that he can be a poet as well as a materialist, a doubting Thomas as well as a priest of faith. In other words, man is, in most cases, a creature of circumstance and as such must go on oscillating and vacillating in his different moods. But I had no idea of the complexity of human nature when, as a boy of fifteen, I could still marvel or rejoice at all the shifting impressions I received at every turn. So, I was not a little bewildered when my father told me that he was both an agnostic and a believer rolled into one.

"Don't confuse me, Father, please!" I pleaded. "How can a man who has no faith in Krishna write beautiful songs about His love and charm—songs to which people respond with tears of ecstasy? And then, when you sing your songs on the Mother Kali or Durga, are you not carried away yourself by your love for Her and don't you enthrall others by your rapture? Have I not born witness to the joy you shed when you sing of them?"

My father laughed and, patting me affectionately, said: "But those songs I composed in a passing ecstatic or poetic mood if you will. Poets, my son, will be poets even as boys will be boys. So, they—the poets and composers—come to praise the gods and goddesses, carried away by a sudden exaltation. But you won't understand all this now: you will have to wait till you grow up and see life as it is—a labyrinth of mysterious lanes and streets in which one lane may lead you into a wood, another into a blind alley, a third into a glade, desert or garden of roses."

I have, of course, put it all in my own language but I have not misquoted or misinterpreted him. He did speak often of life's baffling contradictions which, weaving a dense web, alas, could shut out the light and invoke dusk at noon.

But I myself did not find life such an enigma, after all. The reason is that faith suddenly descended into me by the Mother's Grace through the soul-stirring message of Her beloved son, the great Messiah Sri Ramakrishna.

3

MY EARLY LIFE

AMONG MY early blessings, I cannot neglect to mention my mother, who was at once sweet and beautiful, generous and loving, truthful and pure. My father thought the world of her and never looked at another woman before or after her passing. His life had been one "long holiday of joy, music and sweetness," to quote from one of his poems, and it was all because of her. But as Sri Aurobindo puts it pregnantly in *Savitri* (Book I, II):

> There is a darkness in terrestrial things
> That cannot suffer long too glad a note.

My father's "holiday" was cut short by the sudden death of my mother at the age of twenty-seven. Indeed, the pain and heartache he went through when she suddenly passed on to the Beyond changed the course of his life. He had to look deeper for a clue to emergence from the darkness that supervened. Before her passing he used to laugh and make all laugh with him, and, shall I add, laugh at all that is sham and pretentious. It is true he had written not a few tragedies which moved our hearts. But he was strong and self-confident and walked always with a song on his lips. After her passing he began to feel at every step that "there hath passed away a glory from the earth."

"Among my early blessings, I cannot neglect to mention my mother, who was at once sweet and beautiful, generous and loving, truthful and pure."

In one of his most beautiful poems on her he addressed thus her departed spirit:

> How can I say—no cloud had ever passed
>   Between us, man and wife?
> For I did err as sometimes it was you:
>   Mistakes must happen in life.
>
> We are but human, a mixture of merits and faults,
>   We are all flawed—more or less:
> So one, at times, must wound or misunderstand
>   The other one yearns to bless.
>
> Yet this I know: you loved me with all your heart,
>   Nor ever once your love waned;
> Rarely, alas, is a husband here on earth
>   So lovingly sustained.

When my mother breathed her last I was a boy of six and my sister only four years old. So I could not possibly imagine how hard my father had taken the blow dealt by the fates— a veritable bolt from the blue. But a child is a nursling of the future and so it did not take me long to forget my mother, especially because father took us in hand and became to us father and mother in one. But that is another story. I will take up the thread where I left off.

We were with my father in Calcutta in a house he had built in 1908 or thereabouts. I was then only eleven years old. As I did not want to go to school, a private tutor was engaged to teach me English, mathematics, history and geography. My mother tongue, Bengali, I had mastered earlier through reading our epics, *Puranas,* novels, plays and my father's famous dramas. I was a voracious reader. Sanskrit I learned to love two years later—especially its melodious meters—when I was sent to a school near our house. In 1913 I matriculated and won a scholarship, getting high marks in Sanskrit and mathematics. But to come to the first impact of Grace which booned me with faith through the agency of a cousin I came to idolize. His name was Nirmalendu. I called him Nirmalda, the suffix *da* denoting elder brother.

He hailed from Shantipur, the home of my ancestor I have already mentioned—the great saint Advaita Goswami. His father, my uncle, was not only a deeply religious man but a saintly soul who, after my aunt's death, had opened himself to Krishna and literally lived for Him, the Lord of His heart.

After passing the matriculation examination, Nirmalda had to go in for the Intermediate in Arts and so was sent to Calcutta where my father invited him to stay with us. On my part, it was a case of love at first sight. He also grew fond of me and we used to read, play and eat together. He was an extremely handsome youth and had marked histrionic talents. As my father had won eminence as a dramatist, Nirmalda used to recite enthusiastically ever so many passages from his dramas, which drew us together in a still closer bond, for I, too, loved to recite noble exhortations and declamations.

But it was not long before I discovered, to my great joy, that Nirmalda was an authentic devotee. I had, indeed, been already initiated in God-love through my father's soul-stirring songs, but as he disclaimed the title of a devotee I prayed for the beneficent contact of a person who loved the Lord from the heart, and lo, here was the blessed answer to my prayer—Nirmalda! As I came to know him more I was delighted to discover that he had the gift also to communicate the light which his father had lit in his heart. Besides, he was an ardent worshipper of Sri Ramakrishna—so much so that his eyes used to glisten when he talked eloquently of the Mother Kali coming in person to Sri Ramakrishna. But though I was a believer at heart I found this a little difficult to accept. No wonder, for in our milieu I had heard my father's intellectual friends laugh at this tall claim of Sri Ramakrishna. They challenged: "How could the Infinite Divine assume a human form and speak to His devotees in a human tongue?" "God may indeed exist," they judicially conceded, "but how could He possibly accept human limitations?

Would not that be absurd? He may guide us mortals from on high but how could He seek birth as a human being or flash before the devotee in the garb of humanity? It would be sheer blasphemy to equate the Spirit with flesh," and so forth.

Years later I read in Sri Aurobindo's *Essays on the Gita*: "Far from the Infinite being unable to take on finiteness, the whole universe is nothing but that; we can see, look as we may, nothing else at all in the whole wide world we inhabit. Far from the spirit being incapable of form or disdaining to connect itself with form of matter or mind and to assume a limited nature or body, all here is nothing but that, the world exists only by that connection, that assumption."* But at that time I was in my teens and found the scoffing repudiation of the Divine seeking birth as, or coming in, a human form to man utterly disturbing.

But Nirmalda was not to be shaken. Had he not borne witness to his father's mystic trance—*samadhi*—and heard him speak of his contact with the Invisible Krishna? So he outscoffed the scoffers, laughing to scorn their pedantic sophistry based on their ignorance of the Divine *lila*, cosmic play. Not that he could parry their thrusts effectively if challenged face to face. But then he was not pitted against them. He had to deal, in private, with me, his beloved ward, who hovered, ill at ease, between faith and disbelief.

But when all is said and done, it is the force of personality which has the last word—as I stressed at the very start. Nirmalda was a tough nut to crack and though not an authentic intellectual was intelligent enough to convince me with his arguments, the more so as they stemmed from his firm faith inspired by the radiant personality of his father who, it was said, walked and talked with Krishna.

Nevertheless my malaise continued or rather visited me from time to time till Nirmalda enjoined me to read *Rama-*

---

* *Essays on the Gita*, Chapter XVI. Pondicherry: Sri Aurobindo Ashram.

*krishna Kathamrita.** "Don't argue from ignorance, my pathetic sage," he bantered. "Be humble and pray for light to repeal the darkness that makes you believe that croaking with reason is more rewarding than singing in rapture." He was wont, as often as not, to taunt me thus. Sometimes I hit back, as I plumed myself on my intelligence, which many a friend admired, but, alas, Nirmalda generally beat me whenever we debated hotly about things of the spirit. His, of course, was the advantage in that he could affirm, with at least a secondhand certainty, that the Lord *does* come to His devotees to efface the darkness of ignorance.

As I have said, I was already versed in the lore of the Spirit, thanks to my study of our epics and scriptures. But the vividness, beauty and simplicity of Sri Ramakrishna's words all but swept me off my feet. Indeed, he spoke like a man with authority (as they said of Jesus), a status with which the Mother Herself had come to invest him, visiting his *samadhi* and explaining at every step how he was to comport himself and deal with his devotees who would come, one after another, a radiant retinue. His laughter, wit, repartees and, above all, his childlike candor alternating with his vibrant testimony about the Divine Reality—all this made a deep dent in my adolescent mind, thirsty for the rain of light in the desert of ignorance.

But though Sri Ramakrishna's words induced in me the will to faith, for the time being the net result was vacillation: to believe or not to believe, to welcome or to reject, to aspire to the epiphany or accept it only tentatively? After a good deal of wavering, I decided to "wait and see," à la

* It means the nectarous words of Sri Ramakrishna. The first part was published in 1902; thereafter four more parts saw the light one after another. Swami Nikhilananda translated these into English and in 1942 published them in one volume in his monumental *Gospel of Sri Ramakrishna*. The original *Kathamrita*, in Bengali, was recorded and published by Sri Ramakrishna's dear disciple whose pen name was "Sri Ma" (Sri Mahendra Nath Gupta).

Asquith, and shook my head. It was at once too good to be true and too true to be dismissed—true because the radiant personality of Sri Ramakrishna declared unambiguously that no sincere call to the Mother's light could remain unanswered; whoever sought Her nectar in all humility must win Her showers of Grace.

I know now, though I did not know it for certain at the time, that it was this, Her Grace, which booned me with the faith I hungered for. Otherwise I could not have been electrified by his mystic assurance that the Mother is not a myth but a vivid and everlasting reality, as anyone who appeals to Her may verify by the response of Her beneficent smile.

Even alternating as it did with my doubts, this certitude gave me not a little relief in my lonely pilgrimage to the Divine, for which I have to thank Nirmalda who came to me in my adolescence to countervail the beguiling falsehoods of scientific materialism. In this way, again and again in my life, the most precious boons were borne to me first and foremost through the personalities I have loved. I mean, my faith in Sri Ramakrishna was buttressed by Nirmalda's assertion that Sri Ramakrishna *was* the Messiah of our age—the *Yugavatar* —and as such could not possibly mislead us by unverifiable or unwarranted pronouncements.

I still recall how Nirmalda upbraided me one day for my hesitation to accept Sri Ramakrishna's testimony. "But how can you take me to task," I complained, "when his statements were not *written* by him, but merely attested to by one of his disciples? How can one be sure that 'Sri Ma' was a faithful reporter? Surely you don't claim that he used to keep a record of it all, in detail, in a diary from day to day?"

Nirmalda leaped up and roared: "That is exactly what he did, you skeptic! Come, I will take you straight to him and prove it to the hilt."

I have mentioned already that "Sri Ma" was the pseudonym of Sri Mahendra Nath Gupta, a favorite disciple of the

Messiah. He was headmaster of a very good school, Morton Institution. I had heard of him and, naturally, my curiosity often goaded me to try to meet him face to face, although when Nirmalda invited me to accompany him to the great chronicler I felt not a little shy. But Nirmalda dragged me into his presence—a willing prisoner in whose heart joy vied with alarm for mastery. Lo, to meet "Sri Ma," an intimate of Sri Ramakrishna! Joy, joy, joy! But how could I stand before him without withering away! A deep fear gripped me.

But "Sri Ma" was not in the least formidable: he was compassion itself. What beautiful eyes, large and expressive, what a light on his face and last, though not least, what a childlike smile which made him despite his beard look so young and eminently approachable!

After Nirmalda had bowed down to the ground at his feet and I followed suit, he asked me kindly who I was. I told him.

"Oh, you are the great D. L. Roy's son!" he exclaimed. "Blessed, blessed boy, to have such a noble father! Come, come! Don't be shy, draw nearer, come, sit here, close to me." He caressed my face with his hand, appraising me with an affectionate scrutiny.

I was delighted, my misgivings just conjured away. I sat beside him with bowed head, my heart going pit-a-pat.

After a while he placed his hand on my shoulder and asked: "Now tell me, my boy, what has made you call on me?"

I met his kindly eyes and answered: "I have come, sir, to hear about *Thakur*"—meaning Sri Ramakrishna.

He was galvanized and shouted: "Prabhash! Prabhash!* Just come, come running! Look, this little boy has come to hear from me about *Thakur*, fancy that!" Then turning to me: "Look, my dear boy, how my hair has stood on end!"

---

* Prabhash was his son and publisher of the *Kathamrita*. They called Sri Ramakrishna *Thakur*, which means a *Divine Being*.

And I looked in amazement: his body was indeed shivering with ecstasy and every single hair on his hand stood on end while his eyes glistened with unshed tears!

"What devotion for the guru!" I said, thrilled, to myself. I touched his feet with my forehead. He gathered me up tenderly.

"You are blessed, my boy! Thrice blessed to have been called by *Thakur's* Grace!"

Then he talked and talked about Sri Ramakrishna, laying stress on his Love Divine and relating incidents about his purity and simplicity which no human being could boast. Thereafter he showed me his treasured diaries, bound in morocco, wherein lay recorded for all time the "nectarous words" of one who had come to appease the agelong thirst of countless way-lost mortals.

I was simply overwhelmed. For such a great devotee to have come down to the level of an unknown teenager and speak to him of his great guru's divinity! For to him, as to millions of other devotees in India and abroad, Sri Ramakrishna was and is still looked upon as an incarnation of Love Divine and immaculate purity. He pointed to a framed picture on the wall, an enlarged photograph of the Master, and said: "Look, it was taken by a devotee when he was in *samadhi*. When, the next day, it was shown to *Thakur* he smiled and said: 'A day will come when this picture will be worshipped by millions.' Now tell me, wasn't he a prophet?"

My eyes filled. He drew me to him and then startled me by an unexpected remark.

"Before you go, my boy," he said, "I would like to make you one request."

Request! I stared at him in blank amazement.

"You are born blessed in having such a great father," he went on. "Promise me you'll keep a record of his jeweled sayings, will you?"

I nodded mechanically, still dumbfounded. He appraised me with his glistening eyes and amended: "And not only

"Faith suddenly descended into me by the Mother's Grace through the soul-stirring message of Her beloved son, the great Messiah Sri Ramakrishna."

your father's sayings. Whenever you meet a great man, you must put on paper any memorable words that fall from his lips. You had best keep a diary, as I have."

I do not know what impelled him to make such a strange request to a mere schoolboy. Can it be that one hero-worshipper knows another? Or had he felt something, some intimation from above? I cannot tell. All I know is that I have never been able to forget my promise to him, which is the genesis of my book *Among the Great,** and later my Bengali reminiscences, entitled *Smriticharan*, in which I recorded my conversations with more than a dozen remarkable men whose contact had enriched my life.

The unexpected encouragement of "Sri Ma" not only thrilled me, it effectively changed the course of my destiny in that I was oriented toward a new call that haunted me. Before I met him I had been quite a normal boy, a trifle precocious maybe—and as such more enthusiastic about whatever I came to love—but *after* my joyous contact with him I went on dreaming about him now and again and woke up often in a rapture. Nirmalda, who slept on a bed next to mine, sometimes awoke to find me praying with folded hands.

"What are you doing, my little saint?" he said, tapping me affectionately on the shoulder. I felt shy, caught red-handed. The reason was that in the *Kathamrita* (the Gospel of the Master) Sri Ramakrishna had said over and over again that one should always meditate alone, stressing that the less other people know about one's prayers, the better it is for one. This I could understand even then. For I had a congenital longing to be appreciated and applauded. But a true aspirant must never yield to such a desire. Sri Ramakrishna said in his homely patois: "One must meditate *moné, koné,*

* Bombay: Jaico Publishing House, 1940. It is a record of my conversations with Mahatma Gandhi, Romain Rolland, Bertrand Russell, Rabindranath Tagore and Sri Aurobindo. This book became very popular and is still available.

boné"—that is, in one's heart, in a corner or in the forest. Nirmalda, who was my monitor at the time, had annotated this with instances of those who, wanting to be praised and admired for their piety, were filled with an egotistical sense of superiority which, for an aspirant, must spell disaster. Fourteen years later, when I accepted Sri Aurobindo as my guide, he emphasized this need for humility which disclaims the flaunting of one's gifts or achievements. He wrote to me in a letter: "Every artist almost (there are rare exceptions) has got something of the public man in him, in his vital parts, which makes him crave for the stimulus of an audience, social applause, satisfied vanity, fame, etc. All that must go if he wants to be a yogi and his art a service not of man or of his own ego but of the Divine."

Of course, all this I did not know then. I only knew that I felt very happy whenever my school friends or teachers or relations lauded my musical or other talents. But Nirmalda was not to be caught napping: he chided me relentlessly whenever he thought an admonition was *de rigueur.* "Not so fast my dear," he would say. "Remember, humility is the key and perseverance the passport. The path is long and pitfalls abound. So one can never be too vigilant . . ." and so on.

He had, indeed, somewhat unconsciously, become my guardian or, shall I say, torchbearer on this path. I was a proud boy but as I adored him I did not mind his hectoring me even when I was restless or somewhat disgruntled. One reason was that he introduced me to a good many sadhus of the Ramakrishna Mission, notably Swami Saradananda, the famous author of the Messiah's monumental biography* which I read again and again in great joy. I read eagerly two other biographies also of Sri Ramakrishna—one by Ramchandra Dutta, the other by Gurudas Burman—and a few books of Swami Vivekananda, the more assiduously as

---

* Entitled *Sri Ramakrishna Lilaprasanga;* subsequently translated and published in English as *Sri Ramakrishna, the Great Master.*

Nirmalda was well read in the Ramakrishna Mission literature and I could not bear to lag behind.

But what enraptured me was Sri Ramakrishna's living room at Dakshineswar, in the famous Kali Temple of Rani Rasmani, situated on the holy River Ganga. The temple was sixteen miles from Calcutta, and as there were no buses or cars in those days (1910-11), we either had to take the train and then trudge two or three miles or go by boat. But these difficulties of transit did not discourage us—for we two fared to the Holy of Holies on winged feet, and the moment I entered his Sanctum Sanctorum I felt a deep heave in my heart and tears of ecstasy leaped to my eyes. I prayed and prayed in simple faith, the faith of a guileless boy, that I might follow in his footsteps, remain a *brahmachari** and dedicate my life to the quest of Krishna and Kali. To me both were one, as I have said already.

In the Dakshineswar temple the priests worshipped three deities: Shiva, Kali and Radha-Krishna. It was in the room the great Messiah had of old sanctified by his own ecstatic presence that I dissolved in tears. The dominant note of my prayer was that I might stay loyal to His call, the call I had heard in my soul, and I faithfully repeated on my rosary his mantra: "The object of life is to realize the Divine." Years later Sri Aurobindo explained to me what dedication implied. "Art, poetry, music, as they are in their ordinary functioning," he wrote, "create mental and vital, not spiritual, values, but they can be turned to a higher end, and then, like all things that are capable of linking our consciousness to the Divine, they are transmuted and become spiritual and can be admitted as part of a life of Yoga. All takes new values not from itself, but from the consciousness that uses it; *for there is only one thing essential, needful, indispensable: to grow conscious of the Divine Reality and live in it and live it always.*"

* *Brahmachari* is a seeker who stays loyal to the call of the Divine and remains a celibate.

I need hardly say that in those days I did not fully realize what my vow imported. It was brought home to me only gradually that it was far from easy to stay pure, a stern *brahmachari*. But as the Grace of Sri Ramakrishna drew me within its aura I did succeed in not yielding to temptations, thanks to the power of prayer. For I discovered to my great joy that whenever I prayed in tears, my weakness gave place to strength. So I resolved to pray more seriously.

But how was this to be achieved in our house? My father was by nature generous to a fault and I had no privacy, as his elder brother Harendra Lall Roy and his family—three sons and two daughters—were our guests. Then there was Nirmalda and another cousin Bhupenda. So we all had to study together in just one room. Fortunately, I could concentrate somewhat easily, but I could not pray or meditate when others were there. Had not Sri Ramakrishna enjoined that one must meditate in solitude? But how was I to find solitude in an overcrowded house? So, with Nirmalda's help, I built with a few planks and a curtain a small cavelike sanctuary on the roof of our house. It was just big enough for a boy of fourteen to sit in, so with the curtain pulled across the front none could see me praying. It was there I prayed to Sri Ramakrishna, Krishna or Kali. And, as often as not, I was filled with joy and a feeling of strength. As I look back in retrospect I can see myself in that curious homemade cave praying fervently for strength, purity and, above all, devotion to the Lord. I well recall the deep peace that used to descend into me and permeate my entire being, especially when my prayer ended in tears of devotion. It was a very simple experience then, but an experience which utterly eluded me after my father's sudden death when my sister and I were taken in hand by my grandfather who lived in a noble mansion on Theatre Road in Calcutta.

But before I turn to this new chapter in my life I must stress that I had grown to love my father passionately and cherished him as one of the noblest of men. His watchword in life was truthfulness which, he said, was synonymous with sincerity. He hated nothing more than falsehood, and though he made allowances for vacillating people who could not always be guided by high principles, he would never have any truck with hypocrites and adventurers. He was wont to recite an oft-quoted couplet of the *Mahabharata:*

Na ca satyāt paro dharmah nanritāt pātakam mahat:
Dharmasy a hi stitih satyam tasmāt satyam na lopayet.

Which means: "There is nothing in life higher than truth and nothing lower than falsehood. The basis of *dharma* [righteousness] is truth: so do not violate truth, come what may."

This noble dictum had been early installed in my heart because of his example. For he always practiced what he preached, not an easy thing to do in this our world of pitfalls and temptations, masques and make-believes.

4

PRAYERS

IN ONE of her chapters my daughter-disciple Indira writes
cogently about the necessity of relaxation when one sits
down to meditate. But I did not know this when I took
the silent vow of *brahmacharya.* So I went on praying, when
nobody was about, before an enlarged photograph of Sri
Ramakrishna in *samadhi.* My father loved this picture and
told me more than once that though he knew nothing of
samadhi he knew for certain that here was an authentic saint.
His certitude was all the more remarkable because he had
never read Sri Ramakrishna's Gospel—*Kathamrita.* He had,
indeed, met a few sadhus of the Ramakrishna Mission but
was not conversant with the teaching and message of the
great Master. It is true that he was a devotee within—though
he professed to be an agnostic without—but beyond rejoicing
in singing the hymns he had composed he did not seem to be
vitally interested in God or Godliness. And his God-mooded
periods were short-lived. A man of tremendous vitality, he
could never sit down seriously to meditate, even though,
inspired by God-love, he wrote lovely songs on the theme
of *bhakti.* In my adolescence I often felt deeply moved by
his intermittent enthusiasm for Krishna, Kali or Shiva, not to
mention his rapturous hymn to Mother Ganga which he
wrote a year before his death. As hundreds of devotees have

37

shed tears whenever he (and later, I myself) sang this song
I append here my own translation:

> O Ganga, who redeem'st all sinners' sins!
> When Narad sang, Lord Vishnu, the Evergreen's
> Compassion dissolved in rapturous music and flowed
> In a million reboant streams that glowed.
>
> And, athrill, alighted on the sky-vast tresses
> Of Shiva, the Yogi. His everliving Grace, is
> Dispensed to earth and ocean in resonant joy
> Through thy chants adown the mystic Himaloy.
>
> To thee, Heaven's daughter, turned through dateless ages,
> For absolution, sinners, seers and sages
> And sang in deep devotion's cadences
> Of thy mission to kindle in flower life's wilderness.
>
> How many a pilgrim, bathing in thy blue
> Billows, attained salvation! Come to woo
> Our dismal din with thy love, song-serene,
> How many a desert hast thou touched to green!
>
> How many a God-forsaken colony
> Has changed to a hallowed city as thy free
> Untrammeled dance with its alchemy of light
> And miracle rhythms transformed to day our Night!
>
> When I shall bid farewell, in my last hours
> Of earth-born joy and pain, O may thy showers
> Rain on my closing eyes thy sleep of sky,
> Croon in my ears thy liquid lullaby,
> Enfold my being into thy heart of peace,
> Redeem death-haunted life with fear's surcease!

My translation does not do justice to his soul-stirring song,
so moving in its sincerity, poetic appeal and imagery. Indeed,
it marked a stage of his evolution as a devotee and is the
more noteworthy as such rapturous deification of a river
cannot be dismissed as a mere passing poetic mood which
just twinkles and goes out. I have often thought that our
worship of the Mother Ganga as a veritable deity cannot but

be incomprehensible to a rationalist. He may, indeed, under-sign the imaginative worship of an image—as a devout Catholic does even today—but he cannot possibly bring himself to equate a river with a goddess who can be worshipped by a suppliant. I do not intend, as did John Milton, "to justify the ways of God to men." For as God is a real, throbbing Omnipresent Entity, His multiform divinity needs no ultra-modern vindication, least of all when He is perceived solely through the devotee's love. One who has love for Him does, in effect, say, à la Descartes: "I have glimpsed God with my Eye of Light, therefore I know what God is."* Similarly, one who has truly come to love Mother Ganga may well claim, *mutatis mutandis:* "Since I feel in her the touch of the Divine I have no qualms about equating her with a goddess." This is not an academic defense, but the acknowledgment of an experiential fact, to wit, that one whose heart has responded to the divine call of Mother Ganga can and does dispense once and for all with the services of an intellectual advocate. For he knows that what seems irrational to the mind may, in the last analysis, be suprarational and thus resoluble in the light of our intuition. Indeed, are not all paradoxes resolved in the harmony of the Divine? To quote once again from *Savitri* (V, III):

> The world is God fulfilled in outwardness.
> The blue sea's chant, the rivulet's wandering voice
> Are murmurs falling from the Eternal's harp.

And necessarily, since:

> His ways challenge our reason and our sense,
> His forms He has massed from infinitesimal dust,
> A greatness founded upon little things.

Or, as a French mystic has aptly remarked:

> *Les yeux sont aveugles: il faut chercher avec le coeur*
> (The eyes are blind, one must search with the heart.)

---

* René Descartes said in his famous *Discours: Cogito, ergo sum*—"I think, therefore I am."

What, then, could be more acceptable to a spiritual aspirant than the testimony of his suprarational experience, an experience, moreover, so rapturously real that once its light is invoked the flickering shadow dance of the senses seems as unreal as a phantom. It was this perception that made my father (like thousands of seekers before him) hail Ganga as the sweet redeemer to whom he prayed:

> When I shall bid farewell, in my last hours
> Of earth-born joy and pain, O may thy showers
> Rain on my closing eyes thy sleep of sky,
> Croon in my ears thy liquid lullaby
> Enfold my being into thy heart of peace,
> Redeem death-haunted life with fear's surcease!

This prayer came to raise its echoes in me—and more and more vibrantly as I grew up. Years later I sang this song at Hardwar, where the blue-scarfed Ganga purls and dances along pauselessly, and my heart was filled with a deep exaltation, so much so that on her bank I went on composing song after song which I sang in ecstasy. Altogether, up till now I have composed more than eighty songs on her blessed beauty. Many of these I have sung in our temple before the Lord with tears in my eyes. In one of these I wrote:

> In my yearning heart, O Ganga, I
> Sing but to appeal to thee:
> Come thou to rend the veil that stands
> Between thy Grace and me.
>
> For then I'll see thy light divine
> In all and love all, Mother mine!
> And learn to harken even in din
> To thy soul's own melody.

5

COLLEGE DAYS

INDIRA WRITES that she aspired to be a nun. I myself prayed to the Lord for strength to be able to dedicate myself to Him. The famous song of Mira's—"Chakar Rakho Ji" (Make me serve, Lord, Thee)—was the refrain of a good many of my own songs. But I differed from Indira in that I did not want to be a monk, cloistered in a monastery. I yearned to bow to the will of the Lord but not to the will of a human being. And yet—paradoxically—I wanted to have a guru! But a guru like Sir Ramakrishna. "No half-baked yogi for me, thank you," I said, jealously guarding my self-will.

En passant, I must pause to pay my grateful tribute to Mother Saradamoni, the radiant consort of Sri Ramakrishna. Nirmalda had presented me to her, praying to her to bless me so that I might shed my proud aversion to the human guru. Mother Saradamoni smiled and said: "My son, one who has loved Sri Ramakrishna need not worry about this and that. He has only to remember him in his heart and cherish him as the final inspirer who sought birth on earth only to give us all his lead of light." With these few words she blessed me, touching my head, as I bowed down to the ground at her feet. I was moved to my depths, and a lump in my throat prevented me from speaking. Besides, what was there to say to her, an incarnation of holy Motherhood? Had I not read about her greatness in Sri Ma's *Kathamrita* and Swami Saradananda's *The Great Master?* Had I not been startled by Sri Ramakrishna's tribute to her when he said he *saw* the Divine Mother in her at the very start? Had I not read about her power of love which had drawn all who came to her to be mothered and sustained by her light? Years later —after she passed on to the Beyond—I wrote a song on her which I have translated into English:

> Could one ever count the myriad souls you drew to yourself
>   to bless
> And take, O Mother, under your wing with heavenly tenderness?
> In our dim hovels of clay like feckless marionettes we play:
> But at your touch we leapt to life, like lightning, day by day!
> And how in that newborn aspiration bloomed your lotus-grace
> In a chiaroscuro of laughter and tears, O rainbow loveliness!
>
> How, too, our centuried pain and ail dissolved at your caress
> And, kissing your twin feet, we attained supernal consciousness!
> Was not that why you came to be hailed by His Love's Deputy,
> Whose compassion blessed us through your virgin Mother-heart
>   sleeplessly?
> And so you sang with your last breath: "None is an alien—none!
> By loving you make all your own—seeing in all the One."

But to resume my thread.

When I came under the guardianship of my grandfather at 34 Theatre Road I was at first very unhappy. I missed my father—his talks and songs, his laughter and debates, his encouragement of my study of the golden lore of the Spirit —and everything that reminded me of his noble personality depressed me. But my native resilience and my college friends —above all Subhash Chandra Bose—pulled me out of my doldrums. After the passing of Subhash in 1945, I paid my tribute to him in a book entitled *Netaji, the Man.* So I will not now dwell on the lasting inspiration he gave me by his idealism, nobility, purity of character and his admiration of Swami

Mother Saradamoni, the radiant consort of Sri Ramakrishna. "Her power of love had drawn all who came to her to be mothered and sustained by her light."

Vivekananda's exhortation to serve our holy Motherland. It suffices to say that due to him I began singing before large gatherings my father's popular patriotic songs, though, of course, for the music lovers I still reserved my favorite love lyrics and devotional hymns.

My college life was happy, with just one fly in the ointment. I had taken up mathematics, physics and chemistry because it was dinned into my ears by the ultramodern world-betterers that only science could deliver the goods. But though I was to graduate with first-class honors, mathematics, physics and chemistry with their acids and test tubes, retorts and galvanometers, bored me to death. But, alas, I had made my bed and so had to lie in it!

Nirmalda I saw occasionally but as he now had other interests we drifted apart. One of the consequences of this was that I lacked the stimulus to prayer and meditation he used to give me when I was a schoolboy. But I did go to Dakshineswar now and again—especially when the worldly talks and amusements palled. Not that I found no joy at all in them. The unregenerate part of me came to rejoice in my worldly-wise friends and relations even though I could not share with them my spiritual aspiration. But the devotee in me was starved and needed an outer support, especially after graduation when my grandparents determined to marry me off before I sailed for England to sit for the competitive Indian Civil Service examination.

My own plan was to proceed immediately, especially as I was to secure a seat at Cambridge University for my friend Subhash who would be following soon afterward. But though I tried to get a berth in one of the P.N.O. ships, I was unable to do so for some months and so had to wait, possessing my soul in patience.

My grandparents, uncles and aunts went on warning me, day after harrying day, that I would be running a great danger if I sailed for England unmarried. They said: "You are a very impulsive boy, and so in England you are all but sure to fall for an English girl." My grandfather was very orthodox and said pointblank that he would not receive any non-Brahmin granddaughter-in-law. I protested and promised to the top of my bent that I would never marry in England, but my grandfather said: "You don't know, my child, the temptations there, so you had better be sensible and accept a safeguard." And so on.

In sheer desperation I ran to Nirmalda and told him of the fix I was in. He wagged his head solemnly. "You are not cut out to prosper as a householder, my dear brother," he said. "Besides, don't you forget you wanted to go into *samadhi* like my father who blessed you with all his heart."

I must pause here to relate my experience with my uncle—an experience eminently worth relating. (I ought to have written about it before, but then it is never too late to mend.)

Nirmalda loved to regale me with stories about his father's marvelous *samadhi* (trance) in which he spoke to Krishna, and finally I implored him to take me with him to Shantipur, a small town about eighty miles from Calcutta. He gladly acquiesced and we went by train to my uncle's, where I stayed for a couple of days.

What I saw was this. My uncle, a physician, rose from his bed very early and after a few hours of meditation and *puja* (worship) went out on his rounds to attend to a few patients. He came back about midday, gave what he had earned to his eldest daughter-in-law, who kept house for him, and from then on he belonged to none but his one Lord, Krishna. He had to earn his living in order to support those who were dependent on him, but as what he earned on his morning rounds just sufficed, he saw no one after midday except some friends who were also devotees of the Lord. With these he talked only about the lore of the Spirit, read the sacred books and heard *kirtans* (devotional songs) for hours. He took no exercise, had no desire for money or fame, hankered for no diversion and indulged in no small talk, not to mention gossip. His *grande passion* was the Lord and he aspired only to concentrate on the Eternal (*nitya*) as against the ephemeral (*anitya*). He admitted no intimacies that were worldly, had no interest in family relationships, went to no social parties—in a word, he had come to be looked upon by all his neighbors and friends as a man who had "gone crazy" about the Divine. Some, who were a little more lenient, said with bated breath: "Nikunja is gripped irretrievably by the Lord!" But all were agreed that he was a kindly soul, albeit without attachments of any kind, a conscientious physician during the few hours he did attend to his patients, still brilliant in his diagnoses, competent in his prescriptions and confidence-inspiring to the ailing. For all that, they said that he was as good as dead to the world, which, indeed, he was, since the center of gravity of his consciousness had shifted from the world and come to rest on an entity that seemed to belong elsewhere. To give a random instance: When he met me he welcomed me cordially enough, but not as his nephew and the son of his renowned brother-in-law, but rather as one who could sing devotional songs. I well remember his first question because it surprised me not a little. "I understand, my child, that you sing devotional songs beautifully," he said, almost wistfully. "Won't you sing me something? Do you know that song Sri Ramakrishna loved: 'Shakali Tomār Ichchhā Ichchhāmoyi Tārā Tumi'?"

I nodded shyly and sang the song, of which I give a few lines in my English translation:

All, all's ordained by you, O Mother!
Naught ever transpires but at your will.
You are the Doer and yet we, fools,
Still vaunt: 'tis we our fates fulfil!
When you bless, cripples scale the heights,
And elephants are trapped in mire.
You coronate some into kings,
While others doomest to Hell's fire.

As I sang, tears coursed down his fair cheeks and he went into a *bhava samadhi* (a half-trance of ecstasy). I was told by his sons, my cousins, that in this state he enjoyed deep communion with the One who sometimes came to him as the Divine Mother, Kali, sometimes as Krishna, sometimes as Shiva and in other forms as well.

It was my first direct experience of a God-lover whose entire being "lived and moved in God." I had heard and read about the saints in hagiography, but so far had never come into contact with one. His whole face radiated joy, thanks to a strange absorption, the like of which I had never witnessed before. My skepticism gave place to veneration for the marvelous mystic whom so many, I felt, had misunderstood, although I do not know how I had decided that I myself was a better judge than those who criticized him. For in this case, I had no precedent to go by, even though I had seen quite a few of India's "celebrities," whose brilliant gifts I wholeheartedly admired. But surely this was an experience of a totally different category! For while those others coruscated in wit and repartee, composed lovely songs and turned out wonderful dramas, novels and essays—in a word, strutted before the footlights of wealth or fame—here was a man who had no special gifts to flaunt and yet his face and eyes radiated a bliss and peace the like of which I had never glimpsed on any living countenance! What was this beatitude, I asked myself, which made him forget my beautiful aunt (whom he had passionately loved and deeply mourned) and lifted him out of the abysmal pain of bereavement to this pinnacle of self-lost ecstasy? What I had read of the breath-taking lives of saints then, were *not* mere fables fabricated by their adoring Boswells! Years later, when I came to yearn for the second sight which would enable me to *see* what this seer had seen and not merely *heard* about it all, I wrote a poem:

> My heart is sated with all my ears have heard
> Of thy far miracle Grace:
> 'Tis time thou gavest me thy boon of eyes
> That leads to blessedness.

Yes, he left an indelible impression on my adolescent mind. For here I had *seen*, and verified personally, something that had stirred me to my very depths and convinced me that such a life could be *lived* in this drab world of ours, a life that throbbed with a consciousness that was as different from our normal consciousness as wings from feet, music from prattle. Prior to this great experience, my aspiration for the mystic life had been more or less inchoate and lackluster, because, do what I would, I could not bring myself to believe with all my heart that what the sacred books claimed as possible was feasible—or, rather, experientially verifiable.

To resume the thread of my narrative once more:

When the citadel of my vow was relentlessly besieged by my well-meaning bevy of aunts led by my grandmother, I had no peace or respite. They opined in unison that it was high time I married a beautiful and cultured maiden who would prove a steadying influence on my life—a ballast I sorely needed. As the onslaughts of their arguments increased I was shocked to the soul to discover how very vulnerable I was *au fond*. For although I prayed fervently whenever I felt weak—and gained thereby just enough strength to maintain my aplomb—I felt more and more tempted as the impact of my loving assailants' coaxing gained in strength and plausibility.

It was not difficult for my shrewd grandmother—the mother of ten daughters and three sons (all but one very much alive and kicking)—to divine my progressive weakening. So, to clinch the argument, she laid a trap for me. "Listen, my child," she cajoled sweetly. "This afternoon at five o'clock I have invited a marvelous girl to tea—so-and-so's daughter. You have got to be here and take a long look at her. And then," she pleaded, "you'll have to sing, remember—she is very fond of music!"

I felt at once defenseless and overjoyed. For I had heard from my aunts that the girl was as beautiful as she was charm-

ing—and cultured to her fingertips. "She is exquisite!" they
sang in chorus, and then, with a cryptic smile: "We know
what is going to be your destiny once she gives you a shy
and responsive look . . ." and so they raced on, giggling.

But it was no laughing matter for me, the less so as I felt
a keen desire to sing to such a paragon. But, as usual, I
vacillated and took alarm. "Suppose," I rebuked myself, "her
beauty and charm should prove irresistible and, in the end,
get around my resolution to dedicate my life to the quest of
Krishna exclusively, what then? Have I not taken a vow
before Sri Ramakrishna's picture that I would never, never,
never marry? How can I, after that, recant and be disloyal to
His call, the very call which inspired my vow?" And so my
self-reproach waxed fast, wrestling with my increasing desire
to stifle the still small Voice in my heart. And each reproach
in its turn deepened my malaise: How could I give in now?
What would Nirmalda say? Should I not look small in my
own eyes . . . and so on till I felt at my wit's end, unutterably
distraught and miserable. After my midday meal I prayed in
my bedroom before an enlarged picture of Sri Ramakrishna.
"O *Thakur!* don't fail me in my hour of need," I adjured.
"You must give me the will-power and strength I so grievously lack. I must on no account be weaned from you by
feminine beauty. You know—I don't want to get married and
lead a self-centered householder's life tied to a wife and children. I want only one thing: to meet my Lord Krishna, face
to face, and live to serve Him alone. And have I not taken
the vow to live the life of a dedicated *Brahmachari?*" So I
went on while tears coursed down my cheeks when all of a
sudden I heard a distinct Voice command from within me:
"Leave at once. Do not be here in the afternoon."

I was thrilled that my prayer had been heard—and not
merely heard but answered in an unforgettably convincing
way. For I felt as if His strength were being syringed into
me till my very blood sang in joy and the fervor of dedication. It was then I realized as never before the import of

Christ's initiation in prayer: "Lead us not into temptation," and the folly of trusting to our own strength before we finally arrive.

I went out noiselessly into the street and hailed a taxi. "Drive to 22 Iswar Mill Lane, North Calcutta," I ordered.

When I alighted at the house of one of my dearest friends, Dr. Satyendra nath Basu and told him all—barring the peremptory command of the Voice—he laughed and laughed, till tears pricked his eyes. But he understood and patted me on the back and wound up with: "Whether you marry her or not, may you retain this sincerity all your life, Dilip dear!"

I had this experience more than five decades ago but I can still almost recapture the thrill of the miracle. For to me it was a miracle of Divine intervention—or, shall I say, Divine Grace coming down in answer to my appeal. I say this advisedly, because it so happened that a few years afterward I accidentally met the girl in Buddha-Gaya at her husband's house where I stayed as their guest. I was so fascinated by her loveliness and poise that I thanked the Lord He had not put me to the test—nay, a veritable ordeal: for I have never met in Bengal a girl more breathtaking in her beauty and charm.

6

SWAMI BRAHMANANDA
NETAJI, ROLLAND

MY GRANDMOTHER sighed and cried and grandfather fretted and fumed because I declined to toe the line. But as I was of age and not dependent on anyone, they could not force me to oblige them by marrying on the eve of my sailing for England at the age of twenty-two.

Now it so happened that at this time Swami Brahmananda, formerly Rakhal Maharaj, was in Calcutta. My grandfather who, as a physician, had treated Sri Ramakrishna during his last illness of cancer had, in the course of his visits, come to know the illustrious disciple quite well. But he never once surmised that I was well posted on the Swami, still less that I had been praying nightly to Sri Ramakrishna for strength, purity and *Bhakti*. I had kept this a jealously guarded secret in my new milieu at 34 Theatre Road. So he thought he would take me by surprise when he suggested I accompany him to Swami Brahmananda, "a mighty saint."

I caught my breath. "Swami Brahmananda?"

"Who else?" he returned. "Since you are gifted with a mulish obstinacy, I am forced to implore him to give you his protective blessing against the deep danger you have decided to run, like a fool. Swamiji," he went on persuasively, "has great powers, real divine powers, as everybody knows, But you, too, must help me by praying earnestly that he may fend off the disaster."

I was overjoyed as I had read all that there was to be read about Swami Brahmananda whom Sri Ramakrishna used to style his *manasa putra*, or spiritual son. But my joy gave place to a palpitation of awe as we entered the house of the late Balaram Bose (another direct disciple of Sri Ramakrishna) where Swami Brahmananda was staying at the time. As we mounted the steps, the fragrant scent of incense filled me with an exaltation which I attributed to the presence of one of the greatest yogis of modern India, a yogi whom Sri Ramakrishna used to describe by the term *nityasiddha* (born emancipated). I recalled his apt simile of the legendary eagle that laid its egg in the sky. Out of this egg the tiny chick is hatched while still falling down from on high, and conscious from birth that the blue is its home, it soars back before it can crash down onto the earth. I recalled, thrilled, how "Sri Ma" had described the deep human-divine intimacy which existed between his mighty Master and this ideal disciple. He was at the time the president of the Ramakrishna Mission and was worshipped by thousands of devotees as a shining example of how a yogi should comport himself in life, dominating it like a king, yet not bound by his kingdom. Such was the man I was now going to meet! "Thrice-blessed am I," sang my young blood. It was with difficulty that I could inhibit my tears.

As we entered the living room of Swami Brahmananda, which was on the first floor, the great yogi, in an ochre-colored robe, turned and greeted us with a simple smile.

"O Pratap Babu!" he exclaimed. "This is, indeed, delight-ful!"

The two old friends talked on for a while in great joy, after which I was brought forward and duly presented. I was aquiver with ecstasy. But then, alas, began my trial, for my grandfather, having once started to complain of me, went on volubly, blaming me for everything with every conceivable epithet. I will recount it briefly. The scene is graven in my memory!

After having given Swamiji all the enlightenment he needed about my character and antecedents, my grandfather may have felt that he had overdone it in his zeal.

"He is not a bad boy, though," he extenuated. "And I will say this for him, he is rather good in his studies—has passed this year with first-class honors in mathematics. But I *am* worried, Swamiji. You see, his father has left him a fairly large fortune. And then as he has already attained majority, there is no holding him. Besides, he is, as you can see for yourself, a handsome boy. But the trouble is, Swamiji, he is too downright by nature . . . and temperamental . . . and impulsive . . . and modern—that is the worst of it— modern. So he refuses to marry . . . God knows why . . . though several beautiful brides are in the offing—one with a considerable dowry into the bargain. But alas," he shook his head dolefully, "he is obstinate as a mule and simply refuses to marry!"

An amused smile edged the great saint's lips.

"I quite understand, Pratap Babu," he said, "But what is it that you would have *me* do about it? Surely you don't expect me to coax him into marrying, I being what I happen to be—a monk, untied to the world. But then," he added, mollifyingly, "why not leave it to him?"

"I would, willingly, Swamiji," explained my grandfather. "Only the trouble is—he insists on proceeding at once to England. And I am—well, afraid for him, don't you see! He is a rather impetuous fellow and has plenty of money, and you know—perhaps you don't but *I* know—how quickly things come to a head there: he will march straight into the snare and come back with a—er minx—all painted and rouged! And that will be the end of everything—sheer ruin, I predict. So I told him: 'Since you are so pigheaded, at least come with me to a great saint: let us at least have his blessings by way of protection and so make the best of a bad bargain.' And, oh yes, I forgot to tell you," he added rue-fully, "he happens to be a musician—simply sings and sings away—and you know how dangerous that is—when young girls are about—"

But he was cut short by Swamiji who addressed me eagerly.

"You sing, my boy? Why, that is very nice! Won't you sing something to us? A song about the Mother, I mean. Do you know any?"

I was overjoyed and complied readily. I chose a song, a famous Kali *kirtan*, of the great devotee Kamalakanta—"Majlo Amar Man Bhramara"—a song Sri Ramakrishna used to love, which I had set to music in the *Raga Bhairavi*. I give below my translation:

> My soul's a honeybee of love
>   The Mother's lotus feet invite:
> And intoxicate, I fly to lose
>   My world and all in Her delight!
>
> Earth's lesser loves have lost their savor:
>   Pledged am I to Her alone
> And, thrilling in Her marvel Grace,
>   All other graces will disown.
>
> Dark the twin blooms and dark's my soul:
> The pilgrim has attained the Goal!
>
> Lo, barriers are overpassed,
>   Desire's snares have alien grown:
> For, basking in Her marvel Grace,
>   All other graces I disown.
>
> Kamalakanta's dream's fulfilled
> At last—when She to him's revealed!
>
> Beyond Time's pleasures and pains he harks
>   To Her blissful Timeless monotone:
> So, thrilling in Her marvel Grace
>   All other graces he will disown.

As I sang, his face became transfigured, almost self-luminous. Then he lost outward consciousness altogether and passed into *samadhi*. I went on singing, my eyes fastened on his trance-still face, till I could see no more, through my unshed tears. When I paused at the end of my song, peace had descended into me—a deep peace which seemed to fill the very interstices of my being. I felt, with a vividness I do not know how to describe, that he had blessed me while I was singing.

My grandfather, too, was moved, for once. Perhaps he had felt, for the first time in his life, that music might, on occasion, avert danger instead of inviting it. Anyhow, the expression on his face had changed and he looked approvingly at me as our eyes met. And all the time the great yogi sat, a statuesque figure, hardly breathing, a beatific smile on his face. Holiness was there and purity and, for *me*, romance! A stray line I had read somewhere recurred to me: "Eternity in an hour!" And it gave me not a mere feeling, far less a sentimental emotion, but a strange experience as of a glimpse —just a glimpse—but of what I could not define. Only one thing I knew, though I can neither prove it nor wish to, namely, that I had received from him something which had purified me in an unaccountable way, and that it was something that belonged to me though it seemed to flow into me from him. But much as I would like to paint it more graphically, I can say no more because such an experience can never be convincing to one who had never felt the ecstasy of an authentic saint's blessing.

We waited in silence till he came back to normal consciousness. Then he looked intently at me in silence. I lowered my eyes, soothed and, withal, a trifle embarrassed under his steadfast scrutiny. Suddenly he turned toward my grandfather and said with a beautiful smile: "Pratap Babu! Have no misgivings: he will come to no harm abroad."

My grandfather stared at him uncomprehendingly. Swamiji

smiled again. "Do you know what I saw while he was singing? I saw an aura of protection around him . . . *Thakur's* [Sri Ramakrishna's] aura, which is an armor, I tell you, and I know what I am speaking about. So let him go where he will—he will come back unscathed. He may, indeed, stumble sometimes—but I can assure you he will not fall." Then, turning his face toward me: "Come my boy—come nearer."

I could hold myself in no more and rested my brow on his feet as tears of joy and gratitude found an outlet at last.

He stroked my head gently; the touch of his palm soothed my entire being as a cool current of deep peace coursed down my body from the crown of my head till it touched the base of my spine. When I lifted my eyes to his he was still gazing at me tenderly.

"Won't you—won't you give me some—some advice?" I faltered, wistfully.

He held my eyes for a few seconds; a gentle smile trembled on his lips.

"Only one thing," he said, his voice hardly above a whisper. "Remember—always."

"Remember?"

He nodded. "Yes, that is what *Thakur* used to tell us so often: *smaran manan*—to remember constantly—that is the essence of yoga. And—remember his Grace—*Thakur's*—and keep reminding yourself: 'I have received His Grace: I must be worthy of it.' And then—all will be well."

These were the only words of advice he gave me and they were etched forever on the tablet of my heart.

I have often wondered whether it was because I was destined to receive this great inspiration I so sorely needed that my sailing for England was delayed over and over again. (Once I had actually come to Bombay but the P. & O. authorities told me that not a single berth was available for months.) I wondered in India and wondered more in England every time I was accosted by a temptation and I told myself every time: "Remember Rakhal Maharaj! Repeat on your rosary: 'I have received *Thakur's* Grace and must be worthy of it.'" This invaluable admonition never once failed to give me the needed strength to quell the temptation, but the *modus operandi* of Divine Grace cannot be described in human terms because it operates from a plane beyond the vital-mental.

I arrived in London in July, 1919, and from the first was delighted. The gorgeous lights, the tremendous bustle, the glorious theatres, the picturesque houses, the lovely gardens, the marvelous Piccadilly Circus with its glittering shows and restaurants and, above all, the incredible underground trains —all went into my blood and intoxicated me.

But, alas, no intoxication comes to stay! So, after a few weeks the charms of London dwindled so that the city almost began to seem homely, although it still remained an enchanting place of pleasures punctuated with outbursts of joy. From time to time, whenever I visited London, I felt a happy glow in my veins, especially when I made new foreign friends, through each of whom I savored, as it were, the beauties of his homeland. They might not be lasting friends, but how could their transcience give the lie to the wonderment which, like an entrancing wave, just rushed me along on its crests of romance to magic islands of glamor and gleam?

But Subhash, who arrived a few months later, came to stay in my heart and grow momently in stature. The more I knew him, the more I loved him, till it became almost an exquisite adoration. Not that we never differed from each other. But even the difference of our individual viewpoints and tastes contributed to the deepening of our intimacy. One thing which I realized more and more through our clashing arguments over men and things was that true friendship actually thrives on differences because even a disagreement can become a grist to the mill of love, founded on the rock of youthful idealism. My ideal was Sri Ramakrishna, who had said that the object of life is to meet and live in the Divine. Subhash said that the object of life was to serve our beloved Motherland, India, by liberating her from the foreign yoke which bled us dry ruthlessly. It is not that I did not love India. I was wont to say to Subhash with a courtly bow and a theatrical smile (paraphrasing Shakespeare's Brutus): "Not that I love India less but that I love Krishna more." He laughed and said: "I duly applaud, my dear, but how can we, famished plebeians, enthuse over Krishna à la well-fed patrcians like Dilip, born with a golden spoon in his mouth? I don't mean to be sarcastic, I only want to remind you of what Vivekananda said about spirituality being unable to thrive on an empty stomach. Remember his noble couplet—the admonition of one of our greatest apostles of *dharma* at its loftiest [*Birbani*]:

> *Bahurupe sammukhe tomar*
> *chharhi kotha khunjicha Ishvar?*
> *Jive prem kare jei jan*
> *shei jam sebiche Ishwar*

(In countless forms God stands before thee: all He does indwell. Why must thou seek Him elsewhere then? Who loves man serves God well.)

"But is it possible to love man," I countered, "till one has first learned to love God?"

My rejoinder was not a lame defense of earth-averse asceticism, still less of any pseudo-piety, but, as I now know, the intuition of a dateless truth of spiritual experience—namely, that true love, by which I mean selfless love, is hardly to be achieved by the egoist, nor egoism eradicated until we learn at last to redirect our love away from ourselves and toward the One from whom all true love is born. For it is only then that the spirit wakens and loves all, seeing in all the One-in-All, as has been so beautifully expressed by A.E. in his poem *Sybil:*

Sri Dilip Kumar Roy and his college friends in England, 1920. *Clockwise from lower left:* D.K. Roy, K.P. Chatterji, Subhash Chandra Bose (Netaji), C.C. Desai.

When the spirit wakens
It will not have less
Than the whole of life
For its tenderness.

But in England, alas, I found no one with whom I could discuss such questions. In Cambridge I made, indeed, a number of friends who were knowledgeable and cultured to their fingertips. But not one of them endorsed the dictum of Sri Ramakrishna and Jesus that the highest fulfillment in life is God-realization.

Still, Subhash was nothing if not inspiring. In our generation I had not met a man so unutterably dedicated to the one ideal of delivering our Motherland from the ignominy of an alien domination. To him India was not a peninsula of rivers and plains, mountains and lakes, but a dreamland to love and be inspired by at every turn, a sacred land—*Punya bhumi* —exploited and bled dry by alien materialists to whom every ideal except that of making money was unknown and unreal.

To put it in the vibrant words of Sri Aurobindo:

India's nature, her mission, the work that she had to do, her part in the earth's destiny, the peculiar power for which she stands is written there in her past history and is the secret purpose behind her present sufferings and ordeals.*

And this purpose, he emphasized, was that of the evolving Spirit:

Man in the Indian idea is a spirit veiled in the works of energy, moving to self-discovery, capable of Godhead. He is a soul that is growing through Nature to conscious self-hood; he is a divinity and an eternal existence; he is an everflowing wave of the God-ocean, an inextinguishable spark of the supreme Fire.†

I need hardly confess that I did not think along these lines in Europe in the twenties, but it will not be an overstatement

---

* *The Foundations of Indian Culture* (Pondicherry: Sri Aurobindo Ashram), Chapter III.
† *Ibid.*, Chapter V.

to claim that I dimly perceived the inviolable truth that man can never find his soul till he finds God in his heart as a living Resident and Guru to be led back home by His "kindly light."

Subhash, too, conceded this but he was so utterly one-pointed and dedicated to the ideal of achieving here and now India's political freedom that he said over and over again that first things must come first, and the first need of the hour was India's final liberation from the stifling alien yoke. And he was wont to add, in complete agreement with Sri Auro-bindo's vision: "Our spiritual message cannot be born home to the world at large till we stand finally on our own feet. For the world at large just will not hearken to the psychic message of a race of slaves who subsist to do the will of a heartless bureaucracy of alien masters." To this I had to be silent—for how could one answer the unanswerable?

Nor did I *want* to answer him, because just at this time—in 1920—I read Romain Rolland's great novel *Jean Christophe* and was so enraptured by his lofty idealism and vindication of the mission of true art—especially music—that I wrote a long letter to him enthusing over his masterpiece and asked him whether he could grant me the favor of an interview. And I was thrilled when he wrote back inviting me to a Swiss village, Schoeneck.

I longed to sing to Rolland as well as discuss with him whether the ideal of music (or of art) could fully satisfy the soul. I did not write about Sri Ramakrishna's asseveration to the effect that the supreme object of human life is to meet the Divine face to face and live constantly under His aegis. I only asked pointedly whether art—literature, music or poetry—was not somewhat self-centered in its very nature and as such disqualified itself as a call to the highest peak in our ascent.

I saw him altogether six times in Switzerland: twice in Schoeneck, thrice in Villeneuve and once (the last time) at Lugano. My talks with him I have recorded elsewhere so I need hardly recapitulate them. I shall only acknowledge here my deep debt to Rolland, for it was he who finally persuaded me to direct all my energies to the cultivation of a musical career.

But he inspired me not in the realm of music alone: I was first initiated by him (and later by Bertrand Russell) into the cult of internationalism. He wrote to me in November, 1922:

No, there is no unbridgeable gulf between the musical art of Europe and that of Asia. It is the same Man whose soul, one and multitudinous like the tufted oak, seeks to embrace in its ramifications the endless and elusive Life. I love the oak in its entirety. Through it all I love to hearken to the soughing of its massive branches. I would glut my ears and heart with their composite and moving harmony.*

And again, on October 1, 1924:

Among the Europeans I find myself rather isolated in so far as my outlook on India is concerned. The majority here repeat blindly and stubbornly: "Asia is Asia and Europe is Europe" . . . And I am persuaded, friend Roy, that I must have descended down the slopes of the Himalayas along with those victorious Aryans. I feel their blue blood in my veins.†

And this vision could flower in him so spontaneously because of his essential responsiveness to a largeness whose ubiquitous roots stretched everywhere to infinity. But catholicity in Rolland's eyes could never justify that perverse usage

* Non, il n'y a aucun fossé entre l'art musical d'Europe et celui de l'Asie. C'est le même Homme, dont l'âme, une et multiple, comme un chêne touffu, cherche avec ses cent bras à entreindre l'innombrable, insaisissable Vie. J'aime le chêne tout entier. J'aime à l'entendre bruire, de tous ses puissants rameaux. Je veux emplir mes oreilles et mon coeur de leur totale et mouvante harmonie."

† "Je me trouve assez isolé parmi les Européens dans mon jugement de la pansée de l'Inde. La plupart répète le mot aveugle et entêté: 'L'Asie est l'Asie et l'Europe est l'Europe.' . . . J'en suis convaincu, Ami Roy, j'ai la certitude d'avoir descendu jadis les pentes de l'Himalaya, avec les Aryans conquérants, et dans mes veines j'ai leur sang."

of ugliness which, even in his own day, under the guise of invigorating realism, had become a canker eating its way into the very core of Western literature.

"Art for art's sake?" he asked rhetorically in his great work *Jean Christophe*, whereupon he rejoined with the noble credo of his own life: "O wretched men! Art is life tamed. Art is the emperor of life."

I rejoiced, as I had never myself believed in the trite shibboleth that art is just a purveyor of life and as such must mirror all the mean filth and ugly tumors of a diseased or morbid craving that meets our eyes, alas, at every turn. Rolland not only rejected such pathological ailments as inappropriate for the canvas, but condemned such delineation as disgraceful. To quote once more from his masterpiece:

> Like those artists who turn to profit by their deformities, you manufacture literature out of your deformities and those of your public. Lovingly do you cultivate the diseases of your people, their fear of effort, their love of pleasure, their sensual minds, their chimerical humanitarianism.

A strong castigation, indeed, but how true to fact! He invaded the modern unhealthy and sordid realism like a purifying gust from the heights which cleared the miasma of his time not a little. Here, too, he can well claim to have been a great boon-giver who came missioned with his indomitable idealism. He believed with Schopenhauer who wrote, "*Von Schlechten kann man nie zu wenig und das Güte nie zu oft lesen.*" Which means: One cannot read too much of what is good and shun too much of what is bad. One of the reasons Rolland admired Beethoven was that his music elevated the soul in a mystic way by taking us on its wings to dizzy heights, giving us thrilling glimpses of an unhorizoned beauty. In his biography of Beethoven he quoted with fervor the great-souled German's tribute to music: "*Musik ist höhere Offenbarung als alle Weisheit und Philosophie.*" That is:

Music grants a revelation greater than that of all wisdom and philosophy. Similarly, Rolland admired Tolstoy not just as an artist, like Turgenev (whom he merely called "excellent"), but as a "gigantesque force de la Nature"—a gigantic force of Nature—the great creator of *War and Peace*, a master portrayer of multitudinous Life.

The point I want to make is that Rolland was born with a rare gift, for he had not only artistic creativeness, but also the ability to feel the impact of greatness and assimilate it no matter where he met it, in whatever walk of life or sphere of activity. That is why we find him belauding ecstatically (for he was never lukewarm about any genius he admired) Sophocles, Euripides, Beethoven, Tolstoy, Gandhi, Shakespeare, Rabindranath, Sri Ramakrishna, Swami Vivekananda, Sri Aurobindo, Russell, Einstein, Lenin, Netaji. . . . He might well have echoed Vivekananda's famous credo: "Wherever greatness in any shape or form has flowered I must bow my head in reverence."

He was great also in his worldwide sympathies. One of his later books is entitled *Je ne Veux pas Me Reposer* (I Will Not Rest). And it was literally true: he never rested till his last breath. In one of his most moving letters to me he wrote, in June, 1933 (published posthumously, in 1951, in his voluminous diary entitled *Journal*):

What use is it to me to know that the One on high embraces and rules all the waves of the present? My first duty as a boatman is to save those who are drowning in these waves or else to perish along with them. Vivekananda's cry of 'My God, the miserables' is engraved in my flesh.*

* "Il nous faut immédiatement courir à l'aide des opprimés, hommes et peuples, qui ne peuvent attendre. Nous ne nous reconnaissons pas le droit de distraire un seul instant de l'action présente. Mon intuition à beau savoir et percevoir que l'Un embrasse et qu'il domine les flots innombrables de ce qui passe: mon premier devoir de batelier est, sur ces flots, de sauver ceux qui s'y noient, ou de périr avec eux. Le mot de Vivekananda: 'Mon Dieu, les misérables' est imprimé dans ma chair."

That was Rolland all over. He could not sit by when he saw oppression or injustice in any part of the world. He lived the last two decades of his life in a Swiss village, seemingly in seclusion, but in reality in almost day-to-day contact with the whole world. People visited him from literally all the continents of the world and his doors were open to all: none were turned away without a sympathetic hearing. He could truthfully claim that he had done his best, all his life, to live up to the motto of the Roman poet Terence: *Homo sum: humani nil a me alienum puto*; that is, I am a man, I count nothing human indifferent to me.

But what endeared him most to me, or shall I say inspired me the deepest, was his fervent love of art. I used to vacillate in those days because serious doubts had crept into my mind whether art could be regarded as a vocation, a call to the heights. Was it not, in the last analysis, a diversion, a delightful pastime, at best an ideal that falls into the category of the second-best, a *pis-aller?* I wrote to him asking for clarification. He generously answered at once:

Never have I been able to regard the life of a real artist as that of a careerist or a mere egoistic pleasure-seeker. I know too well that in Europe all the greatest artists—like Michelangelo, Rembrandt, Beethoven, etc.—had to be, like Christ himself, *Hommes de Douleur* [Men of Sorrow]. It is almost a prerequisite of real genius. Genius must first pass the test of misery, solitude, doubt and general miscomprehension. Tolstoy in his letter to me goes so far as to assert that it is the test which distinguishes the *real* artist from the mountebank: the real artists must *sacrifier à leur foi, à leur art, leur bonheur terrestre* [sacrifice their worldly happiness to their faith and their art]. The life of a real artist, being made up of renunciations, could be little short of intolerable for the commonality. If the artist missed his inner joy and faith in his creative genius, he would not be able to breathe: he would succumb—asphyxiated. He must, anyhow, create for himself the air necessary for respiration. There again is the call to heroism—the heart of a lion.

You seem surprised at the incredible impression made by *Othello* on Malwida von Meysenburg. But do you know that the impression produced on the general public of the Théâtre Française (in this very Paris, called so superficial) by Sophocles' grim tragedy *King Oedipus* was something very similar in nature? Pain at a certain intensity is transmuted to exaltation and all the great tragic poets of the Occident know it. Thus it is by no means a mysticism which is peculiar to the Orient. Only one must crown it by the sovereign harmony—the natural concomitant of a great art. The most beautiful quartets of Beethoven towards the end of his life, the sighs of Amfortas in Wagner's *Parsifal*, are instinct with the same mortal anguish of the soul, but the sublimity of the crucified soul becomes a divine boon for those who can aspire. One comes out of such ordeals like steel purged through fire. Nurse no doubts about the element of moral energy which is at the source of all great souls and all great achievements. For us the first thing needful in the world is Energy. (It is not only Beethoven who said this, but your Vivekananda as well.) Without energy there can be nothing great, with it—nothing feeble. *Ni vice, ni vertu.*

Je vous serre affectueusement la main,

> *Croyez-moi*
> *Votre devoué*
> *Romain Rolland*

7

THE CONTINENT

A NUMBER OF my friends and well-wishers lustily deprecated my resolve to take to music as a career. Originally I had intended to sit for the I.C.S. examination in 1920—the year Subhash passed it. But when he confided in me that he was determined to resign, quoting the Bible that one cannot serve two masters, I was deeply stirred by his idealism and decided to accept music as my ideal. So after passing Mathematical Tripos, part I, I sat for and passed Music Special, part I. It was at this psychological moment that both Rolland and Rabindranath Tagore (about whom I shall have more to say presently) urged me to vacillate no more. It was a pat of encouragement I sorely needed at the time, for in those days —the early twenties—it was, indeed, unthinkable to "sober, sensible judges" that a young man of promise should be so mad and senseless as to embark upon music as a vocation. "But then," I told myself, "art as a profession was never deemed *comme il faut* by the worldly-wise *bourgeois gentilhomme* who branded the artist as a Bohemian. Was not Michelangelo chastised by his parents when he said he wanted to be a painter?" It is true that there were a few geniuses in Europe who had made their mark in music as composers, but in India fifty years ago music was regarded as a pastime, at best a diversion that soothed the frayed nerves. At any rate, none of my practical guardians and well-wishers approved of my aspiration to become a musician. That is, none save Rabindranath and Rolland, who both told me that I should not waste my talent in following the "sober and sensible" professions. Subhash had been of two minds at the start; but afterward—when I told him about Rolland and Rabindranath's categoric seal of approval—he became a powerful and invaluable ally. "Yes, Dilip," he was wont to say, "we must not aspire only to shape ourselves into humdrum lawyers, doctors and clerks, You will be able to wake up your countrymen from their slumber and lethargy by your patriotic songs. And now I fully endorse Rolland's advice to you to study the art seriously." With this he left for India, throwing himself with his marvelous vitality and one-pointedness into the vortex of the noncooperation movement under the aegis of C. R. Das. Subhash had also exhorted me to "burn my boats," which, in the end, I did, if only to follow in the illustrious footsteps of one who had burnt his boats to court the prison over and over again. An idealistic elder, Sri Sarat Chandra Dutta, came also to contribute his fuel to the flame lit in my heart, by eloquently spurring me on with "One who calls himself a friend of the great soul Subhash dare not play safe." So, in the end I sailed for Germany and began to take lessons in violin and singing. I wanted to learn also the European method of voice production and duly found an excellent teacher in Jukelius, a marvelous Hungarian singer who joyously taught me German and Italian songs as he urged me to undergo the regular arduous training, since I had it in me, he said, to flower into an "Opern-Sänger." But I shook my head determinedly: "Nothing doing, *mein Herr !* I am learning European music not to become a professional "Sänger," but only to be able to import into our music something of the vitality of German and Italian songs, which I admire wholeheartedly." He was shocked to the soul that I should decline to dedicate myself to European music, especially the great operatic tradition. He was wont to sigh:

"*Es ist ewig Schade, mein Herr !*" reminding me of Othello's "The pity of it Iago, O Iago, the pity of it!"

Rolland, in the capacity of musicologue, had asked me more than once not only to sing to music lovers on the Continent but also to explain to them meticulously the structure and evolution of our raga music. It was at his suggestion also that I was invited to deliver a lecture on the classical music of India before the Society for International Peace and Freedom, at Lugano. The Society's secretary wrote to me that Bertrand Russell would speak on China and Georges Duhamel on the War.

So I duly arrived at Lugano via Geneva with my lecture carefully typed, a copy of which I had previously sent to Mademoiselle Madeleine Rolland (Rolland's sister) who very kindly got it translated into French and later read it out for the benefit of those who did not know English. The audience responded warmly to my lecture and demonstration and the lecture was published a few months later in Calcutta in the famous quarterly *Rupam.*

It was at Lugano that I met Georges Duhamel, about whom I had already heard glowing reports from Rolland. During the First World War the celebrated physician-turned-litterateur had worked with the Red Cross, as a result of which he was a trifle obsessed with the spectacle of avoidable human misery and the moral decline of humanity. Often enough, when I asked him to tell me about his deeper experiences, he heaved a sigh and said: "It is folly, *monsieur*, sheer folly, stemming from the ego's obstinate refusal to admit the Light of His Grace on high."

From the first I was charmed by his elegant French, beautiful courtesy and, above all, his warm response to the fascinating personality of Mahatma Gandhi, about whom he was well posted. So it was a sheer joy to me to converse with him about men and things and sing to him our raga melodies. He reacted with spontaneous enthusiasm to our lovely modes and improvisations, and paid a warm tribute to Indian music.

Among other things, he wrote that our raga melodies (which I had the opportunity to sing to him again in Paris in 1927) "go as far as it is humanly possible to go in their impassioned appeal and profundity."

At Lugano I also met Rolland's friend Hermann Hesse the Nobel Laureate, whose book on the Buddha had created a stir in Europe. Rolland, too, attended though he did not take any active part. But the person who gave me the greatest thrill was Bertrand Russell. He gave a series of three lectures on China, whence he had just returned—splendid lectures which we all heard with bated breath. As I have already written about my long talks with him,* I need only add here how profoundly he continued to influence me with his tremendous courage, sincerity and, of course, scintillating intelligence. In fact, the avidity with which I used to pore over his books sometimes proved an obstacle to my spiritual aspiration in that Russell encouraged the will to doubt at the expense of the spiritual discrimination which alone is the true touchstone in yoga. But as I have dealt with this long-drawn-out struggle in my *Among the Great, Kumbha* and other books, I will conclude this chapter with a relevant letter my guru, Sri Aurobindo, wrote to me to cure me of my excessive admiration for Russell's advocacy of doubt and "debunking" of spirituality:

Dilip, I have not forgotten Russell but I have neglected him, first, for want of time: second, because for the moment I have mislaid your letter; third, because of lack of understanding on my part. What is the meaning of his "taking interest in external things for their own sakes?" And what is an introvert?† Both these problems baffle me.

---

* *Among the Great;* also *Bhavan's Journal,* this written after his passing.
† I had quoted from Russell's latest book, *The Conquest of Happiness,* the following passage among others: "We are all prone to the malady of the introvert, who, with the manifold spectacle of the world spread out before him, turns away and gazes upon the emptiness within."

The word "introvert" has come into existence only recently and sounds like a companion of "pervert." Literally, it means one who is turned inwards. The *Upanishad* speaks of the doors of the senses that are turned outwards absorbing man in external things ("for their own sakes," I suppose?) and of the rare man among a million who turns his vision inwards and sees the self. Is that man an introvert? And is Russell's ideal man "interested in externals for their own sakes"—a Ramaswami the chef or Joseph the chauffeur for instance—*homo externalis Russellius* an extrovert? Or is an introvert one who has an inner life stronger than his external one—the poet, the musician, the artist? Was Beethoven in his deafness, bringing out music from within, an introvert? Or does it mean one who measures external things by an inner standard and is interested in them not "for their own sakes" but for their value to his self-development, psychic, religious, ethical or other? Are Tolstoy and Gandhi examples of introverts? Or, in another field—Goethe? Or does it mean one who cares for external things only as they concern his ego? But that I suppose would include 999,999 men out of every million.

What are external things? Russell is a mathematician. Are mathematical formulae external things even though they exist here only in the World-mind and the mind of Man? If not, is Russell, as mathematician, an introvert? Again, Yajnavalkya says that one loves the wife not for the sake of the wife, but for the self's sake, and so with other objects of interest or desire—whether the self be the inner self or the ego. In yoga it is the valuing of external things in the terms of the desire of the ego that is discouraged—their only value is their value in the manifestation of the Divine. Who desires external things "for their own sakes" and not for some value to the conscious being? Even Cheloo, the day-labourer, is not interested in a two-anna piece for its own sake, but for some vital satisfaction it can bring him; even with the hoarding miser it is the same—it is his vital being's passion for possession that he satisfies.

What then is meant by Russell's "for their own sakes"? If you enlighten me on these points, I may still make an effort to comment on his *Mahāvākya* [great message].

More important is his wonderful phrase about the "emptiness within"; on that at least I hope to make a comment one day or another.

Sri Aurobindo

8

RABINDRANATH TAGORE

I RETURNED HOME in November, 1922, after about a three-year sojourn in Europe. In Cambridge I had not taken any degree or diploma and so had only three achievements to show to my credit: I had learned to speak French fluently, German less fluently and Italian still less; I had won a great many friends and met world celebrities; and last, though not least, I had greatly improved my voice, thanks to the Italian method of voice production. But none of these accomplishments had any market value. Among my old friends only a few like Subhash, Satyen Bose or Dhurjati Mukherji encouraged me.

True, I could now hold an audience singing songs in Bengali, Hindi, Sanskrit, German, French and Italian. But music, as my guardians had argued, was merely decorative, if that; it could not serve as a gainful profession, still less a respectable vocation. The virtuosos who in those days eked out a miserable living through music were indeed invited to sing on festive occasions—sometimes even applauded for their virtuosity—but one never dreamed of hobnobbing with them. A *ustad*—that is, a professional musician—was just paid to amuse his audience, never greeted as a respectable member of society.

Fortunately, I did not have to earn my living as a professional. For though my grandfather had died before my return home, I still lived at 34 Theatre Road where my loving Uncle Khagen was now my guardian and adviser. But I was born under a lucky star in that my voice and singing style appealed to all who cared for music, especially in Bengal, the land of music. The musicologist Professor Fox Strong-ways writes in his well-known book on Indian music that the euphonious Bengali language is so appropriate for music that it could well claim kinship with the Italian language in Europe.

But though I soon became popular in Bengal as a singer, I was nothing if not ambitious. So I engaged a number of first-class musicians to train me fully in the art of Hindustani music. I also began to travel the length and breadth of India, scouring our land for musicians of note from whom I was to learn a great deal, including the devotional songs which were later to become the staple of my musical life. I wrote a well-documented book entitled *The Diary of a Roving Minstrel* which earned me the blithe epithet of a "musical vagabond"—*bhramyaman*.

One of the greatest boons that my kind destiny conferred on me was the love with which Rabindranath Tagore greeted me on my return. He invited me to teach music to his students at Shantiniketan (which has now become a full-fledged university). But though thrilled by his affectionate invitation, I decided instead to learn more about the technique of our music—in particular the classical music. When I told him this he was a little disappointed, but he blessed my aspiration nonetheless.

I was so attracted by his magnetic personality that I felt overjoyed whenever he invited me to be his guest in his country home in Bolpur, Shantiniketan.* I recall how on one such occasion, in January, 1927, to be exact, I asked him

* Though I have written at great length about him in my *Among the Great*, I must still add a few words here about his mysticism, which was as beautiful as it was profound in its essentially Indian outlook, or, shall I say, inlook.

Sri Rabindranath Tagore, "the poet and mystic who drew us all to his aura of exquisite beauty and opulent vitality."

whether he believed in destiny. I had quoted Hamlet's:

> There is a divinity that shapes our ends
> Rough-hew them how we will.

He mused for a while, then said: "I believe we are free, within limits, and yet there is an unseen hand, a guiding angel, that somehow, like a submerged propeller, drives us on."

"Will you be a little more explicit, please?" I said.

The king of similes gave a beautiful one.

"Let us suppose," he said, "that there is a master flutist who has fashioned some flutes. Naturally, each of these has a different timbre. But you find that a few flutes surpass the others and, somehow or other, emit deeper notes of a perfect pitch. The flutist no doubt plays on all his flutes, but he likes best to play on these exceptional ones. The same with regard to men. The Supreme Molder of personalities has cast them in different molds, fashioning them each with a different stuff of experiences, sensibilities and capacities. Yet some will always excell the rest. These, if you study them closely, are not unlikely to give you some glimpses of a special design of the Designer."

He was somewhat apologetic about thus seeming to claim to be superior to his fellows. But none who ever met him could possibly misunderstand, still less blame a colossus like him for being conscious of his genius. For—to exploit his own simile—the Supreme Flutist who *had* chiseled him into the exquisite flute he was must have done so because he could play through him some of his melodies to better advantage than through the others.

In a beautiful poem entitled "Jivan Devata"—written more than sixty years ago—he had asked the "Lord of his life":

> *Apani baria niyechile more*
> *na jani kiser ashe!*
> *Legeche ki bhalo hey jibananath,*

Amar rajani amar prabhat,
Amar dharma amar karma
  tomar bijan base?

'Tis thou, O Lord, hast welcomed me
I know not for what end!
Didst thou, from thy lone heights,
  Smile on my days and nights,
My plays and strivings,
  O my life's one Lord and Friend?

That he was missioned to sing of what he had seen had
been a constant theme of his self-exploration on which he
improvised to the end of his days; and, thrilling again and
again to the marvelous discoveries that he came upon at
every turn, he went on singing of what he had glimpsed in
Nature, Man, Love, Faith, the world as it is and, lastly, the
world as it might have been had we but lent ourselves to be
willing flutes in the hands of the Supreme Flutist. For then,
he sang, each of us would spontaneously acquire the blessed
status of a creator, partaking in his own way of the one
illimitable creative joy.

He was, indeed, a born votary of all that his beloved
Mother Earth spread before his eyes from day to day in
ever-new and endless carnivals of rapture. His heart, mind
and senses could never be sated with her glorious plenitude
of blossoming beauty, mystic murmur and fairy fragrances.
The more he received of her lavish blandishments, the more
fervently he sang of her supreme beauty:

Thy gifts to us mortals fulfil all our needs and yet run back
to thee undiminished.
The river has its everyday work to do and hastens through
fields and hamlets; yet its incessant streams winds towards
the washing of thy feet.
Flower sweetens the air with its perfume; yet its last service
is to offer itself to thee.
Thy worship does not impoverish the world.

From the words of the poet men take what meanings please them; yet their last meaning points to thee.

(*Gitanjali*, p. 69)

He had spoken of this "last meaning" in one of his earliest poems, "Nirjharer Swapnabhanga," a poem inspired by a revelation. In his *Reminiscences* he said of it:

One morning as I was looking out from my verandah . . . a veil seemed to be lifted off my eyes and I saw the world aureoled with an ineffable glory, billowing out everywhere on the crests of bliss and beauty . . . and I wrote:

How my heart has opened suddenly, O bliss!
Where visits me the world to embrace and kiss.

The experience was a twofold one in that—to quote his own words—"I saw as if with my whole consciousness . . . that deep down in the fathomless womb of the universe an inexhaustible fountain of quintessential delight was outspraying spontaneous laughter on all sides."

It was this total acceptance of the world of laughter and tears, song and silence, light and shade—a world which gleams in tremulous beauty in the heart of fathomless pain—that made him testify to the gifts of Divine Grace, the thirst for which could never be appeased even though he had received them at every step from the Lord of his destiny. And it was this acceptance also that brought him so exhilaratingly close in spirit to Sri Aurobindo, who viewed the world not only as the *lila*, cosmic play of the Divine, but, even more significantly, as the progressive manifestation of Divinity through a supreme act of evolutionary self-discovery. In other words:

A heavenlier passion shall upheave men's lives,
Their minds shall share in the ineffable gleam,
Their hearts shall feel the ecstasy and the fire.
Earth's bodies shall be conscious of a soul;
Mortality's bond-slaves shall unloose their bonds,

> Mere men into spiritual beings grow
> And see awake the dumb divinity.*

It is well known how moved Rabindranath was when, nearly seventy years ago, Sri Aurobindo first startled us with his hortatory articles, staking his all for the independence of our Motherland. When the latter was subsequently imprisoned on charges of sedition, the poet wrote one of his greatest poems, hailing him as a heaven-sent Messiah of freedom.

> Rabindranath, O Aurobindo, bows to thee!
> O friend, my country's friend, O voice incarnate, free,
> Of India's soul! No soft renown doth crown thy lot,
> Nor pelf or careless comfort is for thee; thou hast sought
> No petty bounty, petty dole; the beggar's bowl
> Thou never hast held aloft. In watchfulness thy soul
> Has thou ever held for bondless full perfection's birth
> For which, all night and day, the God in man on earth
> Doth strive and strain austerely; which in solemn voice
> The poet sings in thunderous poems; for which rejoice
> Stout hearts to march on perilous paths; before whose flame
> Refulgent, ease bows down its head in humbled shame
> And death forgetteth fear. . . .†

I recall how I once recited to Rabindranath this magnificent poem of his and told him how, while reading it, I had grown to thrill to Sri Aurobindo. To my surprise, the poet only smiled without making any comment. I again visited him after my first interview with Sri Aurobindo. I related all that Sri Aurobindo had told me and how profoundly I had been impressed by his radiant personality. Rabindranath was pleased but, after a pause, said that he had lately come to entertain some misgivings about Sri Aurobindo's deep seclusion.

"You see, Dilip," he sighed, "Sri Aurobindo used to sweep

---

* *Savitri*, "The Book of Everlasting Day."

† The poem was translated at my request by Justice K. C. Sen. I have quoted here only the opening lines.

us off our feet in those unforgettable days. His articles and exhortations, his visions and aspirations, his flaming speeches and reckless courage did electrify Bengal. But alas, since his mystic retirement in his ivory tower he seems so aloof and . . . shall I say nebulous? . . . I don't know, Dilip, but I wonder. . . ." And so he went on, ruing Sri Aurobindo's inaccessibility.

I stood my ground and returned: "But I have seen him with my own eyes. He seems light incarnate, I assure you. Why not pay him a visit and see for yourself?"

I then quoted from memory a passage from Sri Aurobindo's *Synthesis of Yoga:*

An individual salvation in heavens beyond, careless of earth, is not our highest objective: the liberation and self-fulfilment of others is as much our own concern—we might almost say, our divine self-interest—as our own liberation.

I had quoted the above to refute Rabindranath's charge about the solitary's "ivory tower." He seemed visibly moved by my ingenuous enthusiasm and said: "All right, I will try to see him if the opportunity ever comes my way."

He kept his word: he visited Sri Aurobindo in his Pondicherry retreat in 1928, and wrote about his conversion in the *Modern Review.* To give an excerpt:

At the very first sight I could realize that he had been seeking for the soul and had gained it, and, through this long process of realisation, had accumulated within him a silent power of inspiration. His face was radiant with an inner light and his serene presence made it evident to me that his soul was not crippled or cramped to the measure of some tyrannical doctrine which takes delight in inflicting wounds upon life.

I felt the utterance of the ancient Hindu Rishi spoke from him of that equanimity which gives the human soul its freedom of entrance into the All. I said to him: "You have the Word and we are waiting to accept it from you. India will speak through your voice to the world: Hearken to me. . . ."

Years ago I saw Aurobindo in the atmosphere of his earlier

heroic youth and I sang to him: "Aurobindo, accept the salutation of Rabindranath." Today I saw him in a deeper atmosphere
of reticent richness of wisdom and again sang to him in silence:
"Aurobindo, accept the salutation of Rabindranath."

As I read his eloquent tribute to the great sage, my heart
sang paeans to the greatness of both. What impressed me
most was the poet's deep humility which made him bow so
readily to one who had been so grievously misunderstood in
his lifetime. But then only a colossus can truly understand a
colossus. Which is why, incidentally, Sri Aurobindo also
recognized his affinity with Rabindranath whom, in a letter
to me, he once called "a wayfarer towards the same goal as
ours in his own way."

In his prophetic book *The Future Poetry*, he added:

And at the subtlest elevation of all that has yet been reached
stands or rather wings and floats in a high intermediate region
the poetry of Tagore . . . in a psycho-spiritual heaven of subtle
and delicate soul-experience transmuting the earth-tones by the
touch of its radiance. The wide success and appeal of his poetry
is, indeed, one of the most significant signs of the tendency of the
mind of the age.*

* Chapter 32, p. 400.

9

MAHATMA GANDHI

I AM AFRAID I have digressed a little, lured away by the radiant personality of Rabindranath, the poet and mystic who drew us all to his aura of exquisite beauty and opulent vitality. So I must remind myself once more that since I have taken up my pen to trace by and large my spiritual aspiration, I must strive as best I can to shove aside such topics as are not germane to my theme.

After my return home, in the heyday of my youthful enthusiasm for the vital life of music and other variegated experiences, I found, alas, my aspiration dwindling day by day. So, to revive my drooping God-love, I repaired now and then to Dakshineswar to meditate in Sri Ramakrishna's living room, because every time I entered it my sleeping *bhakti* woke up with a start, and I prayed to him in tears that I might never forget his memorable gospel that the ultimate goal of a pilgrim of the stars is the starland of divine love, bliss and light.

But as our scripture has it, a *karma*, or action, must entail its consequences, a doctrine I have found to be irrefutable in my life's strange ups and downs. Only, thank God the Merciful, I have discovered that the undesirable consequences can be obviated—partially, if not altogether—if the heart's aspiration is sincere and strong.

Do what I would, however, I simply could not keep up my aspiration to stay loyal to His call amid the growing din of encomiums. I did try by fits and starts, but it was a sporadic outbreak of the spirit which declared obstinately: "I am His even though I have to live in the world and accept my bonds as Rabindranath has done." But it was of no avail, for the bonds only grew with time till they hampered me grievously at every turn. Thanks to my virtuosity and ability to sing songs in different languages, especially Hindi, I was sought after everywhere—at fêtes, conferences, meetings and assemblies—with the result that I grew overfond of appreciation and popular applause. I could see how this was affecting my spiritual peace. But alas, there is a song of the Poet, full of pathos, whose opening lines are:

> *Jarhaye achhe badha, chharaye jete chai*
> *Chharhate gele byatha baje*

which is to say:

> My shackles cling, I long to be free,
> But it hurts, alas, to disown them.

It was at this time that I met two great souls who gave an impetus to my spiritual aspiration: Mahatma Gandhi and Yogi Krishnaprem. Although I have written at great length about both elsewhere I must say a few words about their greatness as I saw it.

Mahatma Gandhi is looked upon by many as a phenomenon. A frail, short man, he attested at every step to the truth of the spirit performing miracles against desperate odds. For it was, indeed, a miracle he achieved with the only equipment he had and believed in, namely, soul-force.

His philosophy was simple in the extreme: God is Truth, and so one who worships Truth is in effect worshipping God, the sum total of all that is or ever will be. And what is Truth? The answer was equally simple: that which is perceived in the light of our soul's aspiration and which, when

Sri Dilip Kumar Roy. "It was at this time that I met two great souls who gave an impetus to my spiritual aspiration: Mahatma Gandhi and Yogi Krishnaprem."

we surrender wholeheartedly to it, takes us under its wing and makes us invulnerable. And this was no mere intellectualizing, not with his emphasis on *brahmacharya* (chastity), voluntary poverty as advocated by Tolstoy and last, though not least, *ahimsa,* or nonviolence and nonresistance. I could go on writing endlessly about what he amounted to, how he disciplined himself with sleepless vigilance year after tedious year, and the why and wherefore of his strange intuitions, sudden decisions, redemptive fasts and what not. But I need only echo one of Rabindranath's poems which hits the target so directly:

> *Tomar kirtir cheye tumi je mahat*
> *Tai taba jibaner rath*
> *Paschate pheliya jai kirtire tomar barambar*

which means:

> You are, sire, greater than all you achieve
> And so your life's rich chariot time and again
> Leaves far behind all your resplendent feats.

Directly after my return from Pondicherry to Bombay, in 1924, Mahatma Gandhi was unconditionally released from prison where he had been held a political prisoner. While convalescing after an appendectomy he was confined to a hospital in Poona, about a hundred miles from Bombay. So, after fulfilling a few musical engagements, I went straight to Poona, not only to pay homage to the saintly soul, but also to convey to him the fraternal greetings of Romain Rolland. I made him my *pranam* and said that I had come to Poona only to see him.

"Oh, that is kind of you, indeed!" returned Mahatmaji with his limpid smile. His whole face softened in gratefulness, another well-known trait of his beautiful nature.

He invited me to take a seat next to his cot and asked my name. I introduced myself.

"Oh," exclaimed one of the visitors, the daughter of a popular poetess, "you are the musician—aren't you?—who has been to Europe studying music? And they say you want to import Western harmony into Indian melodies?"

"It is true I have studied a little European music in England and Germany," I said. "But I am afraid I have never been guilty of the dark design you so playfully suggest."

"But you *are* a musician all the same, aren't you?" put in Mahatmaji with his solvent smile. "So why words instead of songs? Won't you sing for a poor convalescent?"

"I shall be delighted, Mahatmaji," I said gratefully after we had selected a time in the afternoon when I would return with an instrument. "But tell me one thing: do you *really* care for music?"

"What a question!" he said. "I have loved music—particularly devotional songs—since my childhood days. Of course, I cannot claim, I warn you, any expert or analytical knowledge of its technique, but I cannot say I regret that very much, seeing that good music always moves me genuinely. After all, that is the essential thing, isn't it?"

The conversation continued for a time and then I left, returning at about five with my instrument, the *tamboura*. I first sang a *bhajan*, a devotional song of Mirabai. I give below the translation:

> Oh, make me serve, Lord, thee
> In deep humility.
> I would fain stay thy slave, and pray: may I thy garland weave!
> Then in my gloom thy beauty's bloom will set my soul a-heave.
> Thine eye's one spark shall quell my dark-rid slumber's undelight
> And my breath repeat thy name flower-sweet when thou thy
>   troth wilt plight.
> Everlastingly I will chase thee—a shadow loyal and true
> And will receive whatever thou'lt give—thee, thee alone to woo.
> I will attend on thee, O Friend, my heart laid at thy feet
> And sing and sing of thy Grace, King, through every lane and
>   street.
> Some, in despair, to thee would fare to win swift boons from
>   thee:

Some long to know, some ache to glow in flame-austerity:
Mira, thy slave, chants: "Nought can save but thine unflawed
    compassion."
She only cries to thy sunrise in love's song-adoration.
In ecstasy, I dream of thee: vestured in gleaming gold,
And crowned with plumes of peacock and blooms, O Flutist
    aureoled!
If thou indwell my heart, why still must yearn my eyes forever?
In my chaos of pain, Oh come to reign on the bank of love's
    blue river.

His gentle eyes glistened as he gave me his beaming smile. I was touched by his response.

"Mira's songs are always beautiful," he said.

"I suppose you hear them often—in Gujerati?" I asked.

"Well—I know a good many of them. I like the members of my ashram to sing to me her lovely songs—so touching in their sincerity and poetic appeal!"

I was delighted, because among the mystic poets my favorites were Mirabai, Tulsidas and Kabir.

"They are so moving," added Mahatmaji, "because they are so genuine. Mira sang because she could not help singing. Her songs well forth straight from the heart—like a spray. They were not composed for the lure of fame or popular applause as are some others' songs. Therein lies the secret of her lasting appeal."

"I feel," I said, encouraged, "that our beautiful music has been sadly neglected in our schools and colleges."

"It has—unfortunately," he agreed. "And it is high time for us to wake up to it. For it would be a tragedy, indeed, if our beautiful music were to die from sheer popular neglect and indifference. I have always said so."

This was corroborated by Mahadeo Desai.

"I am very glad to hear this, Mahatmaji," I said, "because, to be frank, I was under the impression that art had no place in the gospel of your austere life. In fact, I had often pictured you as a sombre saint who was positively against music."

"'I do maintain that asceticism is the greatest of all arts. For what is art but beauty in simplicity, and what is asceticism but the loftiest manifestation of simple beauty in daily life?'"

"Against music—I!" exclaimed Mahatmaji, as though stung. I was startled. "Well, I know, I know," he added resignedly. "It is not your fault if you should have drawn such a picture of me. There are so many superstitions rife about me, that it has now become almost impossible to overtake and gag those who have been spreading them all over the place. As a result, my friends' only reaction is almost invariably a smile when I claim I am an artist myself. Indeed, they take it to be a first-class joke," and he burst out laughing, like a child.

"I feel so relieved, Mahatmaji," I said, laughing, having caught the contagion of his mirth, "but may not your asceticism be somewhat responsible for such popular misconceptions? For surely you wouldn't blame the people too much if they found it rather difficult to reconcile asceticism with art?"

"But I do maintain that asceticism is the greatest of all arts. For what is art but beauty in simplicity, and what is asceticism but the loftiest manifestation of simple beauty in daily life shorn of artificiality and make-believe? That is why I always say that a true ascetic not only practices art but lives it."

Such was the great Gandhi. Even now, when I think back on his one-pointed yet loving asceticism and how it united the hearts and minds of millions upon millions of Indians to disarm one of the mightiest empires on earth, I catch myself wondering: did such an incredible manifestation really happen in our drab world of hate and strife, envy and greed, chicanery and opportunism? Did such a being really come to bless our earth—a great lover of man and God, who trod with us the thorniest paths of life, the while singing:

> O Lord, who art Truth! may Thy inviolate Grace
> Give me the eye through Truth to vision Thy Face.

I have given a brief account of our first meeting in Poona in 1924 and will now end with another, this covering the last time I sang to him in New Delhi on October 29, 1947. It was at one of his open-air prayer meetings in which devotional songs would be followed by Mahatmaji's comments on current topics.* I sang a song of Kabir's which I have translated thus:

> No fires devour nor tempests swamp
>   Nor robbers hurt that devotee
> Who in the Lord's inviolate Grace
>   Is cradled everlastingly.
>
> For this great guerdon ever aspired
>   The sages and saints who won to His Light:
> Blessed are they on earth who reach
>   His Midnight Sun beyond the Night.
>
> Ponder, O King, the irony:
>   Thine is vainglory's carnival,
> While Kabir's is the immortal bliss
>   Of tramping with the Lord of all.

After my song Mahatmaji said: "You have heard a very sweet song. But you ought to know something about the singer. His name is Dilip Kumar Roy. I met him first, years ago, in the Sassoon Hospital at Poona where I was convalescing after an operation for appendicitis. He then sang two *bhajans*, accompanying himself on a *tamboura*. This morning, too, he sang to me two famous national songs: the *Vande Mataram* and *Hindusthan Hamara* set to his own music. I liked them very much, specially the first one whose music, I felt, was very fitting to the spirit of the noble anthem. He has, as the saying goes, retired from the worldly life to practice yoga at the feet of his great guru, Rishi Aurobindo, to whose ashram he, and many others besides, have dedicated all they had in order to follow the gospel of their guru. You should know that in Sri Aurobindo's ashram

---

* These were published in *Delhi Diary*, Ahmedabad: Navajivan Publishing House, 1948.

there is no distinction of caste or creed, race or religion. I heard this from the lips of no less a person than the late Sir Akbar Hydari who told me that he used to go there every year as on a pilgrimage. Naturally, Dilip Kumar is a chip off the old block, having no prejudices, religious or sectarian. And though I am no connoisseur of music, I may, I think, make bold to claim that very few persons in India—or rather, in the world—have a voice like his, so rich and sweet and intense. And today his voice struck me as having grown even sweeter and richer than before. But I want now to draw your attention to the message of his song which you would do well to ponder deeply. For the song emphasizes that the wealthy may possess everything on earth—wealth, glory, pomp and equipage—and yet remain intrinsically poorer than the pauper who has everything because he possesses God, whom we only call by different names in order to quarrel with one another fanatically. If you will all take a leaf out of this Book of Supreme Wisdom you will be able, by dint of brotherhood, to shed all prejudices that must mar the harmony of peace and universal happiness."

He then went on to dwell at some length on the fratricidal war that was being waged in Kashmir and wound up with: "Let us all sing in our hearts the refrain of the *bhajan* which has been sung just now: that we all derive from one God who presides in us all, no matter by what name we choose to worship Him."

On the last evening, November 1 to be exact, I sang to him a Sufi song he loved. So I will give here my translation:

> The land where lies our home of homes
> Is a land of blooms without a thorn:
> Proscribed are Fear's dark forests there
> Nor ever is Sorrow's harvest borne.
>
> All day Love's rivulet ripples blue,
> Creation is a thrilled delight
> And visions celestial soothe the earth
> As dateless streams appease our sight.

There every prayer is self-fulfilled,
None bargains when he gives away,
There life is poured in molds of Truth
Enfranchised from Illusion's play.

Outlawed are selfish clamorings
And exiled thoughts of thine and mine,
No owner rules, no slave obeys,
Nor scorch ever mars the Light Divine.

'Tis not a poet's fairy tale
This world of love's sweet ecstasy,
But resident in every heart
Awaits our soul's discovery.

When the last line trailed off into silence, his eyes glistened as he said, commenting on the message of the song:*

Sri Dilip Kumar Roy sang the *bhajan* whose first line meant that the devotees belonged to the blessed land where there was neither misery nor sorrow. In my opinion it has a double meaning. The one is that they belonged to a country—that is, India—in which there is neither misery nor sorrow. But I cannot recall a time when India was in such an ideally blessed state. The first meaning, therefore, I regard but as an aspiration of the poet, first and last.

The second meaning has reference to the soul and the body. The poet sings that the body, being the temple of the soul, cannot possibly be the dark arena of men's fleeting passions and evil impulses. Lastly, he assures us—bless him—that when the body becomes the playground of the soul we shall win through to His bliss, peace and harmony. And then the poet's dream of India will come true, *Om shantih, shantih, shantih* [*Om* peace, peace, peace].

I was invited by the postgraduate students of Calcutta University to give a lecture-demonstration under the aegis of the vice-chancellor. The subject was: "Points of Contact

---

* Mahatmaji's comments on my songs were printed in full in *Delhi Diary,* pp. 118, 122, 124 and 125.

between Indian and Western Melodies." The date: January 30, 1948. I had just sung a German *Wiegenlied* (lullaby) by Curschmann:

> *So schlaf' in Ruh! so schlaf' in Ruh!*
> *Die Sterne leuchten hell und klar.*
> *Es kommt von dort der Engel-schar*
> *Die Äuglein zu,*
> *Mein Kindlein du!*
> *Nun schlaf' und schlaf' und schlaf' in Ruh!*

I then began to describe how close in spirit this melody was to the plaintive and otherworldly vein so dear to the Indian soul when suddenly the shocking news came, a bolt from the blue: Gandhiji had just been shot in Delhi by a Hindu. The meeting was dissolved and a student fainted, screaming hysterically. Gloom descended on us all.

On my way back home I was struck by the fact that the song I had composed and was intending to sing before the news of the assassination came was a mystic duologue between Mother and Child:

> CHILD:
> "I will now sleep in thy love's deep
> And toy no more with things that pall.
> I have at last heard thy far call:
> Without thy dream naught will redeem
> Nor hearts sing like a waterfall."

> MOTHER:
> "O come to me: I'll croon for thee
> My coral-cadenced lullaby
> And heal thine ail with rain of sky.
> For thee I wait at Heaven's gate
> For which I made thee pine and cry."

> CHILD:
> "I never knew—thou wouldst endue
> My life of dust with thy star-shine

And shower thy boons, O Mother mine!
And deemed remote thy Grace Divine."

MOTHER:

"But I knew still what thou must will,
And so I lingered day and night
To help thee home—my way-lost sprite!
When darks now loom thou cleave the gloom,
O hail!—reclaim thy deep birthright!"

In the middle of the night I heard myself singing again and again in my dream:

When darks now loom thou cleave the gloom,
O hail!—reclaim thy deep birthright . . .
Deep birthright . . . deep birthright. . . .

10

KRISHNAPREM

IT WAS, I believe, in 1923 that I first met Ronald Nixon, a professor at Lucknow University. He had come to India to be initiated in yoga as he had lost faith in the scientific-materialist gospel of Europe. Afterward he was named Krishnaprem by his guru, Yashoda Ma, the wife of the then vice-chancellor of the university.

As I have already paid my grateful homage to him in two books* I find it somewhat difficult to write about him without repeating myself. But as these are our reminiscences (Indira's and mine), I feel it incumbent on me to devote at least a brief chapter to his luminous memory which no passage of time can ever dim. Incidentally, it was he who introduced me to Sri Aurobindo's mystic ideology. "Read his *Essays on the Gita*," he said. "Every Indian who loves the Gita should read it. For his commentary breaks new ground and is more inspiring than any other, thanks to his resplendent intellect and yogic intuition."

Before I met Krishnaprem I had read a few of Sri Aurobindo's speeches and articles, mostly political and patriotic, but though I found them brilliant my heart was not moved to its depths because I was seeking *spiritual* pabulum as against the intellectual.

---

* *Yogi Sri Krishnaprem* in English and *Chhayapather Pathik* in Bengali, the latter in the garb of a novel.

It was in September, 1923, that I was invited by Sri J. N. Chakravarti, the then vice-chancellor of Lucknow University, to stay for a few weeks with him. He lived in a sumptuous mansion with an annex which served as a guest house, and was an extremely hospitable man who kept an open house. Ronald Nixon, the most beloved professor of the university, had made his home with him and his wife, Monika Devi, the famous *dame de salon*, as many people dubbed her in those days. I accepted Sri Chakravarti's invitation with alacrity, the more so as Nixon was there to keep me company.

My bedroom was next to his living room. Every morning we had breakfast together, after which I was asked, more often than not, to sing for an hour or so to my host and hostess in their beautiful salon. Krishnaprem never failed to attend, for he, too, loved my singing, especially my hymns to Krishna and Radha. Then, in the afternoon, he would often ask his colleagues and other friends to tea in his large living room which had books scattered pell-mell all over the place. His friends used to call his tea parties *conversaziones*, if only to make themselves feel important. His debates were sometimes attended by outsiders also, as he simply scintillated with brilliant arguments and repartees.

He had two dear friends in Lucknow: one was Dr. Joygopal Mukherji (who later became a great friend of mine as well) and the other was the redoubtable professor and skeptic-cum-rationalist-cum-iconoclast, Dhurjati Prasad Mukherji, an old friend of mine.

One day, while we sipped tea together, Dhurjati suddenly started inveighing against "divine miracles" which, he asserted —thumping the table like a magniloquent orator—"had ceased to happen altogether ever since Science [with a capital S] began to 'debunk' them. . . ." Krishnaprem laughed genially, and took up the gauntlet. "Science," he said, "was born only yesterday whereas miracles are as old as the hills, and an infant could hardly 'debunk' an elder who, besides, had refused to age for ages." And then he related a personal experience, which he repeated to me many a time subsequently.

He said: "I was, as you know, a pilot in the First World War. So I had to drop bombs over the enemy territory. One day, as I was reconnoitering, I was about to steer to the right, where half a dozen fighter planes whirred and zoomed, thinking that they were ours—that is, RAF planes. Just then some force simply caught hold of my wrist and made me veer right around to the left. I was quite bewildered, the more so as the force was too incredible to be doubted. In a few minutes I returned to our base and was told that I had done well to come back so promptly as a number of enemy planes had just come into action. It was then I realized, with a shock of thankful delight, that I had had a miraculous escape. Believe it or not, dear Dhurjati, I am as certain as certain can be that the miracle had been wrought by a power beyond our ken. Only the difficulty is that, though seeing is believing, hearing is not—especially if the auditor luxuriates in pooh-poohing everything he fails to plumb with his little mind's puny plummet."

As Monika Devi loved my songs, she sometimes asked me to sing to her alone—when only Krishnaprem attended.

Little by little, I began to notice in my hostess something which struck me as rather remarkable. Let me explain.

I have given Monika Devi the epithet of *dame de salon*, for so she had, indeed, appeared to us all—that is to say, as a great lady of birth and breeding with the innate personal charm of a born hostess, aristocratic to her fingertips. But gradually it dawned upon me that she was *not* what she seemed. She had, in fact, a mystic personality which, though it defied immediate recognition, soon became apparent to anyone who could delve beneath the surface of things. This came home to me primarily because she responded to devotional songs, especially Bengali *kirtans* and Hindi *bhajans*, with an astonishing warmth, so much so that tears coursed down her cheeks when I sang of the Lord's magic flute and cosmic play—*lila*. I noticed, next, how reverently Krishnaprem gazed at her and prostrated himself before her every time she greeted him as her *Gopal*, heart's darling (the name by which Krishna's mother, Yasoda Rani, called her little son). I was no less impressed when I saw that in her presence the leonine intellectual turned in a moment into a docile lamb! I had, however, no inkling, at the time, that he had already accepted her as his guru. This I came to know only after a year had glided by.

One day, after the *bhajan*, I remarked to Krishnaprem about her being two disparate personalities in one and went on to add: "When I see her in a social mood, laughing, smoking, cracking jokes—a veritable 'cynosure of neighboring eyes,' I do, indeed, admire her scintillating repartees and her native talent to make a party go, but then, as soon as I sing a song on Krishna before her—well, doesn't she look completely transfigured in her ecstatic tears? I don't know, Krishnaprem, but at such times I cannot help feeling that she is a denizen of the deep, a citizen of an utterly different world, as it were!"

"I'm glad," he returned with a loving pat on my back, "that you have learned the wisdom of not judging by appearances. For many a judge has, as you know, summed her up merely as a brilliant *dame de salon* and nothing more. But she is not a person easy to plumb or decipher. In fact, she has to be seen to be believed, if you know what I mean."

About a year had gone by when Dhurjati wrote to me from Lucknow that Krishnaprem had been initiated into Vaishnavism by Monika Devi, exchanged his English dress for the ochre-colored habit and flowered into an imposing Indian sadhu. Joygopal wrote, a few days later, that Monika

Monika Devi [right] when she was the famous *dame de salon* at Lucknow University.

Monika Devi after she had taken full *sannyas* and received the name Yashoda Ma.

Devi had taken full *sannyas*,* changed her name and shaved her head at the instance of her guru, an old Goswami of a Brindaban temple. Naturally I was startled, but I was moved to my depths as well. It was, indeed, incredible! For had she not been born and bred in the lap of luxury, an aristocrat and progressive out and out, an ultramodern who went every two years to England, a resplendent leader of fashion in her set and, above all, a loving mother and wife? Aye, I had to concede that she was, indeed, a lady "who had to be seen to be believed!" (A few years later Krishnaprem was to divulge to me—in their sylvan retreat at Almora—that he had accepted her as his guru because she could talk of Krishna and the gods and goddesses from intimate personal experience.)

A few months after Krishnaprem had retired under the aegis of his guru (now known as Yashoda Ma), I invited him to spend a few days with me in Calcutta in my grandfather's luxurious mansion on Theatre Road. He readily complied and we had a marvelous time together. I used to hang on his words, the more so as he had become an authentic devotee of Krishna, and I started keeping a record of some of his memorable sayings to quote in self-defense before nonbelievers.

He went out of his way now and again to have a fling at my anglicized friends. He held that India was the only country in Asia that had remained unconquered by the materialistic civilization of the West because her sadhus' holy aura still guarded her like armor. Sometimes, when the detractors scoffed at the sadhus as social parasites, he would retort with a smile that if Europe had such an army of parasites the next World War might be staved off; and then he would add provokingly: "The ones you call parasites I would rather endow with the epithet *salt of the earth*."

They would sometimes go for him in a body, espousing

---

* The vows of a *sannyasin*, or Hindu monk.

the cause of the intellect as the best antidote to blind faith. Whereupon he would calmly enjoin: "But the proof of the pudding is in the eating thereof, my friends! If blind faith could dower us with the *Shivanetra* [the Third Eye], I would gladly be blind to the drab chimera of this world." And so he went on, undismayed by their concerted attack, like a veritable "Abhimanyu encircled by seven charioteers," as he often described himself with a chortle. And even they had to give him his due, to wit, that he had a remarkable grasp of our epics and scriptures. Nevertheless, a firebrand challenged him one day: "But Mr. Nixon, how can you possibly subscribe to these dangerous superstitions which no wise man should believe?" Pat came the rejoinder: "My dear wise friend, when you will have outgrown your wisdom, it will dawn on you that it is far more dangerous for you not to believe what you should, than to believe what should not be believed. For though in the latter case you may, indeed, land in a pitfall, you can, nevertheless, see it as such and so climb out to resume your journey. But when you disbelieve what you should believe, you topple over into an abyss and break either your neck or limbs or both."

I regret I cannot go on writing about Krishnaprem's swift flowering into a harmonious man of God. Those who want to know more about him I must refer to my books already mentioned. But I must write a few words about his constant encouragement and loving advice in my repeated crises at Pondicherry because I do not think I could have overcome my self-created difficulties had he not infected me with the contagion of his yogic light to instill hope in my hours of dark despair.

What helped him most was, of course, his fundamental sincerity wedded to an astonishing single-mindedness which tided him over many a crisis in his lifelong quest for the goal of *Nitya Vrindavan*—the eternal City of Love where Krishna plays his eternal flute of flame in an eternal garden of beauty.

His devotion to Krishna was not merely breathtaking, it actually bordered on the incredible. In the course of my roaming over four continents I have met a variety of remarkable aspirants but I have never met among foreigners such a single-minded devotee of Krishna with such passionate ardor to win through to His feet. In the pilgrimage of the spirit it is the steadfast aspiration to meet God face to face (*Ishvar-sakshatkar*) that is the pathfinder first and last. His aspiration, which was at once unwavering and incandescent, came to dower him with mystic vision. He not only loved but knew *how* to love. Once he wrote to me: "He who says he knows but does not love does not know and he who says he loves but does not know does not love." That is why Raman Maharshi called him a rare *sadhak*, an aspirant who not only knew at every bend how to tread the thorny wood, *kantaban*, but also how to invoke Krishna's light to illumine the Way, revealing the hidden crevices and pitfalls. So miracles of the Lord's Grace came to his aid at every turn to help him traverse the pathless deserts to reach the oasis sustained by the Lord's loving welcome.

I do not know how to write convincingly about what was so convincing to my vacillating mind—to wit, Krishna's Grace which revived my drooping faith time and time again. Or was it his radiant face that inspired me and dispelled the invasions of God-hostile darkness? Or his unfailing love for an unworthy aspirant like Dilip—a love that, like a floodgate, suddenly opened to wash away in an instant the silt of centuries? I cannot tell. One who gropes in the dark seldom knows how light responds to his *cris de coeur*, or why. All that he knows over and over again—because he forgets, alas, over and over again—is that every aspirant is, in the last analysis, in Tennyson's words:

> An infant crying in the night,
> An infant crying for the light
> With no language but a cry.

Before he received initiation from Yashoda Ma, Yogi Sri Krishnaprem
(Ronald Nixon) had been a professor at Lucknow University.

Krishnaprem told me many a time that this "language" can never fail to move His heart provided one stakes one's all for the All-in-All. It was this reassurance of his that enabled me time and time again to steer clear of the pitfalls on the seemingly endless way that spiraled upward like a mountain path, to quote Goethe's simile.

And then his amazing *gurubhakti*—loyalty to the guru! How to describe the ineffable? It had to be seen to be believed. For such *Bhakti* is not to be had by the practice of austerities, however arduous. It can come only if one prays for it in tears with one's spirit and flesh made one—a divine boon that descends like beneficent rain when the parched earth cries out for it. As a Sanskrit poem has it:

> *Krishnabhakti-rasa-bhavita matih*
> *Kriyatam yadi kutopi labhyate*
> *Tatra lauly amapi mulyam ekalam*
> *Janmakoti sukritair-na labhyate*

> True God-love is not won in a million births
> Merely by dint of deep austerities
> Only he wins to it—the way-lost child
> Who in his heartfelt yearning cries and cries.

It was his final renunciation of worldly life which drove me ultimately to take refuge at the feet of my future guru Sri Aurobindo—but of that I will have more to say later; let me conclude this chapter with four of his heart-warming letters, revealing exhortations which will speak for themselves.

He wrote to me numerous letters—for well over four decades—from 1924 to the end of 1965, when he passed away. A few of his earlier letters I have, alas, lost, but happily I began in Pondicherry to get all his letters duly typed up and preserved. The earliest letter, which is quoted in my book *Yogi Sri Krishnaprem*, refers to my projected visit to Europe for the second time on the way to America. He wrote it from Lucknow on January 22, 1927, my thirtieth birthday.

My dear Dilip,

So you are off to Europe once again. Well, I wish you all luck. . . . I do not, I confess, feel altogether clear about the nature of the *adesh* [Divine Command] spoken of by Sri Rama-krishna. I am not at all sure that the greatest work is not done unconsciously and for no other reason than that the doer intensely wants to do it. Of course, this intense desire may be said to be the *adesh*, but then doesn't the discussion become some-what pointless? Many poets have, no doubt, felt some sort of injunction laid on them, for example, Shelley, Blake, Words-worth and others, but there are many others of whom one doubts it, for example, Shakespeare, Scott, Byron, Chaucer. In one sense I think the doctrine is a dangerous one (whatever sphere it be applied in) as it leads to the intensification of egoism and the idea "I'm going to do something." After all, do we not find "the man with a mission" one of the most tiresome types of humanity and is not our instinct probably right in the matter? Of course it might be replied that the man with a mission to whom I refer means a man with a pseudo-mission—*mithya adesh* —but this is a difficult point. . . . Then of course there is a further question: Were not Sri Ramakrishna's remarks made in reference to a man seeking to "help others" or influence others or serve others or some such phrase? Does the great artist con-cern himself with "others" at all? Does he not create because he must, in order to relieve himself of what he has in him? I agree with you: now-a-days we tend to overestimate the power of art, and take the view that art is *sadhana*, or spiritual initiation. But is it? Of course great art can, to a certain extent, take one out of oneself and render one (though perhaps only in a mild and metaphorical manner) independent of space, time and circum-stance. However, so can many other enjoyments if pursued ardently enough. Doubtless *all* activities can become part of a *sadhana*, if suitably engaged in. But when all is said, the fact remains that there *is* a difference between Yoga as a *sadhana* and Art as a *sadhana*. Artists, you will say, or at least some artists, urge that art can be *used* as a *sadhana*. But to this platitude the only reply is a counter-platitude: that anything could be taken as a *sadhana* (e.g. battle of Kurukshetra). To this the art-enthusiasts will reply in an injured tone that art enriches our spiritual life. I wonder. I fancy it would not be difficult to maintain that art is a substitute—a surrogate for spiritual life: in Bacon's words, "the shows of things are submitted to the desires of the mind." Shelley has defined poetry as "the record of the best and happiest moments of the happiest and best minds." This is not a bad definition, much better than many more pretentious ones. But can one seriously maintain that the keeping of such a record amounts to a *sadhana*? Isn't it as vague as Rolland's pale internationalism? I used once to believe in such vague consolations, but I am now beginning to have my doubts whether all this is as satisfactory as is claimed. For myself, though I can be tolerant to all countries, I have only one, and that, strange to say, is not England but India. What I feel is, that the wealth of tradition which *is* a nation is too precious a thing to be merged into a common hotch-potch the same from London to Yokohama. If we confine ourselves to Europe (at least Western Europe) the case is somewhat different as the traditions are more or less common; but can England and India, say, be mixed so philanthropically without doing vital injury to both? When the traditions of a nation die, then that nation is dead, and even if it persists as a great Power in the world, yet it is nothing but an aggregate of meaningless individuals determinedly pursuing their contemptible aims. . . . History is a symbol, and what that symbol signifies is something infinitely more precious than a mere piddling adherence to a sequence of so-called "facts." There is only one root fact anywhere, and that is the Eternal One. Whatever helps to reveal Him is a fact, and whatever tends to hide Him is a lie even if all the fools in the world affirm it.

To come now to Russell's delightfully vague and confident panacea. He has a clear mind, I grant you, but what is the good to you or me of all this stuff about education and atheism? Even a mediocre seeker after truth who really believes seems to me nearer the truth and also more of a real man than all Russell's enlightened, free-thinking, cosmopolitan "humanist" sceptics.

Yours affectionately,
Ronald

The second letter dates from many years later, after I had taken refuge at the feet of my guru, Sri Aurobindo. The context is that I felt very unhappy because a few of my *gurubhais*, brother disciples, warned me against worshipping Krishna as that would amount to being disloyal to my guru. So I wrote to Krishnaprem that though Sir Aurobindo had reassured me that there was no incompatibility between his Integral Yoga and Krishna-worship, I could not help but feel a deep malaise, swimming against the current. But what on earth was I to do? Give up my guru? Impossible! Give up Krishna? Unthinkable. And so I went on with my jeremiad, asking him to give me a clue to light in my half-lit labyrinth of indecision. He replied with his characteristic clarity and understanding:

Almora
January 17, 1942

My dear Dilip,

I was very glad to get your letter and poems. I do, I think, understand the special difficulties under which you work and if I have never alluded to them it was rather for fear of seeming to criticise in any way than because I did not realise their existence. However, as you ask me to write as frankly as possible, I will do so.

To my thinking, it is quite out of the question for you to "give up wanting Krishna and using His Name." There can be no question of disloyalty to your Guru in so doing and I am glad that Sri Aurobindo's letter has set your mind at rest on that point. The traditional names and acts of those great figures of the past are, every one of them, windows through which the Real is easily evolved. . . .

There is only one complete Yoga: all so-called different Yogas are partial aspects of it which represent only the partial aspirations of certain people. He who would go the whole of the Way must find the whole Yoga, whether he starts from the *Upanishad*, Patanjali's *ashtanga* Yoga, Vaishnavism or from anywhere else. *Krishnat param kimapi tattwam aham na jane* [I do not know what Truth there can be beyond Krishna]—the

words are not mine but those of the great Vedantist Madhu-
sudhan Saraswati. But Krishna can be seen in many ways and
under many partial aspects. It is certain, however, that He will
never fail anyone nor leave him, saying: "Thus far with me but
no farther." Presentations of *Yoga* may vary; inadequate ones
may have to be criticised; new words may have to be found to
replace those that have become stereotyped in time; but Yoga is
one and eternal. When man first appeared on this earth it was
down the Ladder of Yoga that he came. When the last man
leaves this Earth it will be up that same Ladder that he will
climb. The Ladder is *one*. There is no other. Ways and means
may and do differ from man to man, each of whom has his special difficulties, but the Ladder itself is one. I speak, however
inadequately, of what I know to be the Truth. Take it or leave
it.

I sympathise with you for your feeling of the lack of personal contact with your *Guru* and can well understand how hard
it must make things. That is a matter, though, which is not in
your power to alter. I, personally, should find it very difficult,
but—as the *Gita* says—"Over that which is inevitable thou
shouldst not grieve." If you can't have it at present, then you
can't, and there is nothing to be done but to set your teeth and
get on with it.

When I read your letter to Ma, she said: "Tell him to look
for Krishna within and not without and that he will see Him
when he cares for nothing else but Him."

Speaking for myself, I know there was a time when it used to
irritate me if people talked too much of "within." I felt I wanted
to see Him without, but I have since understood that one must
first see Him within and then only He is seen everywhere. For
the rest, it is quite true that one's heart must be full of the desire
for Him. It is hardly my place to say it, but as you have asked
me to, I would say that you still perhaps care for too many
things besides Him. For instance, music and poetry in themselves
and the admiration they bring you. As expression of your feelings for Him they are admirable. They can even be admirable
things in themselves for some people but not for you. You have
made progress in music and poetry and all your friends are
delighted? But what will it profit you if, in the process, your
egoism should have increased? I am not speaking *de haut en bas*

[as a superior to an inferior], as they say, for I speak of my own difficulties. Except in relation to your Goal all these things— music, poetry, philosophy, et cetera—are empty, thrice-empty. Read the passage in Tennyson's "Holy Grail" where Percival describes the Waste Land where everything turned to dust and the Bridge that led far out into the Sea. We should not, like Percival, potter about dismayed by the Waste Land nor even spend our time wringing poetry out of the evanescence, but, like Galahad, leap for the Bridge. Don't tell me that in your *Yoga* this world is not the Waste Land but the garment of the Divine. When the Grail was reached and the wound of its Keeper healed, then and only then did the waters flow once more over the Waste Land, fertilising as they flowed.

"All is not phantom," you say in your poem. I tell you all is phantom unless He be seen who is the only Real. See Him and all is His garment: see Him not and all is the merest phantom. What is Maya?—you ask. To see anything whatsoever apart from Him: that is the Illusion—the source of sorrow. There are no "emanations," no "creations"—no things at all apart from Him. All those are so many words which describe deluded ways of seeing. See them and you do not see Him. See Him and you see that all is Him—nothing has vanished, nothing is lost, nothing is rejected: seeing Him you see that all is Him and, He is all. What we call the beauty of the sky, the great spaces of air, the life-giving flow of water, the bright power of fire—all these are Him. See them as separate and you find yourself in the arid desert of scientific nonsense. See Him and they are seen to be the ever-living Gods who form His limbs, eternal as He is eternal.

You say you find it hard to go on. That is a good sign. This path is the hardest path in the world and as long as we find it easy we may be sure we are not getting very far but just free-wheeling easily along a level road. Oh yes, we may be happy and peaceful for a time but that happiness or peace is illusory: anything can disturb it and we achieve nothing. *His* peace is something quite different, something that has its being in the very heart of tremendous winds, winds which would shatter us to atoms. It is only when the strain begins to tell on us, when the breath comes short, that we can know that we are really climbing. Till then all that we have done at most is to go over rapidly the ground we covered in a previous life. This life begins when the strain comes on—scarcely before. There is no attainment of Him, until the egg-shell of self is broken. Why then should we complain when the breaking-strain begins to come on? With pain we are born both physically and spiritually, but it is the inner life that we seek and not the self-enwrapped bliss of uterine existence.

Fill yourself with Krishna, occupy your thoughts with Him and let all your actions be for Him. Surely you will find Him. Do not think that this will be disloyal to anyone, for this is the "surrender" of which you write and he who teaches you will teach you this.

Why worry over what your fellows around you say or do? Each of us has his own egg-shell cracked. Some are cracked one way, some another, but all are broken in the end. As for the "personal independence" of which you write—that is a dream. You can never have it and even if you did, it would be hell, for it means separateness.

As for those who say that seeking Krishna has no part in their *Yoga*—that is the ignorant talk of those who do not know who Krishna is and vainly plume themselves on their own vain ignorance of "all that old stuff." Paris fashions in *Yoga!*

See Krishna, think of Krishna, act for Krishna, and, if you believe me, you will find Krishna with the utmost certainty though the world should crack and open up beneath your feet. This is the Truth. All else but Him is nothing, absolutely nothing.

Love and blessings from Ma. Moti also sends love and *Pranams*.

Love always from,

Yours affectionately,
Krishnaprem

Now for his last two letters. Here is the context:

I received in April, 1965, a letter from his disciple Ashish that Krishnaprem was very seriously ill due to a dread intestinal infection. I wrote back at once suggesting he come to Poona to be treated by the best doctors here. If necessary I would send somebody to fetch him via Delhi and Bombay by air. To that he replied:

Almora
April 26, 1965

Dear Dilip,

I am much moved by the love and concern expressed by you and Indira in your letters received yesterday, and of your invitation to come to Poona and be looked after. What can I say except that I know how deeply it comes from your heart.

But do not be anxious. The Hands that have brought me so far are still holding the wheel of my life. I think its course is not yet run, the voyage not yet finished. Anyhow, my dear, *let us trust Him—we have no other, first, last or in the middle.*

My love to you both and may His blessings be with us all.

Affectionately yours always,
Krishnaprem

Now to append his last letter four weeks before his passing:

Almora
October 17, 1965

Dilip dear,

First of all, all loving Vijoya embraces to you, all affectionate blessings to Indira.

We came back here a few days ago and are carrying on the treatment that the doctor—a very experienced man and an old friend—has prescribed. Your offers of paying for my treatment, check-up, et cetera, at Poona or Lucknow and of sending me and Ashish air-passage from here to your Guest House are, my dear, just what could be expected of your loving heart and touched me very much and I would have loved to come, if only to see you, but I really don't feel that I could undertake a long journey. As for treatment—as you see, I have not refused to go to a doctor—but I do not find any inner sanction for wandering further afield. When Ashish wrote that I didn't expect to be "well" again, he meant that I don't expect just to "get over" it and become again my former self in robust health. The hookworm was merely what brought it to a head and the actual trouble—the ileitis—goes back in its origin some twenty-five years or more. That sort of thing with its resultant organic changes doesn't just clear up and vanish like a thunderstorm in a summer sky, though one may certainly hope for improvements and a build-up of some strength again. In any case, all is in the hands of our Friend and all is well.

In this outer conflict, too, His hand is over all and *satyam eva jayate, nanritam**—that which is based on mere propagandist lies must crumble away. No doubt we have to pay for the mistakes that we or our elected representatives have made in the past but, whatever the difficulties, I personally have full confidence in the outcome. I think that it is the duty of all of us, who have come to know that it is He who is our life, to hold our minds steady that they may be firm platforms from which He can fight. *Jai Chakradhari.*

What more shall I say except, once again, my love to you always,

Affectionately yours.

Krishnaprem

I hoped against hope, but in vain, for he left this earthly vale of tears on November 14, 1965. His final words were "My ship has sailed at last." This phrase, as beautiful in its realization as it was poignant under the circumstances, occurred to me again and again as I wrote in tears:

* *Satyam eva Jayate, Nanritam* is cited from *Mundaka Upanishad*, 3:1-6. It means: Truth alone wins through to victory, not falsehood.

Context: I had written to him about the fine performance of our soldiers in turning back the aggressive hordes of Pakistan, adding that I had often caught myself praying for them in our temple before the Lord and Radharani, not because I am a patriot at heart but because I agree wholeheartedly with Swami Vivekananda when he said in his famous Colombo speech which made history (January 1, 1897): "Formerly, I thought, as every Hindu thinks, that this is the *Punya Bhumi*, the land of Dharma. Today, I stand here and say, with the conviction of Truth, that it is so. Hence have started the founders of religions from the most ancient times, deluging the earth again and again with the pure and perennial waters of spiritual truth. Hence have proceeded the tidal waves of philosophy that have covered the earth—East or West, North or South—and hence again must start the wave which is going to spiritualise the material civilisation of the world. Believe me, my friends, this is going to be. . . ."

Sons of an intellectual age, we scan
And weigh the heart's findings with our mental measures,
Surmising never once that no mind can
Win even a clue to the soul's resplendent treasures.

The more we probe, the more must thought mislead
Till even the meaning of our spirit's birth
Is buried in the din of words that plead
For the reign of trifling truths of temporal worth.

You diagnosed this fatal malady
With an insight born of loyalty to love
And so disowned our reasoned revelry
Whose dire discord your heart could never approve.

O Reason's elect, withal, a citizen
Of stellar climes no mind has ever trod:
Who saw your radiant Face could never again
Doubt faith's deep power of leading us back to God.

11

MY FIRST MEETING WITH
SRI AUROBINDO

K RISHNAPREM'S CONTACT had given a filip to my spiritual
aspiration. But I found, to my dismay, that it came to be
opposed over and over again by my earth-avid proclivities,
to say nothing of the advice of well-meaning friends like
Rabindranath who favored conjugal life and urged me to
get married. The result was that my inner conflicts increased fast till they all but pullulated wherever I looked.
After reading Sri Aurobindo's *Essays on the Gita*, I sought
further guidance from his *Synthesis of Yoga* and other books,
all of which served to further deepen the gulf between me
and my intellectual friends. In the end, emboldened by my
very desperation for the haven I had glimpsed, I wrote
directly to Sri Aurobindo imploring him to give me some
advice about the spiritual quest as well as about its com-
patibility with marital life. He wrote back, or rather one of
his disciples, Suresh Chakravarti, took down what the great
sage had dictated. But as it was a long letter I will give here
only a brief excerpt:

In your own case, everything depends on your ideal. If it is to
lead the ordinary life of vital and physical enjoyments, you can
choose your mate anywhere you like. If it is a nobler ideal like

that of art or music or service to your country, the seeking for a life-companion must be determined not by desire, but by something higher and the woman must have something in her attuned to the psychic part of your being. If your ideal is spiritual life you must think fifty times before you marry. . . . You are given here the general principles only. From their complexity you can easily imagine how difficult it is to give a clear-cut answer. With these data before you, you must decide for yourself.

At the time I was athirst for light—especially light on his yoga. I was then on a musical tour, gleaning data on different styles of our music in different provinces. Though the work still interested me, I could not but admit to myself that my old zest was waning. So my thoughts turned again and again to Sri Aurobindo with the result that I yearned to meet him face to face.

Yet, if I were drawn to yoga, my fanciful conceptions of *sadhana* made me not a little apprehensive. For example, I imagined a life of solemn solitude, awful austerities and desiccating discipline, all of which spelled for me an utter stultification of life. Nor was this mitigated by the fact that mine had been a life of travel, music, laughter and robust optimism which, in Sri Aurobindo's language, support the "vital egoistic life" of worldly activism. Gradually, however, I felt myself being won over by Sri Aurobindo's analysis of our world and his idea of evolution from the spiritual point of view. In his masterpiece *The Life Divine* he wrote:

The universe and the individual are the two essential appearances into which the Unknowable descends and through which it has to be approached; for other intermediate collectivities are born only of their interaction. The descent of the supreme Reality is in its nature a self-concealing; and in the descent there are successive levels, in the concealing successive veils. Necessarily, the revelation takes the form of an ascent; and necessarily also the ascent and the revelation are both progressive. For each successive level of descent to the Divine is to man a stage in an ascension; each veil that hides the unknown God becomes for the God-lover and God-seeker an instrument of His unveiling. Out of the rhythmic slumber of material Nature unconscious of the Soul and the Idea that maintain the ordered activities of her energy even in her dumb and mighty material trance, the world struggles into the more quick, varied and disordered rhythm of life labouring on the verges of self-consciousness. Out of Life it struggles upward into Mind in which the unit becomes awake to itself and its world, and in that awakening the universe gains the leverage it required for its supreme work,—it gains self-conscious individuality. But Mind takes up the work to continue, not to complete it. It is a labourer of acute but limited intelligence who takes the confused materials offered by Life and, having improved, adapted, varied, classified according to its powers, hands them over to the supreme Artist of our divine manhood. That Artist dwells in Supermind; for supermind is superman. Therefore our world has yet to climb beyond Mind to a higher principle, a higher status, a higher dynamism in which the universe and individual become aware of and possess that which they both are and therefore stand explained to each other, in harmony with each other, unified.

The ascent to the divine Life is the human journey, the Work of works, the acceptable Sacrifice. This alone is man's real business in the world and the justification of his existence, without which he would be only an insect crawling among other ephemeral insects on a speck of surface mud and water which has managed to form itself amid the appalling immensities of the physical universe.*

It was in January, 1924, that I saw Sri Aurobindo for the first time. I enjoyed the rare privilege of having a long talk with him on the 24th. The next day the duration of the talk was shorter. I kept an elaborate record of all that had passed and this report I sent him subsequently for revision. He approved of it substantially and made only a few minor corrections. Here is the report:

It was about eight in the morning. Sri Aurobindo lived then in the house which stands at the main entrance to the

---

* Chapter VI, "Man in the Universe."

Sri Aurobindo. "A deep aura of peace encircled him, an ineffable yet concrete peace that drew you almost at once into its magic orbit."

ashram. He was seated in a chair on the front veranda. I bowed before him and took another chair in front. An oblong table stood between us.

"A radiant personality!" sang the very air about him. A deep aura of peace encircled him, an ineffable yet concrete peace that drew you almost at once into its magic orbit. But it was his eyes that fascinated me most—shining like beacons. His torso was bare except for a scarf thrown across.

"The greatest living yogi of India!"—my heart beat fast. Hitherto I had seen but a few sadhus and *sannyasis*, but here was a real yogi, who lived thus for years in seclusion and yet took some interest in my doings.

He appraised me with his soothing yet penetrative gaze. It would be impossible to adequately portray my reactions. After a time, with some effort, I pulled myself together.

"I have come," I stammered out, "to know . . . to ascertain rather . . . if I can be initiated . . . I mean I want to practice your yoga to start with, if possible."

He answered simply: "You must tell me first what it is exactly that you seek, and why you want to do *my* yoga."

I was lost! Why? Did I know myself? How, then, to put it all clearly and cogently? I strove hard to find some light in my bewilderment.

"Suppose," I found tongue at last, "I suggested—or rather suffer me to ask if you could help me in attaining, or shall we say discovering, the object of life?"

"That is not an easy question to answer," he said, "for I know of no one desideratum which is cherished equally by all, any more than I know of an object of life equally treasured by all. The object or aim of life cannot but vary with various people, and seekers, too, approach yoga with diverse aims. Some want to practice yoga to get away from life, like the *mayavadi* [illusionists]: these want to renounce life altogether, since this phenomenal life, they contend, is an illusion, *maya*, which hides the ultimate reality. There are others who aspire after a supreme love or bliss. Yet others want from yoga power or knowledge or a tranquil poise impervious to the shocks of life. So you must first of all be definite as to what, precisely, you seek in yoga."

"I want to know," I proffered desperately, "if yoga could, in the last resort, lead to a solution of the anomalies of life with all its native sufferings and humiliations."

"You mean transcendent knowledge?"

"If you like—but then, no—for I want bliss, too, crowning this wisdom."

"You can certainly get either from yoga."

"May I, then, aspire to an initiation from you?"

"You may, provided you agree to its conditions and your call is strong."

"Couldn't you give me an idea about the nature of these conditions . . . and about this call you speak of . . . may I ask what you mean exactly? I gathered from your booklet *Yogic Sadhan*," I pursued before he could reply to my question, "that you call yourself a *Tantrik* who believes in *lila* [play, as the ultimate reason for cosmic manifestation], and not a follower of Shankara believing in *maya*. You have written for instance: 'To fulfill God in life is man's manhood.' And if my memory doesn't fail me, you said in your *Life Divine:* 'We must accept the many-sidedness of the Manifestation even while we assert the unity of the Manifested.'"

"It is true that I am a believer in *lila*," he nodded. "But why exactly do you refer to that?"

"I wanted to make sure whether you really meant what you wrote in your *Yogic Sadhan*. I hope, too, that your yoga doesn't make it binding on one to live like a cave-dweller who disowns the many-mooded active life or, shall we say, like a passive pensioner whose day is done? This hope, happily, has been fostered by your repudiation of *mayavada*."

"I see what you mean," he said, giving me an indulgent

smile. "Well, yes, I am not a *mayavadi*, happily for you as well as for me. But incidentally, I am not the author of the book *Yogic Sadhan*."

"How do you mean?"

"Haven't you heard of automatic writing?"

"Planchette?"

"Not exactly. I merely held the pen while a disembodied being wrote off what he wished, using my pen and hand."

"May I ask why you lent yourself to such writing?"

"At the time I was trying to find out how much of truth and how much of subliminal suggestion from the submerged consciousness there might be in phenomena of this kind. But let that pass," he added. "To return to your main question. You asked about the active life. Well, it isn't binding on you to renounce all that you value in your active life. What you must be ready to renounce is attachment to *everything* on that plane, whether you live within or outside the wheel of *karma* [action]. For if you keep these attachments, the Light from above will not be able to work unhampered to effect the radical transformation of your nature."

"Does that imply that I must forgo, say, all human sympathy and true friendship, all joy of life and fellow-feeling?"

"It doesn't. Absence of love and fellow-feeling is not necessary to the Divine nearness; on the contrary, a sense of closeness and oneness with others is a part of the Divine consciousness into which the *Sadhaka* enters by nearness to the Divine and the feeling of oneness with the Divine. An entire rejection of all relations is, indeed, the final aim of the *Mayavadin*, and in the ascetic yoga an entire loss of all relations of friendship and affection and attachment to the world and its living beings would be regarded as a promising sign of advance toward *moksha* [liberation]. But even there, I think a feeling of oneness and unattached spiritual sympathy for all is at least a penultimate stage, like the compassion of the Buddhist before turning to *moksha* or *nirvana*."

The conversation then turned back to my *grande passion*, music. To put it in a nutshell, I felt that I was ready to renounce everything for yoga *except* my music. He smiled and said that in his yoga the surrender must be unconditional —in other words, if I were asked to give up music I must be ready to jettison it at once. He added: "The truth of the matter is this: so long as the joys which belong to the lower planes continue to be too vividly real and covetable, you will find ready enough reasons why you shouldn't decline them. You can forgo them only when you have had the call of the higher joys, when the lower ones begin to pall, sound hollow. The Promised Land of the Spirit begins from the frontier of worldly enjoyments to start with."

"But why is it," I asked after a pause, "that one can't expect to have even a glimpse beforehand of this Land? Because of the thick walls of our worldly desires?"

"Your premise is not quite correct," he objected. "For even when we live in the world of these desires the glimpse, the call, comes to us, through chinks and rifts of dissatisfaction and surfeit. Only, it doesn't last long until you are somewhat purified, for then only do you really begin to be open to it. The darkness returns intermittently after the light because it takes a long time to get our whole being open to the light. That is why yoga pushes us urgently upward to altitudes where the light can be shut out no more by clouds. And it is just because yoga is such an ascent of consciousness that any attachment to or desire for lures and laurels on the lower planes, material, intellectual or aesthetic, must eventually prove a shackle."

"Why, then, do you write so appreciatively of materialism as also of the intellectual and aesthetic delights? And why are your own writings so illuminating intellectually? Why have you praised art? Why write that 'The highest aim of the aesthetic being is to find the Divine through Beauty'?"

"Why not? Intellect, art, poetry, knowledge of matter,

et cetera, can all help our progress appreciably provided you direct them properly. It is, at bottom, a case of evolution. That is why I once wrote: 'Reason was the helper, Reason is the bar'; which means simply that our intellect can be a help in our evolution only a part of the way. But when it presumes to judge what is beyond its domain, it must be put in its place. Besides, different recipients are differently constituted for different disciplines—seeking different fulfillments, each approaching Truth in *swabhava* [the way of his nature]. In other words, those who are the best recipients for the light of the intellect are *mentally* more evolved than those who are not so gifted intellectually. But it doesn't mean that there are no realizations higher than the mental ones. Assuredly there are, as we can concretely verify as we open ourselves to the realizations of the Spirit, when we find mental joys no longer inadequate, aesthetic joys no longer satisfying. With this opening we glimpse worlds higher than those we have been used to. Do you follow?"

"You mean that yoga enlarges our consciousness more and more?"

"That is my view of evolution," he nodded, "this gradual unfolding of the consciousness ascending to its higher reaches. It is yoga which is to bring down further light and power in the next step of the evolution of human consciousness."

I reverted to my difficulty: "But what about my taking to yoga?"

"Everyone can practice some yoga or other, suited to his nature," he replied noncommittally.

"But my question was about your Integral Yoga—of self-surrender."

"Ah!" he said slowly as though weighing his words. "About that I can't pronounce here and now."

"But why?"

"Because the yoga that I have been pursuing of late—whose aim is the entire and radical transformation of the stuff and fabric of our consciousness and being, including our physical nature—is a very arduous one, fraught with grave perils at every step. In fact, so great are these dangers that I would not advise anybody to run them unless his call is so urgent that he is prepared to stake everything. In other words, I can accept only those with whom yoga has become such a necessity that nothing else seems worthwhile. In your case, it hasn't yet become so urgent. Your seeking is for some sort of partial elucidation of life's mysteries. This is at best an intellectual seeking—not an urgent need of the central being."

"Allow me to explain a little further," I said with a keen sense of disappointment, "for I am afraid you haven't quite seen where the shoe pinches. I can assure you that mine is not merely a mental curiosity."

"I said *seeking*, not *curiosity*," he amended. "And I referred to the present only: I did not mean this could not develop later on into a real need of your central being."

"Let me make it more explicit all the same," I insisted. I then gave him a fairly long recital of my woes and doubts, at first personal, but concluding with the widespread misery and fears of humanity.

"I quite see your difficulty," he said softly. "For I, too, wanted at one time to transform through my yoga the face of the world. My aim was to change the fundamental nature and movements of humanity, to banish all the evils which afflict helpless mortality."

I felt a heave within—in my very blood. For one like him to talk so intimately to a stranger! Gratitude surged within me and I hung on his words, eager to imbibe the sweet cadences of his serene voice.

"It was with this aspiration that I turned to yoga in the beginning," he added, "and I came to Pondicherry because I had been directed by the Voice to pursue my yoga here."

"I read in the famous letters you wrote to your wife that you had turned to yoga to save our country."

"That's right. I told Lele when agreeing to follow his instructions that I would do his yoga only on condition that it didn't interfere with my poetry and service to the country."

"And then?"

"Lele agreed and gave me initiation. But soon afterward he left, bidding me turn solely to my inner guidance. Since then," he went on, "I have followed only this inner Voice which has led me to develop what I named the Integral Yoga. It was then that my outlook changed with the knowledge born of my new yogic consciousness. I found, to my utter disillusionment, that it was only my ignorance which had led me to believe that the impossible was feasible here and now."

"Ignorance?"

He nodded. "Because I didn't realize then that in order to help humanity out it was not enough for an individual, however great, to achieve an ultimate solution individually: humanity has to be ripe for it, too. For the crux of the difficulty is that even when the Light is ready to descend it cannot come to stay until the lower plane is also ready to bear the pressure of the Descent."

I was reminded of what he had written in his *Essays on the Gita:*

No real peace can be till the heart of man deserves peace; the law of Vishnu cannot prevail till the debt to Rudra is paid. . . . Teachers of the land of love and Oneness there must be, for by that way must come the ultimate salvation, but not till the Time-Spirit in man is ready, can the inner and the ultimate prevail over the outer and immediate reality. Christ and Buddha have come and gone but it is Rudra who still holds the world in the hollow of his hand.

"Consequently," he went on, "the utmost you can do, here and now, is to communicate only partially the light of your realization, in the measure that people are receptive. Even this is not very easy, mind you; for the fact of your having received something does not necessarily make you capable of making a free gift of it to others. You see, capacity to receive is one kind of aptitude, capacity to give—quite another. Indeed, the latter is a very special kind of gift. Some there are who can only imbibe but not communicate, because, for one thing, what you communicate, everybody cannot receive, even when they earnestly want to. To sum up, the number of those is very limited who are capable of both giving and receiving. So you can understand the problem is by no means a simple one. What is one to do? Everybody does not want bliss or enlightenment: men are at different stages of development and this makes any universal panacea for life's evils an impossibility, as the history of human experience has proved again and again."

"But what about the widespread misery and fear and suffering?" I said after a pause.

"How can you help that so long as men choose as they do to hug ignorance, which is at the root of all suffering? As long as they cherish the darkness of attachment rather than the light of liberation and knowledge, how can they expect to see? How would you evade the inexorable law of *karma?*"

"What, then, are you striving for through your yoga?" I insisted. "For your own liberation or fulfillment?"

"No," he said, "that wouldn't have taken so long. But," he added, "it is not possible to answer you more convincingly just now, for if I were to tell you why I am doing yoga, you would either not understand or misunderstand. Suffice it to say that I want to invoke here on earth the light of a higher world, to manifest a new power which will continue to exist as a new influence in the physical world and will be a direct manifestation of the Divine in our entire being and daily life."

"Is this what you have named the Supramental Divine?"

"That's right—though the name is immaterial. What matters is to remember that for a variety of reasons the direct action of the Supramental has never yet been brought to bear on our earth-nature and consciousness."

"Because the time was not favorable for such a descent?"

"Partly. But there were other reasons also which I can't go into as they cannot be communicated through mental language, and so, if attempted, may only lead to fresh mystification."

"But tell me at least if the yogis of yore knew of this Power."

"Some did. But—how can I put the truth of the matter to you?—what happened was that they used to rise individually to this plane and stay there in union: they didn't bring it down to act upon our terrestrial consciousness. Perhaps they did not even attempt to. But I would rather not tell you more about this because, as I said, the mind cannot even glimpse the Supramental Truth, to say nothing of understanding it."

"But on whom and what will this Supramental work?" I asked.

"Why, on our life-material, of course—down to matter and the physical."

"Didn't the ancient yogis attempt this either?"

"Not with the Supramental instrumentation. Their preoccupation was not so much with our basic material-physical, because to transform it with the spiritual force is the most difficult of all achievements. But that is precisely why it must be achieved."

"But does the Divine seriously want such a tremendous thing to be achieved?"

"As to whether the Divine seriously means something to happen, I believe it is intended. I know with absolute certitude that the Supramental is a truth and that its advent is in the nature of things inevitable. The question is as to the when and the how. That also is decided and predestined from somewhere above; but it is here being fought out amid rather a grim clash of conflicting forces."

"Forgive me, I don't quite follow this."

"I know," he intervened, "for it is somewhat abstruse. It is

"At the time I was athirst for Light. Yet, if I were drawn to yoga, my fanciful conceptions of *sadhana* made me not a little apprehensive."

like this. In the terrestrial world the predetermined result is hidden and what we see is a whirl of possibilities and forces attempting to achieve something, with the destiny of it all concealed from human eyes. This is, however, certain: that a number of souls have been sent to see that it shall be achieved here and now. That is the situation."

"Please be a little more explicit."

"To say more would be going beyond the line."

"But tell me at least when the miracle will happen."

"You don't want me to start prophesying. As a rationalist, you can't."

"But tell me one thing," I said, flying off at another tangent. "Didn't any of your predecessors make this attempt—I mean what you call the integral transformation of the physical consciousness?"

"The attempt might have been made, it is not certain. But what is certain is that nothing decisive was achieved on the physical plane."

"How do you infer that?"

"Because all achievements leave some legacy of traces for posterity to follow up. A spiritual realization once completely achieved could never be wholly obliterated afterward."

"You must, then, realize it yourself first?"

"Obviously. Be it a new realization or light or idea—it must first descend into one person from whom it radiates out in widening circles to others. Doesn't the Gita, too, say that the ways of the best of men act as models to the rest? In the Integral Yoga, however, the work starts *after* the realization, whereas in most other yogas it *ends* with the realization. The reason is that I aim primarily at manifestation, for which I must, obviously, reach the Supramental myself before I can bring it to bear on our earth-consciousness. For this, ascent has to be the first step—descent is the next."

"How will the descent work, to start with?"

"When the Supramental touches our being, our consciousness will overpass its twilit stage of the mental, where the

Divine Truth is distorted, into the upper regions where light has free play, that is, where there are no such distortions. This will in its turn bring about the transformation of mind, life and body, as that will be one of the functions of the Force at its inception in the world of matter, generally—to usher in subsequently the new era in man's living. You must not misunderstand me. What I want to achieve is the bringing down of the Supramental to bear on this being of ours so as to raise it to a level higher than the mental and from there change and sublimate the workings of mind, life and body. But this is not to say that Supramentalization will be effectuated overnight so that all will be completely transformed. That is hardly feasible."

"Because we are not mature for such a transformation?"

"Not only that—there are other obstinate impediments and hostile forces to reckon with. This world of matter has been for ages the bulwark of darkness, falsehood's most redoubtable citadel where, hitherto, inertia has reigned supreme. To carry there the message of Truth, to make it responsive to the shock of Light is far from easy. Yet the Supramental power can work its way if once it can descend there; that is to say, if once the earth-consciousness can bear it to start with."

"Suppose it does, on whom will the Force be dynamic in its inception?"

"On those who have acquired the power to be its medium or vehicle. Each of these will serve as an indicator of what humanity is potentially capable of becoming, once it is transformed. Do you follow?"

"After a fashion, I suppose," I said. "But tell me, please, if this power or influence will benefit many or only a handful of isolated individuals here and there."

"Many, certainly. My Integral Yoga would be of little use if it were meant for one or two individuals. For you must remember that my object is not the abandonment of the phys-ical-material life to drift by itself but the fundamental transformation of it by the power of this higher light and seeing."

"But I hope your followers and successors won't have to emulate you in your superhuman *sadhana* if they are to arrive?"

"No." Sri Aurobindo smiled. "And that was what I really meant when I said a little while ago that my yoga was meant for humanity. The first that hews his way through a trackless jungle acts necessarily as the pathfinder, clearing the way for his followers. He faces much to make it easier for his successors."

I was reminded of a saying of the great yogi Sri Ramakrishna: "The man who makes a fire has to take a lot of trouble but, once lit, all who come near may safely reap the benefit of its warmth." As I pondered the significance of this simile, a deep sense of reverence pervaded my being. I wondered how few of us even imagined that such a man was living in our midst! But then, hasn't it always been so from time immemorial? How many truly appraised the greatness of Sri Ramakrishna during his lifetime? I felt suddenly a strong impulse to make Sri Aurobindo my obeisance once more. I restrained myself with effort.

His gaze was on me, unwaveringly. Suddenly I felt a curious upsurge of skepticism so utterly out of tune with my nascent adoration.

"But are you convinced it will be possible—really feasible?" I said.

"For a single individual I have *seen* it to be possible," he emphasized. "For I have *seen* the working of this tremendous victorious Force annihilating at a sweep the forces of darkness and inertia which conspire to keep the spirit under the thrall of matter and flesh. To give a concrete instance: a yogi could here and now achieve complete immunity from the forces of disease if he could isolate himself completely from his surroundings."

"But why does he fail when he reverts to the world?"

"Because of the universal suggestion of disease when he comes out of his seclusion."

My skepticism took yet another line. "But do you think this to be such a great achievement, after all, seeing that even the great Buddha attached so little importance to the physical aspect of our suffering?"

"You forget Buddha had a different outlook on life, a different object. He wanted through *nirvana* a final exit from this phenomenal world of the senses. It may be that at that stage of our human evolution man was not mature enough for a greater realization. But whatever the reason, you cannot get away from the fact that Buddha wanted fulfillment by turning away from all play of expression which is life's mode of self-manifestation, whereas I want its transformation, complete transformation. My aim is not to disown life but to transmute it through the alchemy of the light of the Spirit."

For some time I did not know what to say next. Then a sort of curiosity—or, shall I say, eagerness—got the better of me in spite of my misgivings.

"But what about my yoga?" I brought myself to say apropos of nothing. The next moment I felt a strange self-questioning: was I really calling for an answer? I could not quite decide.

His glance cut into me like a knife. "Yours is still a mental seeking," he said. "For my yoga something more is needed. Why not wait till the time comes?"

"When it does, may I count on your help?" I asked anxiously.

He gave an affirmative nod and smiled.

12

MADAME CALVÉ AND
PAUL RICHARD

So it turned out that my petition was rejected by Sri Aurobindo because I did not yet feel the urge to stake my all for the One-in-All. But paradoxical though it may sound, I felt an intense relief for days on end that he had not accepted me as his disciple. I told myself that as my hour had not yet struck, I might browse and graze far afield to my heart's content. When I told Krishnaprem this he pondered a little and then said that he felt that Krishna's flute-call would come to wean me away from my bondage once and for all sooner than I expected.

I left it at that and went on with my musical peregrinations, singing and learning and reading and giving charity concerts to help the derelicts, political *détenus* and artists who wanted to cross the seas to study art abroad.

But the void remained a void till, in January, 1927, an invitation came from America to make records in New York.

Subhash, who had an inkling of my growing nostalgia for the unattainable and feared that I might make a beeline for Pondicherry, acclaimed the invitation enthusiastically. He urged me to accept and convened a great meeting at the University Institute to give me a spectacular send-off. The great novelist Saratchandra Chatterji—who likewise disapproved of yoga in cloistered seclusion—consented to preside, and Rabindranath himself came to bless me publicly.

I disembarked at Marseilles, having decided to visit Nice, Paris and England once more. Lord Russell had written to me that he would be pleased to meet me in England. I wanted to ask him about the place and function of reason in life, for doubts gnawed at my heartstrings about its claim to be the master light in our quest for Truth.

I reached Nice in March, 1927, and found the Côte d'Azur lovely and soothing. I spent most of my time reading the books of Russell and Sri Aurobindo and, morning and evening, strolled, musing, along the promenade by the blue Mediterranean. Blue has always been my favorite color because Krishna's aura is blue, as has been attested by all the great sages who have visioned Him. So the call of the azure induced in me a keen and sweet nostalgia for Krishna; but there I had to cry halt, for I did not, in 1927, want as yet to stake my all. The vacillation was unpleasant, to put it mildly. I often caught myself wondering whether I should go to America at all. Rabindranath Tagore had told me that he had not felt happy in New York, a dampening remark which recurred to me again and again.

I came to know in Nice a hospitable Swedish countess who invited me to sing in her beautiful salon. I complied and at the end of my songs discoursed in French about our Indian music. But, to my sorrow, I found very little pleasure in being applauded. Their acclamation did titillate me, but only for the nonce. Thereafter, again, the nostalgia resumed its sway. It was an *impasse véritable*.

At the salon of the countess I met an unforgettable character: Madame Emma Calvé, the beautiful and famous prima donna, known in India as an illustrious devotee of Swami Vivekananda.

She related to me how she had met Swamiji. Briefly, she had been passing through an emotional crisis when someone told her that a Hindu saint who was a remarkable savant and spiritual healer had come to America. Madame Calvé was skeptical; nevertheless, prompted by curiosity, she had gone to see him.

When she entered Swamiji's room, he was still absorbed in meditation and seemed unaware of her presence. This was a novel experience for the prima donna who, pricked by her old doubts, grew momently more restive. Just as she started up, however, he said to her: "Please don't leave, mother, I will be with you in a little while." Madame Calvé was so struck by the innocence of his address that she silently resumed her seat and began to contemplate the mystic whom she now perceived to be a marvelous and radiant personality. And such was the miracle of his presence that, overnight, the course of her life was entirely changed as though by the flourish of some magician's wand.

Her eyes glistened whenever she talked of him. "He was indeed a wizard, Monsieur Roy," she said, "a divine wizard such as rarely comes to our world of dust and din, strife and hate. Do you know that he at once told me everything that had been troubling me, intimate things such as no one else could possibly have known."

And then she went on talking ecstatically about how "he was wont to awaken in his audience the dormant divinity. Yes, *monsieur*," she averred, "he was a true Illuminate. No wonder he had the mystic power to kindle in my heart the light by which I could see my path and follow the clue to deliverance from my deep heartache. . . . And it was not a mere flashlight. When he talked about the ultimate realities as against the illusions of our phantom world of desires we used to hang on his every word. Was there a subject he could not discourse on felicitously? The ancient civilizations and their contributions; faith's periodic decadence and revival; the power of the sages to create the ardency of devotion; the epiphany of the Infinite manifested hourly through miracles —and, above all, the greatness of his divine Master, the Guru of gurus, Sri Ramakrishna. Yes, *monsieur*, Swamiji stressed time and again that his great guru was Truth, Love and Purity incarnate who came to us uninvited to show us the Way to Love Divine. . . ." Her voice quavered when she talked of "Swamiji's deep emotion for the sinless Saint of saints whose worship of Truth in the temple of Love led to Bliss everlasting which laughed to scorn 'the slings and arrows of outrageous fortune,'" and so she raced on in raptures while reminiscing. I have put it all in my own language and idiom but she did break out into ecstasy in her lovely French, which sounded like music to my beauty-avid ears. And I may truthfully say that the unshakable flame Swamiji had kindled in his devotee's heart enabled me to glimpse some new aspect of his greatness which had not occurred to me before.

Once when she was talking in this ecstatic vein, I was moved to my depths by her childlike urge to worship Swamiji as a *vibhuti*, or missionary power of the Lord.

"I was greatly relieved by this urge, Monsieur Roy," she said, "because I had inhibited it, afraid of the titter of my fashionable friends who dubbed it an anthropomorphic superstition. Why, they went so far as to brand it a blasphemy, if not indeed a crime against humanity. Can you imagine that?"

I smiled and commented: "But, *madame*, very few people really understand the profound truth which ensouls such worship. That is why Swamiji once admonished his disciple Nivedita: 'You do not yet understand India! We Indians are Man-worshippers after all! Our God is man. . . . You may always say the Image is God: the error you have to avoid is to think God the Image.'"*

Madame Calvé unwittingly deepened my clinging regret that I was straying away from the path of this true worship. I grew more and more listless when a strange coincidence thrilled me to the core:

I was out, brooding, on the promenade by the sea and

---

* Sister Nivedita, *My Master As I Saw Him*, Calcutta: Udbodhan Office.

thinking of Vladamir Vanek, a dear friend I had not seen since my previous trip to the Continent. Vladia, as he had asked me to call him, was an idealist and mystic seeker though outwardly very much engaged in worldly duties. When I had last been in touch with him he was living in Paris where he served as the vice-consul of Czechoslovakia. I wondered if Vladia and his wife Marthe were still in France and whether I should try to see them for a few days before flying to England. I had just decided to send him a wire when, amazing to say, Vladia's dear voice startled me: *"Mon Dieu! C'est notre Dilip!"*

The next moment he enfolded me in his warm embrace. Then he said accusingly: "Why didn't you let us know you are here? Suppose we hadn't run across you thus accidentally, we might never have met in Nice!"

This coincidence did quicken my mystic tendency to marvel. For Vladia had endeared himself to me primarily by his Slavic mysticism, which is not far removed from our Indian mystic's *Weltanschauung*. Years later I was to read in Sri Aurobindo's *Savitri*:

> The world is not built with random bricks of chance,
> A blind God is not destiny's architect,
> A conscious power has drawn the plan of life,
> There is a meaning in each curve and line. (VI, II)

When I look back on my second visit to Europe I can almost visualize again my earth-averse mood (*vairagya*) waxing steadily through everything I encountered: my visit to Nice where peace reigned in the realm of beauty, my discoursing again and again on devotional music (the songs I used to translate into French with the help of Vladia and Marthe), our discussions on the Indian outlook on life and last, though not least, the sudden visit of Paul Richard. Vladia and Marthe suggested that I stay in their hotel and use their suite as my own. It was rather an expensive hotel but I consented because I wanted to be with them all the time. It was, indeed, delightful and we "tired the sun with talking and sent him down the sky," to the soothing accompaniment of the subdued song of the mystic deep. I was delighted, but paradoxical though it may sound, I grew, withal, more listless because our discussions constantly hovered around our beloved query: how to find a short cut to the soul's awakening. We did not go even once to the cinemas or casinos or dance halls which abounded in Nice. Our life was truly austere in the sense that sense pleasures gave us little relief from our painful nostalgia.

"But then, why are you going to America, Dilip?" Vladia asked.

"Well—er," I stammered, "I don't know." Then with a grin: "Suppose I said it's destiny?"

Marthe bridled.

"No, Dilip, such superstitions should not be encouraged even in jest. Fatalism is the defense of weaklings and weaklings are uninspiring. Anyway, *you* do not belong to their ilk. You belong to the elect, the strong, the robust—those who believe in world-affirmation as against world-negation." And so she went on, fulminating affectionately.

It was rather strange that Marthe at this stage of her evolution should have shed much of her erstwhile feminine charm. She sang now mostly the refrain of Danton's masculine *audace*. But when she heckled us what could we do except hem and haw? For Vladia, too, like me, had a sneaking sympathy for those who believed in destiny—not unqualifiedly but with reservations. But I could not help asking myself often why on earth I was attracted to an outlook which had no affinity with the rationalist philosophy I loved? Why did I vacillate whenever I was called upon to take a definite stand? Last, though not least, why are men constantly called to flock to a flag other than the one under which they are born and to which they owe allegiance? We vaunt indeed, in season and out of season, that we are born free. But are we really free even in our thoughts not to mention our actions? Do not invisible forces sway us at every turn and drive us along paths we never once chose to tread? Here Vladia supported me but not Marthe. She felicitated me on my bold decision to cross the seven seas. But why then, in the name of good sense, did I still hesitate—waver? I quoted Shelley with a defensive smile: "We look before and after and pine for what is not—"

"There again!" she cut in, frowning. "You mustn't. Don't fritter away your splendid energy in looking back, pining and sighing. A gifted musician and strong idealist like you must always look ahead. Don't look down when mountain climbing. It will only make you dizzy, which is dangerous." And so she went on in her hortatory vein which effectively silenced us both.

It was at this time that the great Paul Richard visited us at our hotel. Here I must pause and go back a little.

A celebrated author and lecturer, Monsieur Richard had written his first book—an English work—in 1920. Its last chapter was an English translation of his lecture on Sri Aurobindo, delivered in Waseda University, Tokyo. In this lecture he had said that the future would be dominated not by Nietzsche's superman, ruling with his titan ego, but by the divine man of India who would inaugurate a new era and create a new world. He concluded his ringing prophecy with "I have looked for this race for years all over the world till I met in Sri Aurobindo their luminous herald and crowned ruler. His message will transform the world, I tell you, because he has been *missioned*, as a world teacher, to lead humanity to its destined fulfillment."

Years later I read in Sri Aurobindo's *Savitri* (XI, I):

> A mightier race shall inhabit the mortal's world.
> On Nature's luminous tops, on the Spirit's ground,
> The Superman shall reign as king of life,
> Make earth almost a mate and peer of heaven
> And lead towards God and truth man's ignorant heart
> And lift towards godhead his mortality. . . .

In a similar vein, Paul Richard had written in his book *Les Dieux:* "If the empire of land, water and air be the common heritage of men and animals, man alone is the sponsor of the flame, the master of the fire."*

When Paul Richard was still a young man with the dreamlight of a new world glowing in his starry eyes, Rabindranath Tagore had chanced to meet him in Japan. He was so struck by his personality and prophetic accent that he paid him an eloquent tribute:

"When I met Monsieur Richard in Japan, I became more reassured in my mind about the higher era of civilization than when I read about the big schemes which the politicians are formulating for ushering the age of peace into the world . . . when gigantic forces of destruction were holding orgies of fury, I saw this solitary young Frenchman, unknown to fame, . . . his face beaming with the lights of the New Dawn and his voice vibrating with the message of a New Life, and I felt sure that the great Tomorrow had already come, though not registered in the calendar of the statesmen."

Paul Richard made such a deep impression on people not merely because he was a radiant intellectual, but because he was, as he was wont to put it, "a dreamer of real dreams" as well. Years later, Sri Aurobindo wrote about such creative dreams in his *Savitri:*

> If dreams these were or captured images,
> Dream's truth made false earth's vain realities. (II, II)

As usual, we kept a record of what Paul Richard said— Marthe often supplemented my notes with hers. But here I will give only a few samples of his brilliant conversation which are likely to interest all who believe in dreamers and idealists.

Marthe served him coffee in our sitting room.

"Did you know Rabindranath well?" I asked.

* "Si l'homme partage avec tous les êtres l'empire de la terre, de l'eau, de l'air, lui seul est gardien de la flamme, mâitre du feu."

"I told myself that as my hour had not yet struck, I might browse and graze far afield to my heart's content."

He (nodding): "I had long talks with him first in Japan and then in his country house at Shantiniketan where I was his guest.

Marthe: "May I know what was your impression of him?"

Richard: "Oh, he is a great poet all right—to his fingertips." And added: "Descended from the world of beauty and harmony of the *Gandharvas*, the perfect angels. But— well, he hasn't come in contact with the unbeautiful, unlovely —I mean in close contact."

Dilip: "So much the better."

Richard (*shaking his head*): "There I differ from you, Sir. For till one has an intimate knowledge of the dreadful and the diabolical one cannot grow in strength. That is why Rabindranath is so weak in the world of action and movement."

Dilip: "May I know what exactly you mean by growing in strength? Or, to be more precise, who are those whom you consider 'strong'?"

Richard: "Why, Gandhi, Aurobindo. Strong as marble rocks."

Vladia: "Do let us have a little more of your appraisement of Mahatma Gandhi."

Richard: "In Ahmedabad when I was his guest I often disagreed with him violently. But the more I came to know him, the less sure I became of my appraisement of him. I can recall how now and again I used to ask myself: 'Is this frail, lovable man really the king and kingmaker of India?'" (*After a pause*) "But though he is great in strength, he is deficient in imagination. It is there the Poet scores. Gandhi is too obstinate—he can't help it because he has a one-track mind."

Vladia: "Say on, *monsieur*."

Richard: "Well, it's not easy to put it all into words—but I'll try. You see, the world of *dharma*, spirituality, has little in common with the world of politics. If you want to drive a nail into the wall, the hammer will give you the best service, isn't it so? I mean, you would have to be a fool if you wanted to use your spiritual force to drive a nail. Similarly, if you wanted to make use of an intelligent man you could get the quickest results by appealing to his intelligence—coercion would not pay. That is why I used to tell Gandhi that Shiva, the Beneficent God, is not the sole deity—there is Rudra, the Lord of Death, also waiting His hour. In active politics you should steer clear of religion as much as possible, because in its arena of confusion what prevails in the last analysis is the foresight of the statesman."

Dilip: "Do you imply, then, that in the field of politics soul-force cannot deliver the goods?"

Richard: "But why on earth must you import soul-force where a lesser force could act more promptly and yield better harvests? Remember my simile of the hammer and nail. Why must you waste the vast energy of soul-force to bring about a result that could be achieved more quickly by a simpler power? Didn't Krishna say expressly that yoga is skill in works? Didn't the Christ also say that we must give to God and Caesar what is the due of each? When martyrs sacrifice their lives they do so assuredly to promote their ideals. In other words, they see that their sacrifice would invoke a divine intervention sooner and more effectively than their deeds and words could do if they were alive. That a force expressed through life may sometimes be expressed better posthumously is a fact to which history has attested time and time again."

Dilip (*after a pause*): "May I put to you a straight question?"

Richard (*smiles*): "You are a born questioner, aren't you? Go on. I mean, it is a good sign—this itch to question. Wasn't that why Krishna encouraged the mortal Arjuna to prod His divine wisdom again and again?"

Dilip (*smiling*): "But my question is a much simpler one. I want you to tell me frankly your opinion of Sri Aurobindo."

Richard (*after a pause*): "I have not met his peer in the whole world. To me he is the Lord Shiva incarnate."

Marthe: "Please go on, *monsieur*."

Richard: "I can assure you, *madame*, that if Aurobindo came out of his seclusion today he would overtop all others as a king of kings. But he has chosen to decline his country's invitation to resume his leadership—a renunciation I look upon as the most convincing proof of his spiritual royalty."

Marthe: "But aren't there many other yogis also who have renounced their all?"

Richard: "Granted. Only their 'all' hardly adds up to much. I mean, supposing they had remained in the world reaching for worldly laurels, what would they finally have achieved? They were cut out at best to score just a little success by their modest capacities or individual talents. But Sri Aurobindo would have risen to the top in any walk of life—as a philosopher, poet, statesman or leader of thought. But he spurned these lures—why? Only because his vocation was to be an instrument of God missioned to fulfill a human destiny which no other master-builder could have achieved. In this world, *madame*, the most difficult thing is not to attain eminence in this or that walk of life. The feat of feats is to drive *all* your aspirations through one single channel—to be wholly one-pointed, exclusively dedicated to one ideal,*vous comprenez?*"

Marthe: "*Oui, monsieur*. But what exactly is his ideal?"

Richard: "It is that Man must not rest content with his humanity, however brilliant or many-splendored. He has to win through to a new vision and follow it up to reach a peak his predecessors never dared to assault. Nietzsche had indeed heard the call—the call to transcend humanity. Which is why he had said: '*Der Mensch ist etwas das uberwunden werden soll,*' that is, Man must transcend himself by repudiating this humanity he has gloried in so long. But the mistake he made, as Aurobindo has pointed out, is that the one who is going to fulfil humanity is not the superman of power but the Superman of Love who expresses his love through power.

Love is necessary because when it is absent Man becomes not a god but a titan. But power is also necessary because without its support he can't help but fail to translate his ideal of Love into a real flower-fulfillment in the wilderness of life. This is the Call Aurobindo has heard—a call that once heard can be unheard no more. But you cannot hear such a fateful Call till you are chosen by the One on high who leads us on. It is He who has coronated Aurobindo as His Messiah. So march on he must, for harking to His Call has transformed him into what he is today—a herald of the Power that never came down to earth, though it was destined."

Vladia: "But why didn't it come down, since it was destined?"

. Richard: "Because the one who was to invoke it had to be created and perfected before he could be missioned to be its harbinger. God acts not in the void but through His agents who have to be chiseled as out of a rock. A deputy like Sri Aurobindo doesn't grow on every bush, *mon ami*. He has to evolve in His Light through a thousand births. Every cup cannot bear the *soma* [wine] of Love Divine which endows us with the status of the Superman. So Sri Aurobindo had to be waited for as the herald of the Power that never came down to earth—or, shall I say, the invoker of the sacrificial Flame that performs the miracle."

We invited Paul Richard to a vegetarian dinner, as he was a vegetarian. We had the dinner served in our sitting room to enable us to converse more freely.

Marthe: "Did you become a vegetarian to practice yoga?"

Richard: "No. I gave up fish and meat because I could not but agree with Shaw that it is shameful to eat the dead bodies of animals."

Dilip: "But haven't the scientists proved by now that vegetables, too, have life?"

Richard: "We summon such evidence, Dilip, to defend our greed for a nonvegetarian diet. We have got to live and to

live we must kill—not only consciously but unconsciously
as well. We kill microbes at every breath; we declare war on
germs with medicines at every turn; we trample millions of
infinitesimal creatures at every step. But is this a valid defense,
rational justification for killing animals? To gorge on poor
birds and ugly beasts—*quelle horreur!*"

Marthe (*smiling*): "Do you imply, then, that gorging on
human flesh would be less abhorrent?"

Richard: "Assuredly. For just think, *madame!* You love a
human being. You kiss him, caress him and thrill to his contact. If you ate such a being after his death it would at least
be understandable. But a beast you loathe, whose very shadow you dread to cross, whose name has become a term of
abuse and curse—*cochon* [swine]—such a creature you do
not only caress with your tongue but dispatch to your interior to be nurtured in your blood—what could be more
revolting on earth, I ask you?" (*With a smile*) "That is
why, *madame*, to expiate for this deep crime of humanity
against the good beasts, I always take my hat off reverently
whenever I pass by a butcher's shop."

And one of the most engaging traits of his magnetic
personality was that he was not only a thinker who opened
new vistas in the course of his brilliant talks but a scintillating
wit as well—a satirist par excellence who could turn out
epigrams with a regal ease. I noted in my diary a few of these:

*Dimanche: le jour où Dieu s'étant reposé, ses fidèles l'en
remercient.* (God rested on the sabbath, so on Sundays His
faithful priests thank Him for His abstention.)

*Le conscience est un juge intègre qui ne tourmente que les
bons et qui laisse courir les mauvais.* (Our conscience is an up-
right judge who tortures but the honest folk and lets the
crooks escape.)

Par ennui Dieu créa le monde, par honte depuis il se cache.
(God, feeling bored, created this our world, thereafter from
deep shame He hides Himself.)

13

CONFLICTS AND
RESOLUTIONS

T HAT THE Divine Wisdom plans things years ahead is a
truth that has been promulgated by the mystics since the
dawn of human aspiration. What man calls chance, accident
or coincidence is but a fanfare of words used to drown his
sad ignorance about the scheme of things. Often enough he
plans ahead to achieve a certain result only to fail egregiously
because the plans miscarry. On the other side, he may have
done nothing to deserve Divine Grace or a saint's love but is
sustained by it nonetheless so that his soul may flower into
fulfilment. Sri Aurobindo had said to one of his disciples (A.
B. Purani, who repeated it to me years later) that I was sure
to come in due course to the path of yoga.

I had also read in some books on yoga that yogis often
work and act invisibly from afar, influencing us mysteri-
ously with their occult powers. But, alas, I had no confidence in myself nor knew how to arrive at psychic certi-
tudes. All I knew was that what went on happening to me
was disturbing, if not disconcerting, and that I was being
pulled all the time in the direction of yoga. There were, for
example, the three "coincidences" that occurred in quick suc-
cession in Nice: Madame Calvé's confidences about Swami
Vivekananda, the appearance of Vladia and Marthe and,
above all, the tremendous impact of Paul Richard's radiant

personality. Moreover, but for the sudden eruption of Vladia and Marthe, out of the blue as it were, I would not have stayed on at Nice. For I had been invited to Barcelona and Madrid to deliver lectures on music and was thinking of accepting the invitation and then flying to Paris from Madrid. In fact, I was about to wire to my kind hosts in Spain when Vladia and Marthe almost miraculously outflashed to bar my way and take me in tow. I was so overjoyed to meet them that I decided to cancel my visit to Spain—a felicitous decision in that I would otherwise have missed Paul Richard and his rapturous discourses on Sir Aurobindo and his great message.

But though Paul Richard gave me a decided push toward Sri Aurobindo, my aspiration once again engendered an opposing fear which sometimes, indeed, waxed into a nameless dread. It was then I turned to Bertrand Russell. I told myself that I must not make a decision hastily on so momentous an issue. Besides, was it not Lord Russell's brilliant wit and powerful philosophy based on reason, science and human sympathy that so often made me rejoice and say "But this, too, is a great ideal!"

I met Lord Russell in Cornwall and for three days had long talks with him which I have related with his full approval in *Among the Great*, so I need hardly repeat all that. I need only comment that while I could respond to his outlook on ritualism and formal religion, I found it impossible to agree with his strictures on mystic consciousness and spiritual experience. Had not Sri Aurobindo himself so clearly distinguished between the two when he wrote in *The Renaissance in India:*

Religion has been a central preoccupation of the Indian mind; some have told us that too much religion ruined India, precisely because we made the whole of life religion or religion the whole of life, we have failed in life and gone under. . . . It is possible, that on one side we deviated too much into an excessive religiosity, that is to say, an excessive externalism of ceremony, rule, routine, mechanical worship, on the other into a too world-shunning asceticism which drew away the best minds who were thus lost to society instead of standing like the ancient Rishis as its spiritual support and its illuminating life-givers. But the root of the matter was the dwindling of the spiritual impulse in its generality and broadness, the decline of intellectual activity and freedom, the waning of great ideals, the loss of the gust of life.

Perhaps there was too much of religion in one sense; the word is English, smacks too much of things external such as creeds, rites, an external piety; there is no one Indian equivalent. But if we give rather to religion the sense of the following of the spiritual impulse in its fullness and define spirituality as the attempt to know and live in the highest self, the divine, the all-embracing unity and to raise life in all its parts to the divinest possible values, then it is evident that there was not too much of religion, but rather too little of it—and in what there was, a too one-sided and therefore insufficiently ample tendency. The right remedy is not to belittle still farther the agelong ideal of India, but to return to its old amplitude and give it a still wider scope, to make in very truth all the life of the nation a religion in this high spiritual sense.

In the end, after a good deal of painful vacillation, I decided to cancel my booking in the ship in which Lord Russell had booked his berth to America. But I decided I needed a reprieve and so visited the lovely Lake District of England where "nature is at beauty's festival" in summer. Next I delivered a few lectures on music in London and Edinburgh, though my heart was not in it. Vladia was wont to say: "*A quoi bon?*" I echoed him and held that it was all a senseless expenditure of our precious life-energy to achieve laurels which slake no deep thirst of the soul.

In fact, the ovation I received from my audience ultimately startled me into a novel sense of awareness. I felt as though I were being cajoled by some invisible powers to stay put in this world of phantom enthusiasts' phantom applause. I pictured myself lecturing in America in crowded houses booked by an impresario, after which there would be no exit till the whirl of the whole program was finished. I would probably receive a substantial fraction of the box-office returns, and then, as my star of luck was ascending, I would be lionized by professors, musicologists and *dames de salon* whose ardency at white-heat would go to my head and make me "miss the last bus that crossed the frontier," to quote a favorite simile of Krishnaprem's.

But I must cry halt. For I have a good deal to write about the last lap of my journey before I took refuge at the feet of Sri Aurobindo at Pondicherry.

My unexpected return disappointed my friends, especially Subhash who took me to task for my sentimentality. "I know, Dilip," he said with a sigh, "that many of us Indians are born mystics. I myself once left my home to hobnob with the sadhus, as you know. But Swami Brahmananda himself sent me back home. 'You have to evolve on the path of works as a karmayogi,' he said, which I, too, realized after my homecoming. Our country is in shackles which won't fall off—*we* have to break them and free our Motherland." And so he went on and on. This time I did not argue with him as I did not want to repeat like a parrot the same words in self-defense. But I felt sad because even music failed to intoxicate me now. I took alarm and began to roam once more resolutely in search of musicians, with this difference: this time I learned mostly devotional songs of famous mystics like Mirabai, Tulsidas, Kabir, Surdas and others.

The only friend who might have helped me with his advice was Krishnaprem but, unfortunately for me, he had taken the final plunge and reached a point of no return at Almora. I felt depressed because I could not emulate him. And a strange fear gripped me: how could I live a cloistered life in Pondicherry where there was no music or laughter? The strange thing was, perhaps, this curious fact that though I sang and laughed and delighted people I myself derived no pleasure from their society! I told none about my inner conflicts: how my aspiration to take to yoga was opposed tooth and nail by my intense reluctance and this nameless fear. How could I possibly renounce my freedom of movement and enter a monastery, a thousand miles away from Bengal? I neither knew anyone there nor had any idea of the technique of Sir Aurobindo's "Supramental Yoga," as many a devotee called it . . . and so my tussle with my crestfallen self went on interminably.

It was in this forlorn mood that I went to Lucknow where I met Krishnaprem's dear friend Joygopal. He told me all about Krishnaprem though there was not much he could tell because in those days Krishnaprem never wrote to anybody about his yoga. So I gathered from Joygopal only tidbits of information about him, all of which conspired to deepen my gloom. What horrified me most was that Krishnaprem was actually begging alms in the streets and sleeping on a bare blanket on the cold heights of the Himalayas, 7,500 feet above sea level. My heart sank every time Joygopal put me abreast of his feats of courage and endurance, and I asked myself again and again, in trepidation, whether all these heroic austerities were incumbent on one who yearned desperately to be havened at his guru's feet. But I found no answer, and so had to live in a void, since I had no taste left for the fleshpots of the world, and even music, my *grande passion*, had, alas, begun to pall.

So, one night, I confided to my friend my deep misgivings and told him that although I felt miserable I could not help but vacillate because I just dreaded cloistered monasticism. But that was not the whole story, as he divined quickly. So, astutely hitting the nail on the head and giving me a quizzical smile, Joygopal hazarded bluntly: "Don't hedge, Dilip. I propose buying a ticket for you the first thing tomorrow morning. You just make straight for your guru's yoga-shram at Pondicherry, where you belong. Surrender all you have and are to him."

"It's all very well to prescribe remedies," I demurred ruefully. "But are you sure of the diagnosis?"

Sri Dilip Kumar Roy and Sri Krishnaprem shared a spiritual friendship that lasted a lifetime.

A medical man, my friend and host smiled appreciatively and prodded: "What is the nub of the trouble?"

"I wish I knew," I answered bitterly. "I only know that I am groping in a maze. You see, it's like this. My guru, unlike Krishnaprem's, has not given me anything tangible yet. Surely, you don't expect me to give up everything for nothing?"

His noble brow clouded.

"Well, Dilip," he sighed. "You *have* let me down! I cherished you as I have because I thought you were a born yogi, like Krishnaprem. I see now that I was mistaken. For what you say amounts to this: that you can't bring yourself to accept a guru unless he signs a contract with you and gives you in advance some delightful experiences—something like what they call in law a 'consideration,' a *quid pro quo* stipulation! Well, if this be your approach—that is, if you start by bargaining with the Lord—then you shall never arrive."

The shaft went home. The whole night I could not sleep. I was *bargaining* with the Lord, whereas Krishnaprem had taken the plunge, staking everything with just one throw of the dice. . . . Oh, how dare I claim him as my friend after this? . . . A medley of self-pity and vacillation, aspiration and fear, longing and diffidence, drained me of all my strength till I started praying in tears—when the incredible miracle happened.

It is God's truth that I got up and in twenty minutes took the next available train to Bombay, en route for Pondicherry. Just before leaving, I dispatched the following telegram to Sri Aurobindo: "I surrender unconditionally to you all I have and am. You must accept me. Wire yes to my friend Justice K. C. Sen, Bombay."

What followed was an unforgettable experience: the whole landscape seemed to have changed in the twinkling of an eye! Once in London I had marveled at two scenes on the stage. In the first there were only thirsty sand dunes without a trace of vegetation. Suddenly the light went out, then click, the stage revolved and I saw in thrilled wonder a beautiful garden house with roses, palms and a fountain. My experience in 1928 was, indeed, far more apocalyptic: directly after my anguished conflicts and dark doubts there flashed a delectable certitude of security, an unutterable euphoria and, above all, a sense of belonging. I had no idea whither I was bound nor how long I would have to trudge on toward a far-off goal, against what odds. I only knew that all my misgivings had been dissolved, my doubts liquidated, my questionings stilled. Yet, outwardly, nothing had changed! The irksome railway journey, the babel of a jostling crowd, the harsh whistles, the railway porters to be dealt with— all this tedium of prose was transformed in a moment into a rhapsody, answering His Flute Call! How can I say after this that the age of miracles has passed? And the most baffling miracle was that my human destiny was decided once and for all, and in just twenty minutes, by a power beyond my ken. I had a rapturous glimpse of myself being carried along on the wave-crest of a light, which though unseen by the eye enthralled my soul.

All this is not an overstatement of what uprooted me from my native soil of art and social intercourse to be transplanted into an alien garden at the feet of my radiant Guru of Grace, the deputy of my Dream-Lord Krishna. I received in Bombay, at the house of my friend Justice K. C. Sen, Sri Aurobindo's telegram from Pondicherry. Thereafter, on November 22, 1928, I submitted to him myself, in an eager and joyous homecoming like a way-lost bird which had suddenly found its nest in the sky of sweet repose, bliss and security.

14

AT THE GURU'S FEET

I CANNOT GIVE here even a brief résumé of my endless spiritual conflicts alternating with psychic bliss. My euphoria only presaged—so my guru told me—what was in store for me with a hundredfold intensity of rapture. Yet, I had to go through much that was painful and depressing thanks to my recalcitrant self-will. At times I felt like "throwing in the sponge," as I wrote to my guru threateningly, fool that I was! But his unwavering love tided me over the crises with a regal ease. He wrote in one of his letters that worldly friends might fail but Divine Grace could never admit defeat and that the love he offered me was of a piece with Love Divine. In one of his most moving letters (quoted in full in my book *Among the Great*) he wrote to me:

I meant that even before I met you for the first time, I knew of you and felt at once the contact of one with whom I had that relation which declares itself constantly through many lives and I followed your career with a close sympathy and interest. It is a feeling which is never mistaken and gives the impression of one not only close to one but part of one's existence. . . . The relation that is so indicated always turns out to be that of those who have been together in the past and were predestined to join again (though the past circumstances may not be known), drawn together by old ties. It was the same recognition—apart even from the deepest spiritual connection—that brought you here. If the outer consciousness does not fully realize, it is because of the crust always created by a new physical birth that prevents it. But the soul knows all the while.

I was on the whole happy in the Pondicherry yogashram but the norm of what is hailed as happiness is not bliss, which can come only when the soul opens to Divine Grace. In Sri Aurobindo Ashram I experienced this "outpetalling of the soul-flower" many a time, but most often through his letters showering love. It did, indeed, seem to me, time and time again, that his letters held magic which soothed the scorch of my heart with their rain of love. I had received loving letters from friends galore as well as world celebrities, but Sri Aurobindo's letters were written in a very different vein. One of my greatest joys—culminating in thrills—was to receive his letters day after incredible day. I stayed in his ashram a little over two decades, assiduously writing letters till the very end.* But he never failed me once, especially when I was tormented by doubts or felt frustrated. And how he went on pouring out his love from his heart of bounty which beggared description! It did, indeed, seem to me at times that his heart's love-treasury was all but inexhaustible. And not his love alone— but also his incredible patience and understanding, especially when we pitted our perverse self-will against his love-lit star-will. I once wrote to him in jest that I had discovered why I had to come to him: to test his patience to the utmost so as to be able to attest that I found his star-lit understanding and compassionate patience superhuman. He agreed and wrote that the love he offered me stemmed from a source which no human consciousness could believe as real. I have quoted a great many letters of his—some of them extending over a dozen pages—in a few books of mine.

---

* Altogether I must have written to him more than two thousand letters and he at least a thousand. Sometimes I even received two letters in one day.

"I stayed in his ashram a little over two decades, assiduously writing letters till the very end."

Besides, a number of his personal letters to me have been published in a half a dozen volumes of his letters. So I will quote here only two of his relevant letters to show how he lighted my way with his love that "passeth all understanding."

It once happened that I decided I must learn to stand on my own sturdy feet. Why must I depend on a guru when I could appeal to Krishna directly? So I wrote to him, somewhat challengingly, that I proposed to meditate at least ten hours a day in complete seclusion. I complained to him that I was tired of brief showers to soothe my frayed nerves and thirsty spirit. I must have a downpour at any cost. He wrote to me very tenderly trying to dissuade me, prophesying that the austere way of meditating in seclusion would only deepen my thirst instead of invoking the downpour. I wrote back that he must give me a long rope and allow me to appeal directly to Krishna's light. He wrote back again trying to cheer me up, stressing that *bhakti* (devotion) and *karma* (action) were the two master urges of my nature. So I would get the best and quickest results if I galloped cheerfully on with my poetry and music. But I was bent on "following my own light" and repeated that I must be given a long rope. To that he had to consent, willy-nilly.

And so, determined to be heroic, I withdrew all at once from my social activities, stopped singing and went into an ascetic seclusion increasing, day after barren day, my hours of meditation and prayer to the exclusion even of reading and writing. This was the most difficult of all feats, but the more difficult I found it, the less I liked to scotch the project; the more I was coaxed by Sir Aurobindo to take "the sunlit path of the psychic," the more I repeated to myself a famous *yoga-vashista* couplet which said:

> Rely on thine own strength and, grinding thy teeth,
> Defy with heroic deeds the Tyrant, Fate.*

---

* "Param pourusham ashritya dantair dantan vichurnayan
   Shubhenashu-bhamudyuktam praktanam poursham jayet."

But, alas, "Krishna" say the Rishis, "assays you by your attitude, not deeds."† Nor is God mocked. So the more I shut myself in, vowing to pluck the stars from on high by dint of my Herculean meditations, the faster receded from me all joy of life and zest for *sadhana* (spiritual disciplines) till I found myself groping in a veritable catacomb, as it were. Life seemed dismal beyond endurance and I did not know where to turn now, having ruled out the guru's help as hearsay. And it was not even the gloom that mortified me most, but its stark irrelevance in the context of my ardor and aspiration. I could neither understand why my heroic attempt to soar should have been rewarded by clipped wings nor explain how a march toward the east could have pushed me back to the sunset of the last gleam of hope. Alas, there was now nothing to do but grind my teeth still harder. And yet, the more I persisted, the less I succeeded in penetrating the mystery of my dire pain, which only deepened till—it happened, the great miracle! What it was, let the good reader judge from the correspondence which passed between us.

O Guru [I wrote after giving him a full history of all that I had gone through, riding my folly] I wanted to achieve it all exclusively by my own effort and so meditated and concentrated as never before, for days and days. But the more I persevered, the deeper grew the gloom and the mental agony till, last evening, when I was utterly shut out from light and felt like one completely stranded, I prayed, in tears, upon my lonely terrace. "O Krishna," I said, "you know I have only wanted you all my life, or at least aspired to want nothing but your Grace. You know also that I decided of late to arrive through *tapasya** because I was told that you never let a sincere prayer go unheeded. Then, how is it that the more I sue you, the more you melt away like a shadow form to my eager clutch? I do not understand your *lila*,‡ Lord, but have mercy on one who is at

---

† *Bhavagrahi Janardana—Janardana* is a name of Krishna.
* Arduous self-discipline.
‡ Playfulness.

the end of his tether! I own at last that my much-vaunted intelligence cannot find a key to the enigma. I have only learned one thing: that there is no ignominy in not understanding it all and that true understanding can come only when one realizes that one is completely impotent by oneself. In any event, I appeal to you in this deep impasse to respond to me—give me a sign that you are not a chimera."

O Guru, as soon as this prayer issued from my heart of humility, I experienced a velvety softness within and a feeling of ineffable plasticity which rapidly grew into something so concrete that I felt almost as if I could *touch* it with my fingers! But even this was not all. As soon as my pride admitted defeat all my piled-up gloom of despair and frustration vanished as though by magic: my restlessness was redeemed by peace and my darkness by a radiance which seemed too incredible to be true and yet too vivid to be dismissed as wishful thinking. And to me it was so utterly convincing because it seemed to descend, like an avalanche, from nowhere—to sweep me off my feet when I had least expected it. Kanai congratulates me and insists that I have had a real and important *psychic experience* without knowing it. What have you to say thereto, Guru? To think that even I should have had an experience and a psychic one at that!

His reply came, duly, the next morning:

It was certainly an experience, and as Kanai very accurately described it, an experience of great value: a psychic experience *par excellence*. A feeling of "velvety softness" and an "ineffable plasticity within" is a psychic experience and can be nothing else. It means a modification of the substance of the consciousness especially in the vital emotional part, and such a modification prolonged or repeated till it became permanent would mean a great step in what I call the psychic transformation of the being. It is just these modifications in the inner substance that make transformation possible. Further, it was a modification that made a beginning of knowledge possible—for by knowledge in yoga we mean not thought or ideas about spiritual things but psychic understanding from within and spiritual illumination from above. Therefore the first result was this feeling of yours that "*there was no ignominy in not understanding it all and that the true understanding could come only when one realized that one was completely impotent by oneself.*" This was itself a beginning of a true understanding: a psychic understanding—something felt within which sheds a light or brings up a spiritual truth that mere thinking would not have given, also a truth that is effective, bringing both the enlightenment and solace you needed, for what the psychic being brings with it always is light and happiness, an inner understanding and relief and solace.

Another very promising aspect of this experience is that it came as an immediate response to an appeal to the Divine. You asked for the understanding and the way out and at once Krishna showed you both: the way out was the change of the consciousness within, the plasticity which makes the knowledge possible and also the understanding of the condition of mind and vital in which the true knowledge or power of knowledge could come. For the inner knowledge comes from within and above (whether from the Divine in the heart or from the Self above) and for it to come the pride of the mind and vital in the surface mental ideas and their insistence on them must go. *One must know that one is ignorant before one can begin to know.* This shows that I am not wrong in pressing for the psychic opening as the only way out. For as the psychic opens, such responses and much more also become common and the inner change also proceeds by which they are made possible.

Upon this I wrote to him once again asking whether a "feeling" could be called an "experience." Was not a mere feeling something too adventitious and subjective to be eligible for the status of an "experience?" To this again he replied promptly:

I doubt whether I am able to answer your question or whether even I quite understand it. There is no law that a feeling cannot be an experience. Experiences are of all kinds and take all forms in the consciousness. When the consciousness undergoes, sees or feels anything spiritual or psychic or even occult, that is an experience (in the technical Yogic sense), for there are of course all sorts of experiences which are not of that character. The feelings themselves are of many kinds. The word "feeling" is often used for an emotion, and there can be psychic or spiritual emotions which are numbered among Yogic experiences, such as a wave of pure *bhakti* or the rising of love towards the Divine. A feeling also means a perception of something felt—a perception in the vital or psychic or in the essential substance of the consciousness. I find, even frequently, a mental perception, when it is very vivid, described as a feeling. If you exclude all these feelings and kindred ones and say that they are feelings and not experiences, then you leave very little room for experiences.

Feeling and vision are the main forms of spiritual experience. One sees and feels the Brahman everywhere; one feels a force enter or go out from one; one feels or sees the descent of Light; one feels the descent of peace or *ananda*. Kick all that on the ground that it is but a feeling, not an experience (what the deuce then *is* an experience?) and you make a clean sweep of most of the things that we call experience. Again, we feel a change in the substance of the consciousness or the state of consciousness. We feel ourselves spreading in wideness (this can be seen also). We feel the heart-consciousness being wide instead of narrow, soft instead of hard, illumined instead of obscure, the head-consciousness also, the vital, even the physical; we feel thousands of things of all kinds and why are we not to call them experiences? Of course it is an inner sight, an inner feeling, not material like the feeling of a cold wind, or a stone but as the inner consciousness deepens it is not less vivid or concrete, it is even more so.

In this case what you felt was not an emotion—though something emotional came with it—you felt a condition in the very substance of consciousness—a softness, a plasticity, even a *velvety softness, an ineffable plasticity*. Any fellow who knows anything about Yoga would immediately say: What a fine experience—a very clear and spiritual and psychic experience!

I have chosen the letter that follows because he explained therein with his luminous clarity how doubts bar the way of most pilgrims of the star like a lion in the path and why one should be on one's guard against the darkness they inevitably entail. In my own case I was hampered most by:

(1) My impatience: I wanted quick results. Sri Aurobindo once wrote to me with a smile that I was "a spoilt child of favor and fortune" and as such wanted to have *siddhi*, realization, without an arduous *sadhana*, self-discipline.

(2) My doubt: I argued that, as Rabindranath had said, he and I were artists and not yogis, so I must conclude I had missed my vocation. This thought made me go through interminable forests of painful gloom. Sri Aurobindo questioned my premise that I was ineligible for yoga and asserted that he knew my real self and *swadharma* (native aptitude) better than anybody else. And he wrote in one of his most beautiful letters that I was bound to arrive if only I stayed loyal to my call and went on singing the mantra: *Have Him I must and have Him I will.* I have written about my first difficulty, impatience, and so will give here his wonderful and inspiring letter on doubt—a letter for which many an aspirant in later times has thanked me from the heart.

Dilip,

I have started writing about doubt, but even in doing so I am afflicted by the "doubt" whether any amount of writing or of anything else can ever persuade the eternal doubt in man which is the penalty of his native ignorance. In the first place, to write adequately would mean anything from 60 to 600 pages, but not even 6,000 convincing pages would convince Doubt. For Doubt exists for its own sake; its very function is to doubt always and, even when convinced, to go on doubting still; it is only to persuade its entertainer to give it board and lodging that it pretends to be an honest truth-seeker. This is a lesson I have learnt from the experience both of my own mind and of the minds of others: the only way to get rid of doubt is to take Discrimination as one's detector of truth and falsehood and under its guard to open the door freely and courageously to experience.

All the same I have started writing, but I will begin not with Doubt but with the demand for the Divine as a concrete certitude, quite as concrete as any physical phenomenon caught by the senses. Now, certainly, the Divine must be such a certitude not only as concrete but more concrete than anything sensed by ear or eye or touch in the world of Matter; but it is a certitude not of mental thought but of essential experience. When the Peace of God descends on you, when the Divine Presence is there within you, when the Ananda rushes on you like a sea, when you are driven like a leaf before the wind by the breath of the Divine Force, when Love flowers out from you on all creation, when Divine knowledge floods you with a Light which illumines and transforms in a moment all that was before dark, sorrowful and obscure, when all that is becomes part of the One Reality, when it is all around you felt at once by the spiritual contact, by the inner vision, by the illumined and seeing thought, by the vital sensation and even by the very physical sense, when everywhere you see, hear, touch only the Divine, then you can much less doubt it or deny it than you can deny or doubt daylight or air or the sun in heaven—for of these physical things you cannot be sure that they are what your senses represent them to be; but in the concrete experiences of the Divine, doubt is impossible.

As to permanence, you cannot expect permanence of the initial spiritual experiences from the beginning—only a few have that and even for them the high intensity is not always there; for most the experience comes and then draws back behind the veil waiting for the human part to be prepared and made ready to bear and hold fast to its increase and then its permanence. But to doubt it on that account would be irrational in the extreme. One does not doubt the existence of air because a strong wind is not always blowing or of sunlight because night intervenes between dawn and dusk. The difficulty lies in the normal human consciousness to which spiritual experience comes as something abnormal and is in fact supernormal. This weak limited normality finds it difficult at first even to get any touch of that greater and intenser supernormal experience or it gets it diluted into its own duller stuff of mental or vital experience, and when the spiritual experience does come in its own overwhelming power, our normal consciousness very often cannot bear or, if it bears, cannot hold and keep it. Still once a decisive breach has been made in the walls built by the mind against the Infinite, the breach widens sometimes slowly, sometimes swiftly, until there is no wall any longer, and there is the permanence.

But the decisive experiences cannot be brought, the permanence of a new state of consciousness, in which they will be normal, cannot be secured if the mind is always interposing its own reservations, prejudgments, ignorant formulas or if it insists on arriving at the Divine certitude as it would at the quite relative truth of a mental conclusion, by reasoning, doubt, enquiry and all the other paraphernalia of Ignorance feeling and fumbling around after knowledge; these greater things can only be brought by the progressive opening of a consciousness quieted and turned steadily towards spiritual experiences. If you ask why the divine has so imposed it on these highly inconvenient bases, it is a futile question—for this is nothing else than a psychological necessity imposed by the very nature of things. It is so because these experiences of the Divine are not mental constructions, nor vital movements, but essential things, not things merely thought but realities, not mentally felt but felt in our very underlying substance and essence. No doubt, the mind is always there and can intervene; it can and does have its own type of mentalizing about the Divine, thoughts, beliefs, emotions, mental reflections of spiritual Truth, even a kind of mental realization which repeats as well as it can some kind of figure of the higher Truth, and all this is not without value, but it is not concrete, intimate and indubitable. Mind by itself is incapable of ultimate certitude; whatever it believes, it can doubt; whatever it can affirm, it can deny; whatever it gets hold of, it can and does let go. That, if you like, is its freedom, noble right—privilege; it may be all you can say in its praise, but by these methods of mind you cannot hope (outside the reach of physical phenomena and hardly even there) to arrive at anything you can call an ultimate certitude. It is for this compelling reason that mentalizing or enquiring about the Divine cannot by its own right bring the Divine. If the consciousness is always busy with small mental movements— especially accompanied, as they usually are, by a host of vital movements, desires, prepossessions and all else that vitiates human thinking—even apart from the native insufficiency of reason— what room can there be for a new order of knowledge, for fundamental experiences or for those deep and tremendous upsurgings or descents of the Spirit? It is, indeed, possible for the mind in the midst of its activities to be suddenly taken by surprise, overwhelmed, swept aside, while all is flooded with the sudden inrush of spiritual experience. But if afterwards it begins questioning, doubting, theorizing, surmising what this might be and whether it is true or not, what else can the spiritual Power do but retire and wait for the bubbles of the Mind to cease?

I would ask one simple question of those who would make the intellectual mind the standard and judge of spiritual experience. Is the Divine something less than Mind or is it something greater? Is mental consciousness with its groping enquiry, endless argument, unquenchable doubt, stiff and unplastic logic something superior or even equal to the Divine consciousness or is it something inferior in its action and status? If it is greater, then there is no reason to seek after the Divine. If it is equal, then spiritual experience is quite superfluous. But if it is inferior, how can it challenge, judge, make the Divine stand as an accused or a witness before its tribunal, summon it to appear as a candidate for admission before a Board of Examiners or pin it like an insect under its examining miscroscope? Can the vital animal hold up as infallible the standard of its vital instincts, associations and impulses and judge, interpret and fathom by it the mind of man? It cannot, because man's mind is a greater power working in a wider, more complex way which the animal's vital consciousness cannot follow. Is it so difficult to see, similarly, that the Divine Consciousness must be something infinitely wider, more complex than the human mind, filled with greater powers and lights, moving in a way which mere Mind cannot judge, interpret or fathom by the standard of its fallible reason and limited half-knowledge? The simple fact is there that Spirit and Mind are not the same thing and that it is the spiritual consciousness into which the Yogin has to enter (in all this I am not in the least speaking of the supermind) if he wants to be in permanent contact or union with the Divine. It is not then a freak of the Divine or a tyranny to insist on the mind recognizing its limitations, quieting itself, giving up its demands, and opening and surrendering to a greater Light than it can find on its own obscurer level.

This doesn't mean that Mind has no place at all in the spiritual life; but it does mean it cannot be even the main instrument, much less the authority, to whose judgment all must submit itself, including the Divine. Mind must learn from the greater consciousness it is approaching and not impose its own standards on it; it has to receive illumination, open to a higher Truth, admit a greater power that doesn't work according to mental canons, surrender itself and allow its half-light half-darkness to be flooded from above till where it was blind it can see, where it was deaf it can hear, where it was insensible it can feel, and where it was baffled, uncertain, questioning, disappointed it can have joy, fulfillment, certitude and peace.

This is the position on which Yoga stands, a position based upon constant experience since men began to seek after the Divine. If it is not true, then there is no truth in Yoga and no necessity for Yoga. If it is true, then it is on that basis, from the standpoint of the necessity of this greater consciousness that we can see whether doubt is of any utility for the spiritual life. To believe anything and everything is certainly not demanded of the spiritual seeker; such a promiscuous and imbecile credulity would be not only unintellectual, but in the last degree unspiritual. At every moment of the spiritual life, until one has got fully into the higher light, one has to be on one's guard and to be able to distinguish spiritual truth from pseudo-spiritual imitations of it or substitutes for it set up by the mind and the vital desire. The power to distinguish between truths of the Divine and the lies of the Asura [demon] is a cardinal necessity for Yoga. The question is whether that can best be done by the negative and destructive method of doubt, which often kills falsehood but rejects truth too with the same impartial blow, or a more positive, helpful and luminously searching power can be found which is not compelled by its inherent ignorance to meet truth and falsehood alike with the stiletto of doubt and the bludgeon of denial. . . . An indiscriminateness of mental belief is not the teaching of spirituality or of Yoga; the faith of which it speaks is not a crude mental belief but the fidelity of the soul to the guiding light within it, a fidelity which has to remain till the light leads it into knowledge.

Sri Aurobindo

15

RAMANA MAHARSHI

Ⅰɴ sʀɪ Aurobindo's ashram I had a good many experiences of the descent of energy (about which I will have more to say presently), but as often as not these were followed by a reaction of listlessness. As this condition showed no signs of abating I finally said to myself: "The Gita advocates equanimity* so I must have it here and now at any price."

Thus it happened that after a few years I once more found myself in the throes of a crisis whose din and discord made me extremely unhappy. I struggled on incessantly, as I badly wanted a respite of peace, the authentic yogic peace, but do what I would, I could not, alas, find peace anywhere on the horizon!

Now just at this time I came by a booklet of the well-known mystic writer Paul Brunton (whom I was to meet later on). He was at the time an inmate of the ashram of Ramana Maharshi. In the booklet he gave the Sage of Arunachala very high praise as a heaven-sent boon-giver who could communicate peace by his mere proximity.

I was overjoyed, for the Maharshi lived in Tiruvannamalai, a village not far from Pondicherry. So, with Sri Aurobindo's permission, I wanted to set out on my pilgrimage to him to win peace if I could.

* *Samatvam yoga ucchate*, that is, "Yoga means equanimity" (II, 48).

But, alas, in our ashram a veteran colleague of mine was aghast and advised me on no account to yield to such a "disloyal impulse." "It is not done," he said emphatically. I felt unhappy but as I longed to see the Maharshi I had an animated dialogue with my conscience and thereafter, subduing my qualms, decided finally to see for myself. "Besides, when Sri Aurobindo himself has given me permission," I argued, "how can I possibly go astray? I am not going to a cinema star but to a mighty sadhu, aren't I?"

Nevertheless, when I arrived at the small house where the Maharshi lived I felt a deep malaise. How could I hope to get peace and inspiration from him if I failed to get it at the feet of my own guru, who was surely no less great? Thus I argued, chiding myself for my imprudence, but it was now too late to return. Besides, the rebel in me spurred me on: why should I attach any importance to the opinions of my colleagues—what must I regret when I have done nothing wrong? Was I not persuaded that I had done well in coming to seek inspiration from the great yogi who was venerated by spiritual aspirants of every category? At the same time I wondered whether this was the proper frame of mind to receive the boon of peace from such a mighty donor. Could noisy eddies of doubt hark back to the diapason of harmony?

It was in the afternoon that I entered the living room of the great sage; it was bare save for the oblong cemented dais on which he reclined. A handful of devotees were sitting on the floor. A few were meditating in a stiff and erect posture while others were gazing wistfully at the sage who sat stonestill, staring straight in front at nothing at all—as was his want. He never spoke unless someone first spoke to him or asked a question. For five long decades he had been living on this hill, feeling no call to leave it even once. In the earlier stage of his yoga he had lived in a cave for about eight years, vowed to complete silence, *mounam*. Subsequently, a number of devotees had built him the ashram where he had thus been living his singular life for the last forty years, blessing all but belonging to none, interested in everything but attached to nothing, answering questions but never asking any. He did give one the impression of a Shiva, the great God of compassion who was there to give but not to ask any favors of anybody. I had, indeed, read what Paul Brunton had written of him and heard a lot about his lovable ways from a dear friend of mine, Duraswami, who had known him for years. He had told me that the Maharshi had been living ever since his renunciation of the worldly life in a state of *sahaj samadhi*, that is, in a state of *samadhi* while still in the normal, waking consciousness. But what I saw personally in his ashram impressed me even more profoundly, though I find it far from easy to portray what exactly I saw or rather experienced. Here was a man who lived like a god, supremely indifferent to all that we worldlings clamored for all the time. Dressed in a bare *koupin* (even scantier than a loin-cloth), he yet sat ensconced in a regal peace and egoless bliss, giving us a glimpse of another "mode of living" we could at best marvel at but never appraise. Kings had come to him with all sorts of rich offerings, but in vain: he had blessed them but never accepted any gifts. One day he pointed at a golden temple which his devotees were building to honor him, and remarked with an ironic smile to Duraswami: "Just fancy, they insist on erecting this for me when all I need is the shade of a tree under which to sit and *be*."

The modern man may criticize him for his lack of initiative and argue that humanity has little use for one who lives thus aloof and isolated. But was he isolated—he who radiated peace which hundreds of visitors have experienced by just sitting near him in silence? Did not the lineaments of his serene face, his beautiful smile, his tranquil glance, convey to all a message of liberation—*jivanmukti?* Did he not blossom like a flower stemming from earth, yet alien to all that was earthly? Did not his frail frame disengage a strength that was more than human, his life attest to an invisible anchorage which made him utterly secure and free from the last vestige of fear? Yes, as the Maharshi told me later, he put a premium on two things: inaccessibility to fear and to flattery, however subtle. Once a snake passed over his body while he lay in his dark cave at night. His friend and attendant (a doctor, who related this to me) jumped up as it passed over his chest. "Why? What is the matter?" the Maharshi asked him.

"A snake!" he gasped.

"I know," acquiesced the sage. "It passed over my body, too."

"It did?" asked the doctor. "And how did you feel?"

"Cool!" came the rejoinder.

Apropos of flattery he told me this story.

"A seeker may go very far," he said, "but not till he has traveled beyond the reach of all flattery can he be said to have arrived. Listen. There was once a rich man who wanted God. He gave up his family, home, comforts and everything and repaired to a forest where he practiced untold austerities for years till he arrived at the Golden Gate. But alas, the portals did not open to his repeated knocking—he did not know why!

"One day an old friend of his came upon him in the forest while he was meditating. When he opened his eyes, the friend fell at his feet in an ecstasy of adoration. 'O blessed one! How great you are—how grandiose your austerities and sacrifice! Accept my homage.' The holy man had, indeed, practiced all the austerities and made all the sacrifices attributed to him. Nevertheless he was pleased when the other paid him homage. And that was why the Golden Gate had not finally opened to his knocking."

I heard of many other traits of his supremely lovable personality, amongst which must be counted his sense of humor and love of laughter. He coveted nothing, but loved to joke freely with those who came to him. One day, while I was sitting near him and some visitors were putting questions one after another, a Muslim friend of mine asked: "Tell me, Bhagavan, why is it that God does not answer my prayer

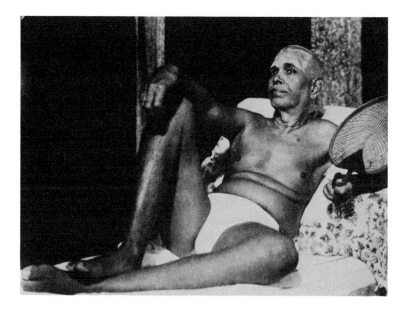

"Dressed in a bare *koupin*, he yet sat ensconced in a regal peace and egoless bliss, giving us a glimpse of another 'mode of living' we could at best marvel at but never appraise."

even when I petition Him for no earthly boon? I only pray to Him to make me humble and pure and selfless so that I may serve Him as I ought. But He simply does not listen. Why doesn't He?"

"Probably because He is afraid that if He did you wouldn't pray anymore," answered the sage readily, with a merry twinkle in his eye.

And we all laughed in chorus.

Many is the time he was asked, even challenged, to prove what he had seen.

"Ah!" he would reply placidly. "I will answer that question if you first answer mine: Who is it that is asking this question?"

"Who? Surely, I—so and so."

"I know. But *who* are you?"

"Me? . . . I . . . I . . . I . . ."

And the Maharshi would laugh. "So you see, you do not even know such a thing as your own identity, yet you presume to challenge others and their experiences. I would suggest you find out first *who* is this challenger and then the truths you challenge will be made manifest to you."

True to our great Indian tradition, the Maharshi did not relish answering merely intellectual questions, or the queries of the curious who were content with mere wordy answers. Again and again he would stress that information was not knowledge and that all true knowledge stemmed first and last from self-knowledge. So sometimes, when he was asked about the worlds beyond or the life hereafter, he would simply evade the question. "Why this itch to know about the other worlds? Do you know even the crucial and basic things about *this* one? If not, why not wait till you do before you start delving into the next? Why do you want to know what happens after death? Do you really know what is happening before your very nose? Why go to an astrologer to be told what you will be twenty years hence? Do you know—truly know—what your are today—this moment?"

Once matters came to a head. A disciple of his intrigued a good many of the members of the ashram, for he was living in perfect bliss in a tiny room, sitting all day on a bare mat, hardly taking the trouble even to eat unless somebody brought him food. Speculation was rife: some thought that he had gone mad; others that he had gone far; while others again said with bated breath that he was living in that super-conscious state which the Gita describes as the *Brahmi sthiti*. In the end a brave deputation waited upon the sage who, after hearing them with his usual patience, gave the leader of the deputation a quizzical smile.

"You want to know about his inner state, do you?" he asked pointedly.

The man fidgeted beneath his disconcerting scrutiny. "Well . . . yes . . . I . . ."

"Wait," he interjected. "First tell me this: do you know what your own state is?"

The other was unnerved. "N—no," he faltered.

"Right," the Maharshi rejoined, pleased. "First find out your own state and then you will know his."

The whole ashram enjoyed it—except the leader, of course.

Exigencies of space forbid my writing about this outstanding yogi and the deep influence his holy life has exercised upon thousands of spiritual seekers all over the world, although he did hardly anything spectacular to enlist the attention of the multitude. Those who wish to know more about him are referred to his published biographies and to the pamphlets about his ashram which are available. A brief account of his call to yoga is all that can be given here.

In 1896, when he had just turned sixteen, he was suddenly drawn to the holy temple of Shiva on Arunachala Hill and, with just five rupees in his pocket, left his home and parents and everything one holds dear. He did not know the way to the temple but somehow arrived there with literally just what he wore, trusting entirely to the mercy of his heart's Lord,

Shiva. He arrived at the temple, went straight to the Image of the Lord and, with tears coursing down his cheeks, said: "I have come at last, Lord!" and at once went off into *samadhi*.

Thereafter he lived on alms, eating but once a day and living most of the time in the bliss of *samadhi*. My dear friend Duraswami, who had lived with him for years as one of his intimates, told me this: Once he was expressing his admiration for the sage's power of concentrating day and night on his *sadhana*, when the other cut in, smiling: "*Sadhana*? Who did *sadhana*? What did I know of *sadhana*? I simply came and sat down in the temple or elsewhere in Arunachala and then lost all count of time." To me he said the same thing in a slightly different way with his characteristic irony: "People call Him by different names, but He came to me with no name or introduction so I know not how to define Him. What happened was that my desires and ego left me—how and why I cannot tell—and that I lived thenceforward in a vast and timeless peace. Sometimes," he added with a smile, "I stayed with my eyes closed and then, when I opened them, people said that I had come out of my blessed meditation. But I never knew the difference between no-meditation and meditation, blessed or otherwise. I simply lived, a tranquil witness to whatever happened around me, but never felt called upon to actively interfere. I could never feel any urge to *do* anything—except to be—just *be*. I saw that all had always been done by Him and Him alone, though we, poor puppets of *maya* [illusion], feel ourselves self-important as the doers, authors and reformers of everything! It is the ineradicable ego, the *I-ness* in each of us, which is responsible for the perpetuation of this *maya* with all its attendant sufferings and disenchantments."

"What, then, is the remedy?" I asked.

"*Just be*," he answered. "Delve down into That which only *is*, for then you will find—you are *That*—there is and can be nothing else but *That*. When you see this, all the trappings of *maya* and make-believe fall off, even as the worn-out slough of the snake. So all that you have to *do* is to get to this *I*, the real *I* behind your seeming *I*, for then only are you rid forever of the illusive *I-ness* and all is attained, since you stay thenceforward at one with *That* which is the immutable you. That's all."

"We shall have to do nothing then?"

"Why? You shall have done the greatest thing—the only thing that is worth doing—after which you may rest assured that all that has to be done will be done through you. The thing is," he added, "not to bother your head about *doing* things: just *be* and you will have done all that is expected of you."

"That is all very well, Bhagavan," I demurred. "But who is to show us how to do this—or rather *be*, as you put it? Is not a guide, a guru, necessary? Or are you against *Guruvad?*"

"Why should I be against *Guruvad?*" He smiled. "Some people evidently need a guru: let them follow him. I am against nothing except the *ego-vad*, the *I-ness*, which is the root of all evil. Rend this illusion and you land pat into the lap of the One Eternal Reality: *That*—the one solvent of all our questionings and ailments."

"But why, then, don't you come out to preach this great message?" I asked. "For most people, you will agree, do not even know that there is this *I-ness* to be got rid of."

He gave me again that cryptic smile tinctured with his characteristic irony and asked: "Have you heard of the saying of Vivekananda, that if one but thinks a noble, selfless thought even in a cave, it sets up vibrations throughout the world and does what has to be done—what *can* be done?"

"Only—forgive me if I presume to ask whether it is being done—in a *tangible* way, I mean?"

He gave me now a bland smile.

"Listen. A spiritual seeker used to attend, religiously, the lectures of a great pulpit orator and feel thrilled by all that he heard from day to day. But after a few years he discovered, to his chagrin, that he stayed put just where he had been at the start—not a single impulse had changed. Then he happened to meet in a hut a silent yogi, who said nothing; nonetheless he felt attracted to something in him he could not define and so went on meditating with him. After a time he discovered, to his great joy and surprise, that things which had worried him before affected him less and less, till he came to feel a deep peace and a sense of liberation he could not account for. And this peace deepened with the passage of time till, at last, he became a different man altogether. Now tell me: which of the two would you name as the doer of something 'tangible'?"

And this was true. After just being near him for a little while my relentless gloom melted away like mist before sunrise. Nor could I myself "account for" why and how it had happened. I only knew—and very vividly at that—that it *had* happened. I shall never forget that night when, after having meditated at his feet, I felt a sudden release from what had been stifling me for weeks. It was such an incredible experience that I did not feel like going to bed. I pulled out an easy chair and just reclined in it under the stars, utterly relaxed and insouciant. Everything around me seemed to drip peace and harmony: the gentle breeze, the murmuring trees, the hooting of an owl, a dog barking, the insects screeching . . . everything enriched my delectable sense of carefree plenitude. And I wrote a poem in the fullness of my heart:

> You came in a pauper's garb and stayed to teach
> The world what only the Illuminate could impart
> And offered a kingdom we could never reach
> By all our science, philosophy and art.
> Someday a light shall dawn and then we'll know
> What you came to give—a King, incognito!

The Maharshi left his mortal body in May, 1950, after having suffered excruciating physical torment for two long

Sri Ramana Maharshi. "After just being near him for a little while my relentless gloom melted away like mist before sunrise."

years. One of his arms had become cancerous. The medical men did their poor best but nothing availed. He died, but with the selfsame mystic smile on his lips. Once the operating surgeon was surprised: the raw wound had to be prodded thoroughly. Declining an anesthetic he stretched out his arm. The doctor caught his breath. The Maharshi's face remained calm and serene—not one groan issued from his lips! Duraswami, who was there, could not bear the sight—the arm was bleeding so profusely—and went away shedding tears. The Maharshi smiled and addressed a disciple who stood before him: "Duraswami is crying because he thinks I am suffering agonies! It is true that my body is suffering. But oh, when will he realize that I am not this body?"

Such was he. No wonder they called him Bhagavan (Godlike) Ramana Maharshi.

And I wrote that night in tears of gratitude for his having healed me with a touch of his divine peace:

> Thou singst, Sage: "Truth wins victory
> Through aspiration's desperate climb;
> Life's din melts in soul's symphony
> Through disciplines which seldom rhyme
> With Reason's feeble yes or no
> Or prudence-prompted whisperings;
> Only strong faith can take in tow
> The storm-tossed minds imaginings."

> We, life's dupes, tremble when comes thy
> Unfaltering courage to tell us this:
> That the soul achieves white harmony
> When it leaves cupidity for bliss.
> Yet thy blue bliss we crave when dark
> Engulfs our world of chains and bars
> And then our gloom implores thy Spark
> That burns the clouds, unveiling stars.

16

YOGIC EXPERIENCES

S<small>RI RAMAKRISHNA</small> once said that what he had heard about yoga was not on all fours with what he actually came to experience when he began practicing it. I was much struck by this pregnant remark of the Saint of saints because it was the same in my own case when I first started to have yogic experiences. I had thought, for instance, that I would begin by seeing divine lights and divine beings and would be visited intermittently, if not frequently, by a peace that passed all understanding and so forth. But my aspiration was answered in a very different way. I will try briefly to explain what I mean by this.

What happened frequently was that I felt a kind of pressure on my head while I meditated, a pressure that invariably dissolved into a kind of concentration in which my mental restlessness and discord were resolved into a delectable silence which I had never bargained for. Peace also supervened sometimes, though not always, but this silence that deepened within me was very rewarding in that it wrenched me effectively from my normal mental consciousness in which diverse thoughts pullulated like mushrooms. On occasions I felt a heave in my heart—or, shall I say, an ascent of my *I-ness* till it became very rarefied and faint. Sri Aurobindo wrote to me on October 13, 1930:

This is a fundamental experience of the yoga—it is the free ascent of the consciousness to join the Divine. When liberated from its ordinary identification with the body, it rises upward to have experience of the higher planes, to link itself with the psychic or the true being or to join the Divine Consciousness, then there is this experience of ascension and of speeding or escaping through space. The joy you feel is a sign of this last movement—rising to join the Divine; the passivity and expectancy of a descent are signs of the openness to the Divine, that is its result; there is also the sense of this openness, an emptiness of the ordinary contents of the consciousness, a wideness not limited by the narrow prison of the physical personality. There is, too, usually, or very often, a massive immobility of the body which corresponds to the silence that comes on the mind when it is released from itself—the silence that is the foundation of spiritual experience. What you have felt (the former experiences were probably preparatory touches) is indeed the beginning of this foundation—a consciousness free, wide, empty at will, able to rise into the supraphysical planes, open to the descent of whatever the Mother will pour into it.

My next unforgettable experience while meditating was that I subsided effortlessly into an exquisite stillness in which peace reigned while I was fully conscious, though seemingly asleep. Sri Aurobindo commented on it on June 2, 1931:

It was not half-sleep or quarter-sleep or even sixteenth-part sleep that you had; it was the going inside of the consciousness, which in that state remains conscious but shut to outer things and open only to inner experience. You must distinguish clearly between these two quite different states, one is *nidra* [sleep] the other the beginning, at least, of *samadhi* (not *Nirvikalpa*, of course). This drawing inside is necessary because the active mind of the human being is at first too much turned to outer things; it has to go inside altogether in order to live in the inner being (inner mind, inner vital, inner physical, psychic). But with training one can remain outwardly conscious and live in the inner being and have at will the indrawn or the outpoured experience; you will then have the same experience of divine immobility and the inpouring of a greater and purer consciousness in the waking state as in what you erroneously call sleep.

I began to have now many a vivid and cogent dream experience when I passed off into sleep while praying or meditating. On one occasion a very curious and thrilling visitation invaded me from without in the form of a luminous serpent. But I did not feel in the least afraid as it drew near and bit me on the crown of my head. I felt electrified and thrills of rapture coursed down me from top to toe. Thereafter I stayed for a long time in a tranquil ocean of bliss. But what amazed me was that I was half-conscious even when my body lay asleep. I wrote in full about it to Sri Aurobindo and asked him why I had such an experience in a no-man's-land—between dream and sleep. To this he replied on November 1, 1932:

Your dreams were very beautiful and symbolically very true. By the way, let me repeat, they were not really dreams; the state between sleep and waking or which is neither sleep nor waking is not a dozing but an inward-gathered consciousness, quite as much awake as the waking mind, but awake in a different plane of experience.

As for the dream of the cobras, it could be taken as an answer to your complaints against the Divine being grim and solemn and refusing to play and your remark that if you could have the faith that the troubles were a part of the Divine plan leading you through them to the Divine, you would be more at ease. The answer of the symbolic experience was that the Divine can play if you know how to play with him—and bear his play on your shoulders; the cobras and the bite indicate that what seems to you in the vital painful and dangerous may be the very means of bringing you the ecstasy of the Divine Presence.

Less generally, the cobras are the forces of the evolution, the evolution toward the Divine. Their taking the place of the legs means that their action here takes place in the physical or external consciousness, and the evolution of the external mind, vital, physical toward the experience of the Divine and of the Divine Nature. The bite of the Cobras (Shiva's Cobras) does

"But to me it was an overwhelming experience of bliss and peace pervading our drab world of fact, a fulfillment which brought in its train a deep sense of liberation from our human limitations."

not kill, or it only kills the "Old Adam" in the being—their bite brings the ecstasy of the presence of the Divine—that which you felt coming upon your head as trance waves. It is this trance ecstasy that has descended upon you each time you went inside or were even on the point of going inside in meditation. . . . It is the universal experience of every *sadhak* that force or consciousness or *Ananda* like this first comes from above—or around—and presses on or surrounds the head, then it pierces the skull as it were and fills first the brain and forehead then the whole head and descends occupying each center till the whole system is full and replete. (Of course there are, or can be, preliminary rushes occupying the whole body for a time or some other part of the system most open and least resistant to the influence.)

I repeat what I have said before (though your physical mind does not yet believe) that these experiences show at once that your inner being is a yogi capable of trance, ecstasy, intensest *bhakti*, fully aware of yoga and yogic consciousness, and showing himself the very moment you get inside yourself, even as the outer man is very much the other way round, modernised, externalised, vigorously outwardly vital (for the yogi is inward vital and psychic) and knowing nothing of yoga or the world of inner experience. I could see at once when I saw you that there was this inner Yogin and your former experiences here were quite convincing to anyone who knows anything at all about these things. When there is this inner yogin inside, the coming to the way of Yoga is sure and not even the most externalised surface consciousness—(not even a regular *homo Russelious* outside and you are not that, only a little *Russelicatus* on the surface)—can prevent final success in the Yoga.

On September 4, 1931, he wrote a long letter (which I have abridged) about another experience of mine—I need not write about my experience as its nature will be easily inferred from his luminous comment:

I have said already that your experience was, in essence, the piercing of the veil between the outer consciousness and the inner being. This is one of the crucial movements in Yoga. For Yoga means union with the Divine, but it also means awakening first to your inner self and then to your higher self—a movement inward and a movement upward. . . . It is, in fact, only through the awakening and coming to the front of the inner being that you can get into union with the Divine. The outer physical man is only an instrumental personality, and by himself he cannot arrive at this union—he can only get occasional touches, religious feelings, imperfect intimations. And even these come not from the outer consciousness but from what is within us.

In your former experiences the inner being had come to the front and for the time being impressed its own normal motions on the outer consciousness to which they are unusual and abnormal. But in this meditation what you did was—for the first time, I believe—to draw back from the outer consciousness, to go inside into the inner planes, enter the world of your inner self and wake in the hidden parts of your being. That which you were then was not this outer man, but the inner Dilip, the Yogin, the *bhakta*. When that plunge has once been taken, you are marked for the Yogic, the spiritual life, and nothing can efface the seal that has been put upon you.

All is there in your description of this complex experience— combining all the signs of this first plunge. . . . First, the sense of going a little deep down which was your feeling of the movement towards the inner depths; next, the stillness and pleasant numbness and the stiffness of the limbs. This was the sign of the consciousness retiring from the body inwards under the pressure of a force from above—that pressure stabilising the body into an immobile support of the inner life, in a kind of strong and still spontaneous *asana*. Next, the feeling of waves surging up, mounting to the head, *almost*, as you say, making you unconscious. This was the ascending of the lower consciousness in the *Adhara* to meet the greater consciousness above. It is a movement analogous to that on which so much stress is laid in the *Tantrik** process, the awakening of the *Kundalini*, the Energy coiled up and latent in the body, and its mounting through the spinal cord and the centers (*chakras*) and the *Brahmarandhra* to meet the Divine above.

* *Tantriks* are yogis who accept life in its entirety, including the body, which they call "The Temple of God." They essay to purify the body by means of elaborate rituals which end in transforming the body's cravings.

Mahatma Gandhi was wont to say that God is Truth. Assuredly. Only one should add that He is also Beauty, Power, Light and Love. In matter He outflowers as Beauty or Harmony, in life as Power or Energy, in mind as Knowledge and Light, in spirit as Love or Devotion. Sri Ramakrishna stressed tirelessly that nobody has ever plumbed God or ever shall. Nonetheless, He meets us in our deepest moments of insight in various lilts and rhythms. In some His touch awakens love, *bhakti*, as happened in the case of Indira over and over again, and most rapturously when she visioned Him in her ecstatic *samadhi*. In some He stirs as the light of knowledge, as happened in the case of Krishnaprem. In my own case, He was sometimes born as *vairagya*, a deep nostalgic yearning intensified by earth-averseness, but more often as a descent of uncontainable energy, *shakti*, which expended itself either in composing (songs and tunes) or in writing mystic prose and poetry. Once, in Pondicherry in 1943, I wrote a hundred-page novel in twenty-four hours. When I disclosed this feat to Sri Aurobindo, playfully quoting Balzac as my model, he replied, reciprocating my playfulness: "A novel in twenty-four hours! A hundred-page novel!! Good Lord, you are the Sir Malcolm Campbell of the Novel Speed, I think!! Congratulations!"

Even when the pace was somewhat slower, my capacity remained undiminished. I worked on my mystic novel, *The Upward Spiral*, from nine to ten hours a day and composed songs with accompanying music from seven to eight hours. Far from this being any strain, I just could not desist from writing or composing once this energy descended into me, most frequently after an hour or two of meditation or telling my beads. But if, at its inception, I thrilled to my sustained work, it also happened that I sometimes felt disgruntled after the energy had fully spent itself. I then regretted having left off meditating, for which petulance Sri Aurobindo had again and again to take me to task, as I have related in the previous chapter.

The long and the short of it is that I thirsted for the Infinite, *bhuma*, which alone can grant beatitude, *bhumaiva sukham*, where "the island ego joins the continent," to quote a line from *Savitri*. All spiritual seekers have aspired for this Refuge, even a fleeting touch of which can redeem the drab spectacle of our common sensibilities. Naturally, when the touch is *only* fleeting, it cannot grant the ultimate fulfillment; but such is the radiant effect of its descent that the soul which has once savored the peace and bliss of such a touch can live no more without it. I will try to make my meaning clear by giving a personal example.

The first time I saw Sri Aurobindo and the Mother* together was on November 24, 1928. But though I felt a great joy, I obtained no glimpse of a higher world. I was a trifle disappointed as I had expected a mystic experience. The second time, however, as soon as they blessed me with their palms upon my head I was given a passport, as it were, into the world of Beatitude—an apocalypse! What happened was a sudden, ineffable descent of bliss like that which Sri Aurobindo has so graphically described in his *Savitri* (XI, I):

> A sudden bliss will run through every limb
> And Nature with a mightier Presence fill. . . .

Savitri was printed in 1949. So I did not know, at least previous to my having the experience, that such was, indeed, possible for us earthlings. For it was not blood, but ichor that seemed to flow through all my veins. Even the landscape was transformed so that it gleamed with a magic light of beauty I could not otherwise even have imagined. I

---

*Madame Mira Richard, wife of the French *savant* Paul Richard. The Richards came to Pondicherry a few months before the outbreak of the First World War and started a philosophical monthly, *Arya*, which was later to become the message-bearer of Sri Aurobindo's masterpiece *Life Divine*, and other books on yoga.

I am not sure about the dates but I think Paul Richard with Madame Mira Richard went for a year or two to France, after which they returned to India. Thereafter he left Pondicherry, leaving Madame Mira Richard the Mother of Sri Aurobindo's yoga ashram.

recalled a lovely line in the *Rig Veda* which says that to one who has had His touch the breeze becomes sweet beyond words and the ocean's waves taste like honey.*

And yet, had I myself never enjoyed this beatitude, what could I have gathered from such a description? Only that its author rejoiced in something he found delectable but beyond the power of any words to portray. He could but babble sweetly like a babe intoxicated with joy. But to me it was an overwhelming experience of bliss and peace pervading our drab world of fact, a fulfillment which brought in its train a deep sense of liberation from our human limitations. I was one with the sky, the tree, the shrubs, the white sands. As I could not bear human company, I went out alone to a distant sea beach where nobody goes in the evening. I sat there stunned, as it were, with bliss and thrilled by a dear Presence, though too elusive to be touched or visioned. But it was not necessary to touch the Elusive Beloved whom I equated with Krishna. I just sat there in an ecstatic half-trance, unable even to sing or otherwise rouse myself from this silent happiness that beggared description.

After a time my analytic mind came to the fore and a voice from within me asked: "Well, supposing a friend inquired, how would you describe what you have just experienced?"

At once another voice within me answered: "I will tell you. What is it that we love most on earth?"

The first voice said: "Well, I suppose it is light and air."

"Yes," the second voice answered, pleased. "And so I would tell my friend that even were I confined for the rest of my days in a dark dungeon, deprived of light and air, such is my bliss that I would want for nothing."

For various reasons, I had not intended, at least in the present book, to touch to closely on recent events. But as

---

* *Madhu vata ritayate madu kshranti sindhavah.*

our dear friend Prashanta would not rest content without at least some more timely narrative, I have decided to append three of my major experiences which I hope the reader will find inspiring, the more so as each stands as a landmark in my own soul's evolution.

It is written that the Lord visits often in our midnight darkness of despair, *adhi rat*. Anyway, He once came to me at midnight, to be precise on January 31, 1969, just when I was lamenting that He had not made me His own. I knew, of course, that I had received from Him ever so many boons I did not deserve. But we in India do look upon "having refuge at His lotus-feet" as the greatest of all boons. Krishnaprem had visioned His feet but, alas, I was not so blessed! So I went on praying till, the Lord be praised, I had my heart's desire: I was granted the apocalyptic Vision and gathered to His lotus-feet! As I can find no words in prose to describe the great miracle, I have written it all in a poem. I will only add that the contrast between the "Trump of Doom" and the outflash of His peerless feet of refuge thrilled me all the more.

The Trump of Doom is sounded in the sky:
"A fairy tale is this your Krishna's story.
O blind suppliant, whom do you beg for alms,
Singing athrill the Nihil's rainbow glory?

"When riding maya's Ferris-wheel you hymn
The grandiose throne of One who is not there:
I, Death, Omnipotent, laugh: O how the gulled
Will nestle in myths, my truth they cannot bear.

"Know fools: 'tis I who made this universe
Moved by a whim—wherewith to blast it all,
None dare defy my sole authority
That kindles and burns to ash beyond recall."

Smiling, I only repeat Lord Krishna's Name;
The mighty roars but make my prayer more sweet:

I fear not even impending death if He
Will grant me refuge at His lotus-feet.

The wrathful titan wields his deafening thunder
Till all's atremble—the earth and seas and sky.
Unmindful I pray on as the phalanxed hordes
Of darkness charge in fury from on high.

His lightning's hurled, a myriad snakes of flame,
Unleashed like the barking myrmidons of hell!
But whose rose-tender arms encircle me
While Indira sings "His Light no storms can quell?"

Whose Grace is this that cleaves the demon host?
Whose midnight Sun relumes the eyes till I,
Lo, glimpse twain exquisite Feet! Are they, Lord, Thine:
The Haven of havens of all who pine and cry?

The heavenly Feet I've meditated on
Since childhood—my last Goal of dream and song,
Whose timeless Refuge seers and saints extoll
In time—the Feet for which the great gods long!

Are they those hallowed Feet—or do I dream?
I reck not—if Thou through its touch to me
Grant Love's last liberation and restore
My lost birthright: Thy peace and harmony.

The answer descends, an avalanche of bliss
To dissipate my agelong questioning,
I have won the asylum coveted of the gods
Where Beauty legislates and Love is King:

Thy Feet—celestial Feet, whose touch transmutes
Our thorns to blooms—the Feet which (when we kiss)
Armor us with thy Grace—O who is there
Would shudder at thunders once he has known Thy bliss?

But where is my physical self? Had death's dark blast
Contrived to annihilate all, how could I see
It now dissolved in infinite consciousness
Sheer, nude and haloed with divinity?

Only thy dawn-rose Feet survive and my
Dear daughter-disciple, I can see naught else!
Have all the cosmic worlds merged in Thy Feet?
Thou answerest with Thy Flute and anklets' bells.

Faith won me in childhood thy compassion's boon:
A sunbeam, clouds of doubt assailed to efface.
Tonight, in the holocaust, that mystic ray
Thou cam'st to rekindle with Thy miracle Grace.

On May 5, 1972, I had a momentous experience in Madras
where I had gone with Indira to teach a few Bengali songs
and Mira-*bhajans*—devotional songs composed by Indira—to
Srimati Subbulukshmi, the prima donna of South India. It
was past midnight.

I found myself ensconced in a blind darkness. All of a sudden, there was a great stir above my head. I could see nothing
in the gloom, but heard a voice distinctly say: "Direct hit,
direct hit, direct hit!" But simultaneously, as the stir swelled
into a crescendo, into a veritable roar, I heard thrice the name
of our Lord Vishnu, the archetype of Krishna. So I waited
in tranquil insouciance with the Lord's blessed name on my
lips till the blow fell, setting up a terrific blast in which my
body dislimned. But it was a delectable dissolution in that I
felt that my ego-sense—the *I-ness, ahamta*—had vanished
completely, leaving a legacy of consciousness of sheer bliss,
delivered from all fear: Who dare harm one poised in Vishnu's name-consciousness and suspended in a Void replete with
His invulnerable peace?

When I wakened Indira and told her in detail about my
thrilling experience she invoked Mira who said that it entailed
the dissolution of the *I-ness* into pure consciousness with no
attributes, or *upadhi*. This is the experience of *Shunyam*, she
stressed, the fecund Void of silence and Bliss apotheosized by
mystics of every clime down the ages. They hold that it is
one of the major experiences in that it betokens a total
annihilation of the surface personality by a supreme blast

Sri Dilip Kumar Roy leading bhajan chanting during satsang.

of the Divine Name which my mind, alas, had equated with a "direct hit."

To conclude with the third experience, and a unique one in all conscience, in that it lasted more than a month: "the peace that passeth all understanding!"

On our return after the world tour in 1953 we stayed once for about four months in Madras with Indira's sister Kanta and brother-in-law, Diwan Narottam Lal Nanda. I could not help wondering now and again how the fates were going to deal with us, as we did not know where to settle down and how on earth we were going to make ends meet when, all of a sudden, a strange thing happened: a deep spiritual peace descended into me on February 28, 1954 to be sustained afterwards in an unbroken continuity! Let me explain what exactly I mean by this. (I could not help but interpret it as a sign that the Lord was keeping me company on my pilgrimage to the Unknown.)

My friend's house was a small one and so I used to go up on to the terrace to meditate on a bare straw mat. On that memorable evening it so happened that as soon as I started praying, a profound peace coursed down my veins in exquisite waves from the crown of my head, *sahasrar*, to the base of my spine, *muladhar!* I had had this lovely experience of peace before on several occasions, but it had never lasted more than twenty-four hours at the outside. This time it lasted, mercifully, for more than a month and seemed to be continually replenished as it were by some beneficent Source above my head—a peace that flowed through my veins in delectable cool waves, that healed life's scorch away everytime I sat down to meditate on the terrace after sunset. When I came down at night for dinner, I felt like a man in a half-trance of bliss. I told Indira and my kind host about the miracle descent. A remark I often made to Nanda (who remembers it still) was that should this peace come to stay I would not know what more to ask of Krishna—it was so unutterably satisfying! And so I went on marvelling, day after incredible day, because the divine Visitant that came to upbuoy me in the form of gracious Peace lingered throughout the night. During the day it did, indeed, wane a little, but only to wax, *de nouveau*, in the evening when my heart was almost dazed with a deep sense of gratitude. And I wrote later in grateful memory of the Grace that came to uphold me in my crucial hour of need:

> How could one hymn the experience of the Light
> Of compassion that descends its troth to plight?

17

SRI AUROBINDO,
THE SEER-POET

To be utterly sure of the evidence of Sri Aurobindo's greatness, I have often of late cross-questioned myself thus: "What was the storm-sweep that uprooted you from your native soil of poetry and music, laughter and popularity, to be flung at his feet in eager self-surrender more than four decades ago?" It is not a question easy to answer because, to quote Nivedita, our deepest convictions often enough spring from data which can convince no one but ourselves. I can only say that in his presence I felt myself gripped by a silent wonder and intense longing to lay my utter self at his feet and lie cradled in his indefinable Grace. As to why I came to feel such a longing, I would humbly offer a simile, to wit, that as a planet is unable to fulfill itself directly by merging its restless star-dusts in the sun, so it sleeplessly revolves around its parent orb waiting its final hour of deliverance. As for me, I often told myself, Sri Aurobindo *was* the sun around which my soul revolved, though in its own orbit traced by its distinct personality. This is not a mere metaphor stemming from a devotee's effusion, for the light in him was not only resplendent like the sun's—whose fire called to the spark of my personality—but also a magnetic pull of love which weaned me irrevocably from my lesser loves. One may contend that all this, boiled down, is little more than a sentimental enthusiasm or, shall I say, a flood which bursts the banks of sober appraisement.

The charge may well be valid. My only defense is that do what I would, after having glimpsed what I had in Sri Aurobindo, I could not possibly write with a critical restraint about him, not only because the Everestian height of his soul's attainments baffled me, but also because to marvel at the incredible outflowering of his intellectual and mystic personality was a rapture that silenced all my questionings. But a truce to ecstasy. Let me now essay to sum him up as objectively as I can within the limited compass at my disposal.

Why does Sri Aurobindo impress us moderns? Having discussed this question with many a friend in the ashram (with visitors as well as disciples), I found that most people were impressed—even overawed—by his marvelous capacity for living a lonely life in an ivory tower for an indefinite number of years. But many is the time I wrote to him that his genius for immuring himself within the four walls of a room had appeared to me as a limitation to be overcome rather than a feat to be panegyrized. Most of my solemn friends were shocked, but not Sri Aurobindo, who possessed an infinite power of understanding and ability to see things from his appraiser's point of view. It was this great trait of his character that endeared him most to me—a trait that amounted almost to a genius for tolerance and imaginative insight. I have always been, personally, somewhat downright and impatient by nature without being, I hope, dogmatic and intolerant, so that I admired his charity and infinite patience all the more. I was moved when once he wrote to me dismissing my denunciation of a friend of mine who got drunk now and then. "Human beings are much less deliberate and responsible for their acts," he wrote, "than the moralists, novelists and dramatists make them. I look rather to see what forces drove him than what the man himself may have seemed by inference to have intended or purposed. Our inferences are often wrong and even when they are right touch only the surface of the matter."

Yes, that was Sri Aurobindo all over, for only he with his experiential knowledge of cosmic and extra-cosmic forces (overt and occult) could bring to bear the sum total of his knowledge of the goings-on behind the "surface" to get at the *real* Truth as against the apparent. In other words, it was because he had outgrown the commonly accepted criteria of judgment that he could, by rights, ask the common judge to pause and recognize his own intrinsically human limitations:

> Impenetrable, a mystery recondite
> Is the vast plan of which we are a part;
> Its harmonies are discords to our view,
> Because we know not the great themes they serve.
> (Savitri II, V)

He was worthy of admiration because he could persevere, in the face of seemingly insuperable obstacles, till he won the clue to the divine harmonies which subserved the "inscrutable work of cosmic agencies"; as also because his restless heart of love saw that

> All we have done is ever still to do:
> All breaks and all renews and is the same (*Ibid*, III, IV)

—but, above all, because his indomitable spirit dared (as he once wrote to me):

To bring down some principle of inner Truth, Light, Harmony, Peace into earth-consciousness. I see it above and know what it is—I feel it gleaming down on my consciousness from above and I am seeking to make it possible for it to take up the whole being into its own native power, instead of the nature of man continuing to remain in half-light, half-darkness. I believe the descent of this Truth opening the way to a development of divine consciousness here to be the final cause of the earth-evolution. . . . It is a question between the Divine and myself—whether it is the Divine Will or not, whether I am sent to bring

Sri Aurobindo. "My humble tribute to his superhuman greatness on the occasion of his centenary celebration (1972):
>   Who once have seen thy Face have known, O Friend:
>   'Tis not a myth that Love is one with Light."

that down or open the way for its descent or at least make it more possible or not. Let all men jeer at me if they will or all hell fall upon me if it will for my presumption—I go on till I conquer or perish. This is the spirit in which I seek the Supermind, no hunting for greatness for myself or others.

The mighty seers in all climes have said with one voice that at the summit of consciousness knowledge is seen to be indistinguishable from love. Nevertheless, it cannot be gainsaid that on the lower plateaus of consciousness, knowledge and love manifest themselves in distinctly different lilts and rhythms. So we would be better advised to "suspend judgment" until—to paraphrase the epigram of Sri Krishnaprem —we grow to love knowledge more and know more of love. For then, our hearts tell us, we shall be able to achieve the great vision which enabled Sri Aurobindo to see God not merely as Love but—as the *Bhagavat* also has put it—as a "Servant of Love":

> Thou who pervadest all the worlds below
>   Yet sitst above:
> Master of all who work and rule and know
>   Servant of Love:

And the vision that made him realize God as a vast Creator seeking humble birth in the lowest of the low is as moving as it is convincing:

> Thou who disdainest not the worm to be
>   Nor even the clod:
> Therefore we know in that humility
>   That thou art God.

Before I met Sri Aurobindo I had, indeed, admired him as a great sage, but I could never get rid of the irrepressible regret that he remained too remote to be sought as a practical guide or help except perhaps in the way a finger post is —to be consulted rather than loved or be loved by in return. In effect, he was—to such as we—more like a lighthouse than a boat. But when I came to know him better I envisioned in him a loving pilot who could address even me as *a friend and a son* and be intimately interested in my fulfillment and salvation. Yes, knowledge is all right, but the heart hungers, first and last, for love and understanding sympathy.

But then, slowly, I came to realize something more: I saw that to know him more was to love him more. That is why I thirsted to know him more as, indeed, I wanted to know Sri Ramana Maharshi more. I can recall how immensely relieved I was when the latter told me in reply to my pointed question as to whether he set as much store by love as by knowledge: "How could I pit the one against the other, since *bhakti* is *jnanamata*," that is, love is the mother of knowledge. I bowed to Bhagavan Ramana Maharshi for having paid this tribute to love, even as I bowed to Sri Aurobindo for having endeared God to us as the "Servant of Love."

In the Vedas I read long ago: "*Brahmavit Brahmaiva Bhavati*"—"one who knows God becomes God." I freely confess that I do not know precisely what this imports. For if it means that he becomes omnipotent or omniscient like God and transcends overnight his human limitations (as is claimed by some fanatics), then it is obviously unacceptable to such as we who cannot equate fanaticism with true faith and wisdom. But if it means that such a man acts from an exalted consciousness which fills us with an ineffable sweetness, lights our path in darkness and goads us to seek one-pointedly and to love selflessly the God of Truth and Love, then surely there can be little objection, since we can testify from personal experience that they do carry us toward the beckoning God, even as wings carry us toward the purer heights. But the wings are not identical with the sky—any more than the sages are with God. For God, to be absolute, must be infallible and emancipated from finite limitations, and no sage, however great of stature, can claim to be utterly beyond the pale of error or of human limitations. This is not to say that he should not be worshipped. On the contrary, no sage can be truly appreciated for what he is till we have offered him our hearts' homage. For only then can he help us with his light in the fullest measure and make us grow in knowledge, tolerance and love, till we come to realize what we have got to realize. More explicitly, while we must, of set purpose, be loyal to his essential guidance, we must not, if we are to stay true to ourselves, follow him blindly, echoing whatever he says. We can—and, indeed, often should—suspend our judgment if and when our hearts cannot fully accept all that he says, but we should not, for that reason, feel obligated to subscribe to what we find unacceptable till we have experientially verified it. Apropos, Guru Nanak said something which, as an admonition, can hardly be improved upon: "You may, indeed, say that such and such a statement you *believe* to be true because your guru says it, but you have no right to assert that it *is* true unless and until you have seen or known it to be true." This, at any rate, is how I myself have come to cherish gurus, to wit, as reliable pathfinders in life's pilgrimage to Truth, to be venerated seeingly but not idolized fanatically. And among such heroic spirits who are intermittently sent to us from on high to relieve our global gloom, Sri Aurobindo certainly stands in a class by himself, not only because of his profound knowledge of human nature and encyclopedic grasp of racial cultures, but also because of his marvelous power of expression both in prose and verse. I stress these three aspects of his personality knowing full well that by themselves they do not mark someone as a spiritual personality. But about his spiritual greatness I need hardly add anything to the tribute I have paid him already and fairly exhaustively.* So I will only say that he gleamed always for those who knew him a little intimately as one of the brightest beacons in the dark and stormy waters of life, a lighthouse that created faith in the

* In my *Yogi Sri Krishnaprem, Sri Aurobindo Came to Me, Among the Great* and *Yugarshi Sri Aurobindo.*

shipwreck of rational hope. It is this faith which made him write to me once: "To me the ultimate value of a man is to be measured not by what he says, nor even by what he does, but by what he *becomes.*"

And he *became* a seer of seers who was thrilled by what he had *seen,* which in its turn made him into what he became: a prophet of the incredible future that is waiting for Man in the next phase of his evolution:

> Night shall awake to the anthem of the stars,
> The days become a happy pilgrim march . . .
> A few shall see what none yet understands;
> God shall grow up while wise men talk and sleep;
> For man shall not know the coming till its hour
> And belief shall be not till the work is done.
>
> (*Savitri* I, IV)

Even those who have seen him only once have known something, were it even a fraction, of the rapturous discovery that impelled him to write:

> A deathbound littleness is not all we are:
> Immortal our forgotten vastnesses
> Await discovery in our summit selves.
>
> (*Savitri* I, IV)

But even those who have never seen or known him have been left the supreme legacy of his mighty vision and message, the last fruit of a *tapasya* (mystic self-discipline) which counted no cost to attain what few even dare to contemplate:

> The Supermind shall claim the world for Light
> And thrill with love of God the enamoured heart
> And place Light's crown on Nature's lifted head
> And found Light's reign on her unshaking base . . .
> Thus shall the earth open to divinity
> And common natures feel the wide uplift,
> Illumine common acts with the Spirit's Ray
> And meet the Deity in common things.
>
> (*Savitri* XI, I)

I must pause here, even at the risk of ending on a note of anticlimax, to speculate a little about how Sri Aurobindo is likely to be estimated by posterity. It will be impressed, I feel, not merely because he was a great poet and a great yogi, but also because he was a paradox, to wit, an earthling who yet transcended the downpull of the earth while loving and blessing it as no earth-enamored poet had ever loved and blessed her.* For in him the paradox was resolved—so will men feel—precisely because he fully believed in the ever-deepening significance of earth-life and what it connoted. This he explained to me in a brief but supremely suggestive letter in answer to my "realistic doubt" as to the possibility of such an inglorious, disharmonious and creaturely thing as our earth being redeemed overnight by a glorious supramental apocalypse:

All the nonevolutionary worlds are worlds limited to their own harmony like the *life heavens*.† The earth, on the other hand, is an evolutionary world—not at all glorious or harmonious even as a material world (except in certain appearances) but rather most sorrowful, disharmonious, imperfect.

Yet in that imperfection is the urge toward a higher and many-sided perfection. It contains the last finite which yet yearns to the Supreme Infinite; it is not satisfied by the sense-joys precisely because in the conditions of the earth it is able to see their limitations. God is pent in the mire—mire is not glorious, so there is no claim to glory or beauty here—but the very fact imposes a necessity to break through that prison to a consciousness which is ever rising toward the heights.

In other words, in Sri Aurobindo's vision is harmonized the last incompatibility, blended the irreconcilable antinomy

---

* Earth is the chosen place of mightiest souls;
  Earth is the heroic spirit's battle-field,
  The forge where the Arch-mason shapes his works

                                                        (*Savitri* XI, I)

  † Sri Aurobindo uses the term to mean the higher worlds of gods and radiant beings, which exist side by side with our world.

between matter and spirit. Not that the ancient seers had missed the supreme clue: their deep intuition, too, had laughed at the misleading *maya* of the phenomenal reality and posited: "*Yadeveha tadamutra*"—"Whatever is there is here as well." But the trouble is that the tyranny of the physical-rational mind has come today to be so universally idolized that such a mystic vision, being beyond its comprehension, is scoffed at by the modern mind as too cryptic to be taken seriously, if not as too good to be true. That is why Sri Aurobindo is likely to be looked upon by posterity as the new Messiah of this postscientific age—a true Messiah because even when he met the challenge of reason with reason, he could asseverate, with the authority of his vision which no mental reason could command:

> This world was not built with random bricks of chance,
> A blind God is not destiny's architect:
> A conscious power has drawn the plan of life,
> There is a meaning in each curve and line.
>
> (*Savitri*, VI, II)

Which meaning must warrant that even death or defeat is not the tragedy it seems, because:

> Arisen from the tragic crash of life,
> Arisen from the body's torture and death,
> The spirit rises mightier by defeat.
> Its Godlike wings grow wider with each fall,
> Its splendid failures sum to victory.

Looking at the world from below—from our plane of the mind and senses—we may be inclined to entertain doubts about our human failures culminating in divine victory, but Sri Aurobindo looked on cosmic evolution from above and so viewed something breathtaking because he saw God himself, descended into the world, slowly but victoriously surmounting obstacles through the miracle manifestation of His

Divine Power—"through Nature's contraries"*—and limned
what he had visioned with poetry that came down like a
torrent of gleaming gold:

> Our imperfection towards perfection toils,
> The body is the chrysalis of a soul:
> The infinite holds the finite in its arms,
> Time travels towards revealed eternity . . .
> In all we feel his presence and his power.
> A blaze of his sovereign glory is the sun,
> A glory is the gold and glimmering moon.
> A glory is his dream of purple sky.
> A march of his greatness are the wheeling stars.
> His laughter of beauty breaks out in green trees,
> His moments of beauty triumph in a flower;
> The blue sea's chant, the rivulet's wandering voice
> Are murmurs falling from the Eternal's harp.
> The world is God fulfilled in outwardness.
> His ways challenge our reason and our sense;
> By blind brute movements of an ignorant Force,
> By means we slight as small, obscure or base
> A greatness founded upon little things,
> He has built a world in the unknowing Void.
> His forms he has massed from infinitesimal dust:
> His marvels are built from insignificant things.
> If mind is crippled, life untaught and crude,
> If brutal masks are there and evil acts,
> They are incidents of his vast and varied plot,
> His great and dangerous drama's needed steps.
>
> (*Savitri* X, III)

And the glorious denouement *will* come because the "archi-
tect of immortality" cannot possibly fail as the omnipotent
leader of human destiny has been urging us onward sleeplessly to fulfill man with the crown of Supramental consciousness on the glorious heights where:

* Our destiny is written in double terms
Through Nature's contraries we draw near God
(Savitri VI, I)

The Spirit shall look out through Matter's gaze
And Matter shall reveal the Spirit's Face.

To end with my humble tribute to his superhuman greatness on the occasion of his centenary celebration (1972):

Knowing thee once, do we not know the Truth,
However fragmentary? For though we may
Still fail to glimpse thy New Dawn which can soothe
Our famished eyes with His unsullied Day,

Yet once thou mak'st our half-lit consciousness
Reverberate thy fire-thrilled melody,
Will not its rapture lead us to His Grace
Resolving our discord with thy harmony?

When in the labyrinthine thrall of Fate
We grope for a Ray, 'tis thy love's benison
Heals dusk with its moon-song inviolate
Our dark-enamoured moods, alas, disown!

Outsoaring our science-fostered strife and din
Thou wing'st the blue—no dragons make thee quail.
Thou hast attained what only the elect could win:
A summit view no clouds can countervail.

Thou hast won through at the long journey's end,
To the Sun-elixir that quells the hordes of Night.
Who once have seen thy Face have known, O Friend:
'Tis not a myth that Love is one with Light.

Dilip

PART TWO

by
Indira Devi

Sri Dilip Kumar Roy and Indira Devi. "Indira was drawn to her guru by his innate power of truth and sincerity."

18

JAI GURU

It is not easy for a spiritual aspirant to write an auto-biography. For in the last analysis, all that hinders her must make her diffident. Shall she be able to rise above these contradictions? Will not the desire to appear better than what she is prevail over the urge to be strictly truthful? How can one write an autobiography without bringing oneself to the forefront all the time? And there is the far more serious problem of exhibiting what is so intimate to one's heart.

Spiritual life and experience is not an academic question with Indira. It is the most precious, intimate and sacred part of her life and the most vividly real. It is what makes her life worth living. It *is* her life. Her love for the Beloved is her very existence. Her search for Him is as essential to her as the air she breathes. Whether or where she shall arrive she does not know. Nor does it seem very important, since she needs only to love and seek her Beloved who is her goal. To seek Him in joy, in pain, in darkness, in light. This search is her fulfillment. What she shall become at the journey's end she does not know; there is no urge to *become* anything, the heart longs just to be His—just to seek and, above all, to love. This love for the little-known Beloved is the one passion of her life.

Indira was drawn to her guru by his innate power of truth

and sincerity. She knows He is her guide and master with the same conviction that she knows God is.

What is Indira's mission in life? Very often this question is asked. Her mission is to seek and to love, love, love, first and last. No power has been given to her to better the world, but the power to love those who come to Indira is her own. And the power to give herself to her Beloved—though it is not she who is the giver. It is this love that has wrenched her from her moorings and swept her into the storm of its passion. It pursued her all through her life. The faint footsteps that she heard walking over memory's lane came closer with time till she felt the touch on her heart, and before she knew she was caught.

19

EARLY SIGNS

A MAGIC HAND balanced the golden disc of the sun on the emerald surface of the lake, tantalizingly bounced it a few times on the waves, and then swept it away from sight into the dark folds of the magician's robe. With the same dexterous movements it threw up a few stars in the sky and they hung there like little lamps with no support.

Night had fallen in the small village of Ziarat in Baluchistan. Halfway on the winding footpath up the hill, a pair of ageless eyes, shining with wisdom, looked kindly into a child's bewildered eyes. The little one had, on an impulse, picked up the fallen stick of a *fakir* (a Muslim saint) and handed it back to him.

"Thank you for helping me, little one! These eyes depend only on the inner light—the outer vision is hazy. The stick is a great help. This is not our first meeting and it shall not be the last. This *fakir* will be there when you need him most, the Lord bless you!"

The child understood very little of what was said and skipped away to resume her play with her little brother.

It was the year 1927 and the girl was just seven years old. The family had come for a picnic from Quetta to celebrate her little brother's fifth birthday. Indira, the little girl, stayed with her maternal grandparents during her holidays. She had been sent to a very selective boarding school at the age of five as her grandmother found her too naughty and intractable. Naughty she certainly was, always getting into scrapes and being hauled up before her beloved Granny, who, in spite of her tender love for her granddaughter, could not help punishing her very often.

Only the other day Indira had let loose a neighbor's calf so that it could have its fill of the mother's milk. But the neighbor's wife had come running to her granny and complained.

"Rani ma, your daughter is a *devi* [a goddess], how come she has given birth to this little devil? She is always up to mischief. Now what shall we do for milk today?"

"Take my share of milk, Auntie," chimed in Indira. "I dislike milk and dislike more the starved, hungry look in the little calf's eyes. After all, the cow's milk was meant for the sustenance of the calf and not us."

Indira's parents lived in Fort Sandeman, a town on the border of Afghanistan. They were a happy, contented couple —very well off, religious and generous to a fault.

Indira's only clear memory of her beautiful mother was of her last moments on earth. She was just twenty-seven and had developed blood poisoning after an accident. Indira remembers being awakened by her nurse in the early hours of the morning and taken to her mother's bedside.

Her beautiful face looked pale and emaciated, but an exquisite smile quivered on her lips. She called her two daughters Indira and Kanta closer and, taking Indira's hand in hers, said: "You are my daughter and son in one. Never forget you are my child. I will watch over you *always.*"

She asked for the time, and being told that it was four minutes to five, requested her brother to read a certain chapter from the Bhagavad Gita. Everyone seemed flurried and restless except the departing one. The servants were called and she spoke kindly to them asking them to forgive her for any hard words she might have uttered to them.

There was not a trace of pain or regret on her face. She looked so beautifully calm and content.

Indira's father came up to her, and taking his dying wife in his arms, wept: "Please say something to me."

"Don't make promises you may not be able to keep. I have lived in joy with you and I go in joy now. Just move away please, so I may concentrate wholly on the Lord."

Her husband clasped her closer to him. Thereafter she just averted her face, uttered the two words: "*Hari Om—Hari Om—Hari Om*,"* and was gone.

A beatific smile still played on her lips. This made such a deep impression on Indira that she could never again feel that death was something dreadful and loathsome. Death to her symbolized something beautiful and inevitable, to be faced with dignity and harmony. Of course, she did not know how she herself would feel when her own time to depart drew near. She prayed that she, too, might pass away like her mother.

There are some incidents which, though trivial in themselves, leave an indelible mark on one's life. Whenever Indira strolls back in memory's lane a few things that happened so long go stand out like little lanterns in a dark alley.

Indira always aspired to be a nun, join a convent and make all the sisters there laugh, as they seemed to her so pure and yet too serious. God did not play a predominant part in her childhood, though she never doubted His existence. There was one strong and lasting feeling she had toward Him. It started as far back as she could remember and is still there as strong if not stronger: the feeling of deep gratitude. Not once in her fifty-two years has she felt that the Lord was unjust or that she was not getting her due. In every calamity, at every setback, whether mental or physical, this conviction is there: "He knows best and left to my *karma* it should have

* In the ordinary sense this can be rendered "Lord, O Lord." An exact translation would require a treatise.

been worse. It is only the Divine Grace that has made it bearable." This sense of gratitude is there when things go right, and more so when they go wrong. She knows that she has always been at the receiving end with the Lord and the guru, received so much undeservingly and unasked that she would be a very petty person not to acknowledge her debt.

It was in May, 1935, that a special sign of His compassion was unveiled to her. She had just arrived at Quetta that evening from Lahore for her summer holidays. Her sister had gone to her parents, her father and her kind and loving stepmother at Muree (a hill station near Rawalpindi—now in Pakistan). Quetta, five thousand feet above sea level, is cold even in summer. The family had gone to bed. Theirs was a large household as her grandfather sheltered a number of poor relatives. The young boys studied in school or college and the women stayed at home helping with the daily chores and reading the scriptures.

At about 3 A.M. Indira saw in a dream that she was making a house of cards when there was a deep rumble and the playhouse of cards toppled down; but, strangely enough, what fell was not cards but brick and mortar. She heard a distinct feminine voice call: "Get up and go out at once." It was repeated again and again till she was compelled to leave her bed and run out onto the veranda, whence she could see one of her aunts bending over her infant son's cradle. On seeing Indira she called out: "Go back to bed! What mischief are you up to now?"

Indira shouted back: "Come out, Auntie! You must. Something dreadful is going to happen."

She did not wait for her aunt's reply and ran out through the almond grove onto the tennis court. No sooner had she stepped onto the lawn than there was a terrible rumble and in less than a minute the whole house came hurtling down before her terrified eyes. Through the dust storm and the screams and wails from all around one thing stood out clearly in her mind: amid all that ruin and rubble a single glass case remained unharmed with the Belgian cut glass all intact.

Thirty people had died in that one house. Indira's grandfather was found in a sitting posture. Death had surprised him while he was at his early morning devotions.

The summer holidays were on again and Indira was back home, this time with her parents as there was no one left in her grandfather's family at Quetta except an uncle who was posted in Rawalpindi and a widowed aunt who was not in Quetta at the time of the great earthquake.

Indira loved animals, especially dogs, but her love had landed her in a hole. A neighbor's dog had bitten her on the wrist, and even though it was known that the dog died two days later Indira was so scared of the antirabies injections that she did not confide in anyone about it.

A month later she felt terribly stiff all over the body and before she knew what was happening lost consciousness as the dread symptoms of hydrophobia appeared. All possible medical aid was summoned but in vain. She was dying, said the doctors who gave her morphine injections to make her end less painful.

As was the custom in the Punjab when anybody is about to expire, Indira's elder brother Jogindar had gone to the beggars' colony to distribute alms. He was accosted by a Muslim *fakir* who asked him why he was weeping.

"My sister is dead, *Baba*,"* replied Jogindar.

"Is she dead or dying?" the other questioned pointedly.

"She must be dead now, *Baba*," Jogindar sighed. "When I left the house the death rattle had already set in and the hiccough was terrible."

"Take me to her, my son, I owe her a debt and I promised to come when she would need me most."

Jogindar reluctantly drove him home, telling him on the way: "The best doctors have been summoned from all over India. But they have all resigned. So what can *you* do, *Baba*?"

---

* A saint is often addressed as *Baba*, meaning father.

When they arrived, the committee of doctors was waiting helplessly in the sitting room. The *Baba* was taken inside unnoticed. He asked everyone to leave the dying girl. Some people who peeped in from outside saw him spit something into her mouth. Then he took a swab of cotton, dipped it in water and moistened her tongue. After repeating this a few times he took a teaspoonful of water and let it trickle in. She swallowed it. The patient with hydrophobia cannot take water, so the doctors had been giving her glucose to counteract dehydration.

Upon this there was such excitement that the astonished doctors wanted to see the *Baba* who had brought the girl back from the maws of death. But he was nowhere to be found, and was never seen again.

Years later, in Pondicherry, Indira saw in her meditation a cave near a mountain stream. There was light in the cave though no lamp or candle was lit inside. The same *fakir* was sitting, resting one hand on a wooden rest. He seemed to look through Indira, his twin eyes glowing like searchlights. He smiled compassionately and then vanished.

Indira was familiar with that hilly land and so her guru wrote to his friend who was the governor of that province to make inquiries at Nainital. The answer came a fortnight later. There was a Muslim saint staying in a hut on the bank of the mountain river Kosi. He came out only after dark and shepherds gave him some milk and bread. It was said that every year when the Kosi played havoc in the monsoon season, and all the villages were vacated because of the flood, this Muslim saint's hut survived unharmed and he never left his retreat. His name was Rajib Sain. Indira contacted him sometimes in her meditation and he always had the same kind smile and sat in the same erect posture.

20

AWAKENING

INDIRA WAS fifteen when the Kosi *Baba* had come to rescue her from the jaws of death.

She was hypersensitive and a proud girl. She was much
misunderstood and it was only when she met her guru that
she realized that pain came through ignorance and through
her attachments. Much to her discomfiture, she discovered
that she did not even understand herself, so how could
others understand her?

Indira was very abnormal where sex was concerned. She
loved her friends very deeply but she felt a deep revulsion
to sex. She shuddered at the thought of being touched by
anyone. Soon after her marriage, even though she loved her
husband very tenderly, she could not bear to live with him
as a wife. Besides her husband she was very fond of one
friend, for he was the only one who unconsciously understood her problem and loved her on *her* conditions and not
his own.

This aversion caused a lot of disharmony and meant a good
deal of heartache for her. Those around her could not understand how one who welcomed men's company, who laughed
and joked with them, could draw the line halfway and say:
"Thus far and no further." She did not think that she was
better or worse than the others, she only knew that she was
different.

It was in 1945, seven years after Indira's marriage, and five years after the birth of her son Anil, that things began to happen which changed the whole course of her life. One of these—she considered it the least important—was her development of the gift of reading thoughts. At first she dismissed it as mere coincidence and then as imagination, but when she verified it again and again she could not help admitting to herself that she had indeed developed this faculty and she was almost ashamed of herself. Every time somebody's thoughts were unmasked to her she felt as though she were peeping into the bathroom of a stranger having his shower. So she locked up this disconcerting secret in her heart, having confided it only to her very close friend Ladli.

At this time she was living with her husband in Bombay while Anil had been sent to the Welham Boarding School in Dehradun. They were staying in one of the lovely suites facing the sea on the top floor of the Taj Hotel. It was the first week of December. They were going out to dinner with Ladli and her husband Akhtar.

At about 8:30 P.M. Indira had just finished dressing. She loved beautiful clothes and jewelry. Her only purpose in coming to Bombay once a year was to select some new saris and jewels. Indira looked in the lifesize mirror to see if her sari was in order but what she saw in the mirror petrified her. She screamed, for staring back at her was not Indira but the hollow eyes of a skeleton.

Her husband came running from the living room. When she told him what had happened he laughed at her and said: "My dear girl, you read too much. So you see skeletons in mirrors. It must be a picture hanging on the opposite wall or the sea breeze playing tricks with the curtains."

She looked at the opposite wall and saw that it was blank. It must be her imagination, she thought—or some shadow falling in a tricky way.

Her husband went back to the living room and before

leaving the dressing room she looked back and there it was—
the skeleton had reappeared!

Indira rushed out of the room and did not say anything
more to her husband. When she mentioned it to Ladli she got
another shock. Ladli, who was much more mature and wiser
than Indira, looked at her for a moment and said: "Don't
you realize that this may not be imagination at all? You *are*
psychic, you know—otherwise how do you read people's
thoughts?"

"Psychic? Me?" Indira pleaded. "Oh Ladli, will I start
seeing ghosts now? Please don't say such dreadful things!"

"What a contradiction you are, Indira!" Ladli said. "You
read thoughts, have prophetic dreams, hear voices—remember the Quetta incident—you feel vibrations—yet, paradoxically, you love fun and clothes and jewels and people around
you. Maybe you'll become like Mother Theresa."

"Please, please Ladli, don't frighten me! I can't even dream
of turning holy—a *World Mother*. Never doing anything
wrong, always sitting on a pedestal. No, no, I'll never be able
to live up to it. I would much rather be your own little
sister. You have such a wonderful sense of humor, the saints
look so serious and superior. If you make me into a saint,
then you will have to come for my blessing and, Ladli, I
promise I'll stick out my tongue at you and shock all the
devotees. Let us talk of more cheerful things."

But even as she spoke, Indira remembered a beautiful vision
she had seen of Christ. She had found herself in a city, walking on a cobbled street. There were high building walls on
both sides. From a side alley the sound of something heavy
being dragged could be heard drawing nearer and nearer; and
then the whole atmosphere changed—the air became sur-
charged with something that cannot be described.

A few men with heavy clumsy clothes and rope sandals
came in front and then there was someone bent double, dragging on his back a roughly hewn tree shaped something like

"'Maybe the Lord expects something else from you. You know, Indira, when you are not up to mischief or fooling around, you do have a very unworldly look about you.'"

a cross. It was too heavy for him and he was bare-bodied except for a sort of Indian *lungi*.* She pushed her way through the crowd, and drawing near the person dragging the cross, cried out: "Oh Lord, why do you allow them to do this to you?" She went down on her knees and wept. He who seemed so frail and weary looked up at her and she saw that His eyes were not sad. They were like two deep pools of clear water, full of compassion. For He understood why men did not understand. He forgave those very unfortunate beings who hated him and offered them Divine Love. He who was pure and sinless was punished by sinners for their own sins. The eyes smiled though the lips were parched. Indira was overwhelmed by the experience. Peace coursed from her head right down through her body.

Why had she seen this vision in the midst of her multifarious engagements and social service? Could such a momentous thing happen for nothing? As she was thinking over these things, Ladli smiled and continued: "I wonder though why you saw a skeleton! Maybe the Lord expects something else from you. You know, Indira, when you are not up to mischief or fooling about, you do have a very unworldly look about you. I often wonder why you who love beautiful things get so quickly detached from them once they are acquired. Why is it that you who love life so intensely and have so few inhibitions feel repelled by sex? Anyway, don't worry, even if one day you do turn holy, we shall have laughter and holiness together—what a blessing!"

Just then Ladli's husband Akhtar came in and said: "Indira, we met a Norwegian priest—a wonderful man. Do you know, the gift of prophecy suddenly descended on him without his reading any books. He can predict your future from your palm imprint."

---

* A wraparound cloth that reaches from the waist to the ankles.

Ladli had a brain wave: "Akhtar, let us send him an imprint of Indira's palm on a smoked paper and see what he says. Indira is very puzzled about something and wants to know what is her future."

"Send it by all means, but you know I have no faith in palmistry and astrology," Indira said.

"But it can't harm you, Indira. Let us have a try just for fun," Akhtar answered.

The palm imprint on a plain smoked paper was sent to this Norwegian monk who in reply wrote to Ladli's brother Sultan:

I herewith send you a brief reading of the hand-print you have sent me. A detailed analysis will take at least a month and as you are anxious to know only certain things I send just a sketch now and the full picture will follow:

1. *Childhood:* Ideal environments—very happy, healthy, highly intelligent, imaginative, supersensitive and playful child. A born leader.

2. *Marriage:* Almost a worshipful devotion to duty is indicated henceforth. The moral strength of character and a complete devotion to mental elevation, the courage and determination to stand by what is right regardless of consequences become the most remarkable features after this at the age of fifteen or twenty. Three male children in the first ten years of married life are a probability. They prove a strong link between the parents.

3. A restlessness and a thirst for truth, knowledge and spiritual peace is a very dominating feature now, this sudden disturbance in the normal life may be due to some sense-shock or the influence of some particular person.

After this there is no sign of real peace or contentment, the struggle and striving for attaining something better and higher grows stronger and stronger. About the age of thirty a complete change is suggested. For the first time the veil falls off and the true and pure soul is revealed. All that the "hand" deserves, it must achieve now. From now on it lives in its own field and deserving circumstances.

It is undoubtedly a most remarkable hand—extraordinary—highly extraordinary, rare, refined, revealing almost complete success in its worldly wants, yet "wanting" more. The owner must necessarily be a wonderful, rare and unique personality.

Character: Extremely honest, clean, refined, philanthropic, very religious, truthful, sensitive, extraordinarily intelligent. Forgiveness and moral strength are rocklike, unfaltering. The love for honor and dignity is remarkable. The lack of interest in worldly goods—and the complete absence of sexual desire are predominant features. It is interesting to note that in spite of the strong distaste for the above, there will always be an abundance of wealth, and the owner of this hand will be a magnetic and irresistible attraction for the opposite sex. The spell cast by contact will be impossible to break for nearly all those the owner wants to keep a hold on. A desire to renounce all will often creep up till such time that there is a complete detachment from all that the world holds precious.

Health: Poor, respiratory organs weak, there is an indication of death due to heart failure or hemorrhage at the age of thirty-four and forty-five when life must end. Though always casting a halo of peace and prosperity on those around, the "Owner" shall never be "happy." . . . Performing all duties religiously and strictly, yet staying miles away from all bondage. A very lonely soul, indeed—wandering alone, striving for spirituality, undaunted yet afraid to take what by right is its own. Doubting its own ability, intelligence and power is the most depressing factor in the hand. Terribly depressing moods another. Demanding little from life, giving all, always struggling against itself. It is hard to say anything about this extraordinary personality in a general tone. It is a hand so unusual—almost from the *books*.

Physically the owner of the hand must be extremely pleasant, charming and attractive. The very embodiment of art, culture and grace.

Forgive me for this hurried note. A detailed reading to the best of my ability shall follow.

In the meantime kindly ask the owner to send me the toe-print, "head measurement" and a photograph. I am proud to tell you about the hidden treasures in the hand of your very dear sister.

Sykelke Reed
23rd March, '45.*

* The Reverend Reed predicted that Indira would turn to the spiritual life at the age of thirty. I met her first in 1946 when she was barely twenty-six. Thereafter she wrote to me a letter that she was groping in unutterable darkness and needed guidance. I invited her to be my guest in my Pondicherry flat—I was then practicing yoga under the aegis of Sri Aurobindo—and she complied in February, 1949. On March 26 she completed her twenty-ninth year and had just stepped into her thirtieth, when I gave her the initiation. So the monk's prediction was correct. His other prediction, about her death at the age of thirty-four or forty-five, was no less remarkable for, in each of those years, the good Lord had to work a real miracle to pull her through the worst possible medical crises. On the general accuracy of his remarkable character reading, I need hardly comment.—D.K.R.

21

DREAMS AND VOICES

INDIRA CAME back from Ladli's place a little confused. She certainly did not take seriously her friend's comment that she was "psychic," but could not solve her riddle about the skeleton. Anyway, she thought it best not to think about it, lest it become a case of autosuggestion.

She went to sleep late after reading a book and woke up with a start, for she was having an oft-repeated dream.

Very often, since her childhood, she dreamt of flying freely and gracefully like a bird, always higher and higher, with a feeling of expanding. On occasion, she came back with a jolt, as she did that night, but just as she was sinking back into slumber, she heard a very clear voice say: "Have you come for *this?* Have you come for *this?*"

She woke up with a start and asked her husband: "Did you say something to me?"

Her husband opened his eyes, still heavy with sleep: "What did you eat last night that has disagreed with you?"

"But I *did* hear the voice," Indira protested, "and time and time again. It certainly wasn't my imagination."

Her husband smiled.

"The walls are thin in a hotel; there must be someone talking in the next room. Go back to sleep. What an unearthly hour to wake up and harass an innocent man!" With this he went back to sleep.

Indira tried to sleep but again the same voice spoke: "Why have you come? Have you come for *this*, have you come for *this*?"

Thereafter she could not sleep anymore. The voice was so distinct and close! Who was it? Could it be a part of her own inner being? Or was the whole thing a figment of her imagination? It was so real and yet so unbelievable. She again decided to forget about it all and suggested to herself again and again: "All this has no meaning. It is a dream and because it was so vivid, the thought-link did not break when I woke up. I must not give in to these suggestions."

But it was easier said than done. Two or three days later, while she was in the midst of a social conference, engrossed in explaining to fellow members about the little orphanage she had taken up and was going to run with her own money, she said: "These little children need a home, love and a feeling of security. They want to feel that they belong and are cared for. They are not little bits of junk dumped together to be sold off later or given away to a charitable person. It is our duty to look after them, but duty is not enough. It should be love tinctured with duty and not duty with an icing of compassion. It is not pity that these little ones want. Pity is an undesirable emotion because it harms the one who gives as well as the one who receives. It only fosters weakness and self-indulgence. If these children are to develop the courage necessary to face this harsh world, they need our respect and encouragement and, above all, our love. Pity, especially self-pity, saps one's strength and induces an inferiority complex. I feel very strongly about it. Children should be encouraged to face reality, they must not waste their lives being pitied and pitying themselves. I will love them and care for them because I have so many to love me and care for me." As soon as she said that she felt as if all the lights had been switched off and she was plunged into complete darkness—all alone and lost! Of course, the electric lights were on, all right. Indira had never had this experience before. It was stifling and she was frightened. She got up from her chair and told her friends: "I am feeling rather funny—maybe I am in for my usual attack of asthma. I must get back home and have my adrenaline injection. I hope you will excuse me." With these words she left the meeting. A feeling of utter darkness and loneliness persisted and she again head the voice: "Have you come for *this*, have you come for *this*? *What* have you come for?"

It stopped for a while and then again repeated the same sentence.

Fortunately, by the time Indira reached home all was well and normal again.

This voice and this sudden experience of groping in utter darkness became more and more frequent, till she became almost frantic. She had not lost interest in her social life or social work but again and again she had the same experience until she was convinced that something very queer was transpiring.

Indira consulted doctors and a psychiatrist who advised her to have another child. At the time Anil, her son, was eight years old. Her husband pleaded with her to accept the doctors' advice, the more so as he was convinced that she was too busy with outer activities—the orphanage, the lepers' home, the school (where destitute women came and learned sewing, cooking, knitting and other crafts), the girl guides and the women's council. He said that running her house efficiently or being a good housewife was not enough, nor did the desire to love orphans and destitutes cut any ice with him. "Charity begins at home my girl! Start with loving your husband and your family members first and then you can go about doling out your love to outsiders."

He wrote to her father, too, that he was worried about her as she was having these fits of deep depression and sometimes had a very far-off look in her eyes.

Her father wired to her to come immediately to Mussoorie where the land was carpeted with snow and the trees stood

"'What a contradiction you are, Indira! You read thoughts, have prophetic dreams, hear voices, yet, paradoxically, you love fun and clothes and jewels and people around you.'"

like white-uniformed sentinels crowned with snow-helmets. It would do her a world of good, he said, and he wrote also to her husband to bring her along.

Indira first went to Lahore to meet her husband's people. Her father had written to her that a dear friend of his, Herr Franz, was in Lahore and they could all motor up to Mussoorie. Herr Franz was visiting India and, as in the past, would spend a few days at Mussoorie before going back to Germany.

She met Herr Franz for the first time in Lahore and asked him to come to dinner with her—she was going to see some friends and telephone them about him.

They were both sitting and watching a beautiful *Bharat Natyam* dance by a Russian dancer. The dancer and her husband were on their way to Mussoorie where, along with the magician Gogia Pasha, they were engaged by the Savoy Hotel. Indira looked at Franz to explain some intricate steps to him (she was a dancer herself) when she read his thoughts:

"Are you a psychiatrist, trying to analyze my frame of mind?" asked Indira.

The other was startled. "Who told you," he questioned, "your father? But he asked me not to mention it to you."

"I just know sometimes, I don't understand how or why —it just happens. I feel troubled about it but I have no control in the matter nor can I read thoughts by deliberate effort. It is as if I were looking through a glass cupboard, and it is not only the thought of the moment, but on rare occasions of the past or future of some person that passes before my eyes. Why does it happen? Why do I happen to be abnormal? You know, I may be just the patient for you." Indira laughed.

"But I, too, am having second thoughts," Franz replied. "For it is you who have started analyzing my mind. You are certainly not mad, as we psychologists know madness, but you are not quite normal either."

"You mean I am on the borderline?" Indira inquired.

"You are an enigma, Indira," he evaded. "I haven't come across such a case before. But tell me: do your people know about this?"

"No, they haven't an inkling," she said: "I have never spoken about it to anyone except my friend Ladli. So please don't mention anything to my father."

He told her then that he was a psychiatrist, though now the roles seemed to be reversed. He became a very dear friend and help to her, especially when the mystic experiences began to descend in an avalanche after her taking permanent refuge at Sri Aurobindo Ashram on February 20, 1949.

Franz stood by her in her hour of need and said: "You know, Indira, what is happening to you is neither hallucination nor autosuggestion; it is something beyond the ken of the mind. I certainly don't understand it, but after knowing you and loving you for four years I am interested in it and do listen to all you say with respect. But don't be afraid and don't analyze it too much. Why don't you let things take their natural course?"

"I can't help thinking about it, Franz," Indira argued, "but my chief difficulty is that I can't even identify myself with these experiences. I am somehow outside them—like a witness—or a spectator, yet they are still happening to me, aren't they? How can I stop wondering and thinking about them with my mind? After all, the mind is all I have."

"Maybe you are wrong," Franz replied. "Maybe you have something else besides your mind or over your mind. It is also possible that another force has come into play—it must have lain latent in you."

"But why me? I am neither a magician nor a yogini. My mind gets restless when it fails to understand. Surely, in this age of reason it is not asking too much to want to understand what is happening to me. I know it is true, it is a reality, but why, Franz? I am afraid. Please help me to get rid of this chaotic condition."

"I can sympathize with you but I can't help you. All I say is: 'Be patient—wait and let us see what happens.'"

"For what should we wait?"

"Wait for tomorrow, Indira. The bud is just in its infancy. Let the warmth of the sun open up the petals and then we shall see its full beauty and texture and perceive its perfumed breath properly. Be patient, don't force the issue; it can only harm this little bud. Since you yourself admit that most of the time you are a spectator, or a witness as you call it, why not remain so a little longer? The audience is hardly expected to jump onto the stage and start directing or questioning while the play is on. This fantastic 'mystery drama' has just begun. Let us wait for the end. Wait for tomorrow, Indira. Don't struggle: just wait."

22

INDIRA MEETS HER MASTER

T HE "TOMORROW" that Franz talked of came a few months later.

It was the 7th of October, 1946. She was to preside at a social function of a college where the chief guest was Sri Dilip Kumar Roy, the famous singer and writer. "The man with the golden voice," the principal of the college told her.

Indira had not heard of Sri Roy, but as she loved music passionately she agreed to come. As ill luck would have it, she had a high fever and an asthma attack on the 7th. So, naturally, she couldn't go, but in the afternoon she felt a great urge to see him. It was an inexplicable but an irresistible urge. She told her husband: "I want to see this great man. Please, invite him to come here." Her husband was non-plussed: "Your fever is certainly very high, for you are getting delirious," he said.

"Please don't, I want to see him, why can't you call him? We have half a dozen of India's top-ranking poets staying with us—he can hear some good poetry or attend the poets' conference afterward," Indira insisted.

"And what exactly do I write to him? 'O Great Man, please come to my house and see my wife who is in bed with high fever and asthma!' No, my dear, you are roaming in the wonderland of delirium now—we'll discuss this when you are back to your normal senses tomorrow."

"But," Indira pleaded, "he may go away tomorrow, he is an extremely busy man, I am sure."

"Exactly," her husband said. "And that is just why I am not going to make such a foolish and inconsiderate request of him. Besides, why do you want him to come? To see your flushed face and gasping breath? Go to sleep, you'll feel better in the morning."

But Indira was not one to give up. She sent her young brother-in-law with a letter to the principal to request Sri D. K. Roy to visit them.

It was about seven-thirty in the evening when someone came into the room and whispered something to the nurse attending Indira. On inquiry the nurse said: "There are a few gentlemen come to see you. One of them is a sadhu."

"A sadhu! O Lord, what have I to do with a sadhu? But, wait, ask their names."

Her husband came in and said: "You have done it, Indira. Sri Dilip Kumar Roy has come to visit you. Shall I bring him in?"

"Why has he brought this sadhu with him?" Indira asked.

"He has not brought a sadhu, it's he who is the sadhu. But don't worry. Sadhu or no sadhu he has a radiant face, a wonderful personality. For once the fluke or your intuition has clicked—for it is a blessing just to look at him. But hurry, he has two engagements after this. Will you come out? Do you know how spontaneously I bowed down and touched his feet? Don't look shocked. You don't have to do that. You can bow to me, that will be enough."

Indira wrapped herself in a warm shawl and stepped into the sitting room. Sri Roy was sitting on a sofa between two friends. He got up when Indira entered the room. An electric current shot up from the base of her spine to her neck. She folded her hands to him and sat down. The first thing that

Indira Devi at the feet of Sri Dilip Kumar Roy, her guru. "In the darkness she could suddenly see her way and Sri Roy was the torchbearer."

struck her was the purity of his face. There was a stamp of sincerity and strength on his exceedingly handsome face. Indira's husband was awed, too, but being a down-to-earth practical man he said to Sri Roy: "I am the president of the Rotary Club. We would feel honored if you would come and speak to the Rotarians on whichever subject you like on any Monday convenient to you."

Sri Roy declined as he had soon to meet Gandhiji and then go back to Calcutta where he was being given a reception on his fiftieth birthday.

"Then please stay with us for a couple of days on your way to Calcutta and speak at the Rotary Club," Indira's husband persisted.

Sri Roy readily agreed and got up to leave for his next engagement.

Indira's husband and the other members of the household all bowed down to him, but Indira stood still, though a storm was raging through her mind.

As soon as she saw Sri D. K. Roy she felt exultantly as if she had been passing through a dark tunnel and a door had suddenly opened at the other end—letting in a cascade of light. In the darkness she could suddenly see her way and Sri Roy was the torchbearer.

It was fixed that Sri D. K. Roy would be their guest for three days in January next and that he would speak at the Rotary Club on "Music and Spirituality."

Indira's husband was in ecstasy. He said: "What a man! This is what I call a real sadhu, he doesn't look the conventional type at all. Do you know that he is Subhash Chandra Bose's dearest friend? They studied at Cambridge together. He is an extremely learned man. What a blessing to meet such a man! I personally think he came here to see me—and by Jove what a woman you are! Standing there so aloof, high and mighty. You didn't utter a word—did not even have the humility to bow down to him. Anyway, I love to meet people like him though I haven't seen many of his stripe. I could see he liked me, otherwise why would he take all this trouble to break his journey and address the Rotarians. A jeweler alone knows the worth of a jewel. Thank me, my girl, for giving you the opportunity of meeting such a man."

"Why should I thank you?" Indira asked. "You would not even send a letter for me and how you laughed at me in the morning!"

"That is exactly why you must thank me, for if I had not refused your request this morning, you would never have obstinately sent the letter to defy me and he would never have come."

"Don't blow your own trumpet—it is vulgar," Indira admonished.

"Vulgar or not, it is the truth and the truth has the courage to assert itself in this topsy-turvy world, where cultured ladies think it refined to call men of Sri Roy's caliber to pay them visits in their sick rooms."

Indira laughed and went back to her bed.

That night Indira had a curious dream: She was climbing up on a zigzag footpath. The way became narrower and narrower. The forest grew darker and the abyss deeper. Her breath was coming short, and just as she turned around another bend, her heart stood still. On this upward spiral a hundred little paths bifurcated, leading in all directions. Some were dark, some were partially lit and some were too small and barely visible. Indira was utterly confused and did not know which road to take. Suddenly, she heard a voice: "I will lead you from darkness to light." She looked up and saw Sri D. K. Roy standing on top of a hill, smiling. He was lighting her path with a torch, there was a light on his face and light coming out of his chest, showing the way.

Indira cried out: "I am breathless and the path is difficult. Please help me up." She woke up before her prayer was answered.

Indira knew now that Sri D. K. Roy had given her his

pledge to lead her from darkness to light, but she must ask for his help. It was all right to plead in a dream but not so easy in real life.

Indira came from the West Punjab. The people of the Punjab are very brave, happy-go-lucky and hospitable. They are very much influenced by Muslim culture. Their language is Punjabi, but the spoken Punjabi is not the written Punjabi. In West Punjab the official languages were Urdu and English. The Hindus and Muslims lived together in very close kinship till the politicians took their destiny in their own hands, whereupon chaos ensued. All Indira's friends were Muslims and she loved them. But West Punjabis (Pakistanis now) are very down-to-earth practical people—they make the finest soldiers in India. There is hardly a family, rich or poor, that does not have a soldier in it, be it a general or an ordinary sepoy. But as far as spirituality is concerned, they take a back seat in spite of the fact that great saints and seers have been born in the Punjab, as well as the Ten Gurus of the Sikhs—the faith to which Indira's people belonged.

Indira had not the foggiest idea what a guru or an ashram was, or what was meant by *Guruvad*. So her turning to Sri D. K. Roy was not consonant with her background, environment and her own nature. She had always believed that she must do what her own conscience told her to do and that nobody could show her the path. She would have to find it herself. She must mold her own life. About spirituality she knew nothing—was not in the least interested in spiritism, etc. This sudden urge to seek the Light was as much to know what was happening to her as to be led out of this impasse. The only two qualities that were predominant in her were contentment and gratitude, which filled her life with joy. How fortunate she was in this respect was revealed to her a few years later in a vision:

Indira was standing in a big marble hall which was filled with blue light. There was a golden seat at the other end of the hall, and someone was sitting there but she could not see who it was. On Indira's side near the entrance door were a lot of effulgent beings—dressed in gorgeous clothes and jewels.

One by one these beings went up to the throne and were asked who they were and how much they were valued on earth. They all seemed happy and satisfied and said that men did need them, they were all indispensable to the earth. Love, Beauty, Compassion, Charity, Nobility, Honesty, Strength, Patience, Bravery, they all came forward and were duly sent back to serve the earth. When they were all gone Indira saw that one beautiful goddess wearing a white dress was standing against the wall. She looked sad and was perhaps wanting to make her exit unnoticed, when she was summoned before the King. Diffidently she moved forward.

"Who are you, my child? And how much does the world need you?" the Great Being asked.

"I am very little in demand in the world, my Lord. My services are the least required or asked for," the little lady whispered.

"What is your name, child?" asked the King.

"I am called Gratitude."

Next morning Indira told the Mother of the ashram what she had visioned, whereupon she nodded and said, "It's all true; I, too, have had a similar experience."

23

THREE YOGIC FEATS

In January, Sri D. K. Roy came at the request of Indira's husband and stayed three days with them. Indira watched him critically and dispassionately. He had engagements all day: singing, lecturing, visiting the helpless and derelict.

Indira watched him but she probed her own self more, but it was lest there lurk some self-deception, something else besides her search for light that was drawing her to Sri D. K. Roy, or "Dada,"* as they all called him now.

He was a great man—a great musician, a brilliant intellect, a conversationalist with a wonderful sense of humor. He literally scattered joy and the house rang with his childlike laughter. All these gifts he had and more but Indira found darkness that gripped her. Her whole being cried out for something to which her mind could not put a name. So she decided that it was time she left off groping with the mind and started searching with the heart.

She must give up her pride and request Dada to show her the way.

But when he told her about Sri Aurobindo, the Mother and the Pondicherry ashram, she felt afraid.

"Do they laugh there, Dada, or are they always grim?" she asked.

* Elder brother.

"Sri Aurobindo assured me once," Dada answered, "that there *is* laughter in the kingdom of heaven even though there may be no marriage there."

Dada left for Calcutta after three days.

The house suddenly seemed silent and empty in spite of its thirty inmates. All her husband's relations were staying with them after the partition of India.

Indira went away to her father's place in Mhow and the day she arrived there she witnessed a breathtaking yogic feat.

A man dressed in ochre-colored robes, flanked by a boy and a girl of about ten, stood at the gate. The children were possibly twins. When the watchman at the gate asked him what he wanted, he said he would like to show some yogic feats. Indira called him in. Just then her father came back from his office. He asked the sadhu what it was that he wanted to show.

The sadhu said: "Three feats: I will be buried underground for twenty-four hours here and you can cement the top and let your car pass over it. Then the rope trick, and lastly, with my daughter's help, I will show you levitation."

He was promised a hundred rupees for all three feats and he was delighted.

A pit was dug immediately nine feet by four feet and nine feet deep. The sadhu uttered a mantra and jumped in. He plugged his ears with some cloth and closed his eyes and nose with his fingers, then recited a mantra in Sanskrit eleven times. Indira noticed that his breathing grew slower and slower till it was hardly perceptible. The sand and earth were shoveled over him, the ground was leveled and the whole area cemented. The two little children took some money and went away.

Next evening, at 6:30 P.M., they were back and a large number of friends had collected to see the buried sadhu hauled up. When all the earth and the thin cloth covering his face were removed, they saw that the sadhu lay there like one dead. His two children who were lowered into the cavity started rubbing his body with some green oil they had brought with them. A few drops were put in his ears, nostrils and eyes.

After a few minutes he opened his eyes and was helped up from the pit. He looked a trifle tired but none the worse for his ordeal. He drank a little hot milk and, promising to perform the other two feats the next day, took his departure.

Indira's husband, who had come with her, said: "But he doesn't look like a sadhu at all."

"You said Dada doesn't look like a sadhu either," Indira commented.

"Dada doesn't look like a conventional sadhu. He looks like a god."

"How do you know what gods look like?"

"Do you know yourself?"

"No." Indira shook her head.

"So how can you contradict me when I say Dada looks like a god? My dear challenger, just as God made man, according to you—man made God, according to me—out of fear, out of love, out of the desire to cling to someone. God is the creation of man. The devotee loves Him and finds Him beautiful and compassionate, the wrongdoer fears Him and calls Him Kali, the Terrible, or Yama, the God of Death. Rational men don't commit themselves one way or the other nor bother their heads about things their minds can't fathom."

"But you just now said Dada looks like a god," Indira protested.

"A human god. The best and the noblest spirits on earth are gods. Don't you ever find anything godlike about me? What a Hindu wife you are! You were in tears a few days back when we went to see the *Story of Ram*. How did Sita behave even when Ram put her to the severest tests and ordeals? She gave up her palace, her wealth and gladly went to live in the forest for fourteen years with Ram. Nonetheless, you will simply go on arguing and getting the better of your husband! Bah!"

Indira smiled and said: "Don't forget that the husband for whom Sita sacrificed so much was not somebody like you but Ram himself. If she had been married to you she would have asked her father-in-law Dasharath to make the period of exile not fourteen years but twenty while she herself would stay back in the palace in comfort."

Changing the subject, her husband said: "But I can't understand why a man of Dada's stature should become a sadhu. He has everything—wealth, genius, good looks, a marvelous voice and, above all, a giant intellect."

Indira considered this for a moment, then answered: "Perhaps he wants peace."

"Why peace? Are we at war with some country?"

"Don't be silly," Indira said. "I am not talking about national peace, but the inner peace that an individual seeks, harmony. Don't you know that wars are but our inner disharmonies projected outside?"

"Let us not discuss it any further as you have started getting that faraway look in your eyes—it is the beginning of your hallucinations. Don't think. For thinking is not your strong point. Leave it to me—I'll ask Dada himself one day."

The next evening at 6 P.M., while it was still daylight, the sadhu and his two children called again. He was a dark, thin man. He sat down on the floor and took out from his dirty cloth bag a thick rope about thirty feet long. He curled the rope into a sort of ball and then, unwinding it, flung one end up in the sky. The rope swayed a little and then stood stiff in the air as though hanging from a hook. The upper end in the air could be seen clearly. He then called the little boy who, at his bidding, started climbing up the rope as if it were a palm tree. He could be seen going up when, lo and behold, his clothes started falling to the ground! He was holding onto the rope with both hands and feet. The sadhu shouted: "Ram, are you all right?"

"Yes, I am all right, Father," the child answered.

"Do you want to come back?"

"No, Father. I am going to climb higher."

Right before everyone's eyes the child started vanishing very fast, till there was only the rope in the air.

"Ram, where are you?" the sadhu shouted.

From a distance the child answered: "Back to earth."

The sadhu now pulled the rope down and started winding it, when lo, Ram's voice rang out from very near: "Let me help you."

There were no setting, lights, stage, curtain effect—just a poor sadhu in torn clothes performing in the garden. There were about fifty people watching.

The boy was sitting back in place and the sadhu was patting him and grinning.

After a while the girl came forward. She was in a dirty flimsy dress, her hair tied up with a rag. The sadhu led her to the center of the audience. The distance between the sadhu and the spectators was not more than ten feet.

He produced a long stick from his bag and made it stand behind her. He pressed her forehead with his fingers and passed his hand over her body all the time chanting some mantras. After about ten minutes he touched with the pointed end of the stick the middle of her back and with the other hand swept her up till she lay on the point of the stick about five feet above the ground. He now mumbled some more mantras and then abruptly removed the stick from under the girl. The girl now lay without any support in the air. Indira's husband wanted to examine her to see if there was some visible support. The sadhu said: "Don't touch her, Sir! But you can pass your hand under her to make sure." He did so, followed by two other investigators—but there was no hocus-pocus. After seven minutes he picked up the girl and laid her tenderly on the grass. She looked utterly exhausted and dazed.

The sadhu gave her some milk to drink and with a smile

took his leave.

He was never seen again. It was said that he was a primitive man—a *Bhil* from the forest—and had probably gone back to his sylvan hut.

24

HIGH STAKES

AFTER DADA'S second visit, Indira had written to him several letters asking him to relieve her darkness. Every time, however, he declined with the suggestion that she turn instead to his guru, Sri Aurobindo. He advised Indira to come to the ashram and that gave her the jitters. She was so ignorant that she did not even know what an ashram was and how the devotees lived there. She thought it would be an austere monastery where everyone went about with rosaries in their hands, lowered eyes and severe holy faces. No laughter, no freedom, no work, only prayers and the reading of holy scriptures and, of course, the women locked up in a separate enclosure. Perhaps it would be wrong even to look at the beautiful dawn or the sun setting on the sea!

She was, besides, busy with so many things and so kept putting it off. But every time she wrote to Dada she got the same answer: "I am a seeker, turn to Sri Aurobindo."

When, finally, she did go to Sri Aurobindo it happened in a curious way. In Pondicherry Ashram Sri Aurobindo gave *darshan*, or audience, four times a year. It was the 18th of February, 1949; on the 21st was the ashram Mother's birthday. Indira just mentioned the fact to the family after dinner, adding that she would have been there at Pondicherry if her little son Premal, who was a year old, were not unwell. Everyone laughed. Her husband said: "An ashram is not a five-star hotel, Indira! There will be no one there to attend on or look after you. I think it is good for you to take to some work."

Indira's brother-in-law chimed in: "It's the best joke of the year: who will make your morning cup of tea there? Who will run your bath and help you dress?"

Indira's sister-in-law added: "Imagine her in an ashram! Prostrating herself before others, saying: 'Yes, Sir, yes, Madam, certainly, my Lord.'"

"Is it a challenge?" Indira asked.

"Yes, it is." Her brother-in-law nodded. "If you can go to the ashram all alone and stay there for seven days, I will give you five hundred rupees."

Indira accepted the challenge, little realizing that she was playing for much higher stakes: her life, her thoughts, her whole being at one sweep. It was not her brother-in-law who was challenging her but the Lord of her destiny. In this game there was only one result: one had to lose all to be the winner. One had to give and not count the cost, one had to be defeated and yet feel the joy of victory, one had to learn the mantra: "Life is to give—give—give."

Indira got up the next morning, took the car and drove alone to Nagpur with just one small bag. She had not even obtained a reservation on the Nagpur-Madras plane, but fortunately a seat fell vacant at the last minute and she got in. At Madras as soon as she alighted from the plane the first person she saw was Dada, surrounded by a big crowd. Someone, evidently, was playing His cards very well, anticipating her every move. All the way from Nagpur Indira had felt qualms and wanted to stay for a day at the Connemara Hotel in Madras and then, after sending a telegram, proceed to Pondicherry. But her die was cast.

Dada took her with him to Pondicherry and on the 21st of February, on the Mother's birthday, she had Sri Aurobindo's and the Mother's *darshan* for the first time. She felt thrice-blessed and her whole body became cool and numb. As soon

"Dada took her with him to Pondicherry and on the 21st of February, on the Mother's birthday, she had Sri Aurobindo's and the Mother's *darshan* for the first time."

as they reached Dada's beautiful flat overlooking the sea, Dada advised Indira and his other guests to sit down and meditate for a while, since after *darshan* it was best not to talk and lose all that the gurus had given by their glance of blessing.

Indira had no idea what meditation was but she sat still and closed her eyes. Her numb body became still and peace came down on her head like a block of ice. When she opened her eyes she saw that three hours had passed. Having no idea what had happened, she did not mention it to anyone, though she saw that people were staring curiously at her.

Next morning Dada wrote something to Sri Aurobindo, who sent a *sadhaka* to Dada with the message: "She is ready for yoga and we are willing to accept her as our disciple." Dada was very happy, but Indira was full of misgivings. A part of her rejoiced that she was called and chosen, but her mind was vexed with doubts about her capacity to stick to this life. She could not persuade herself that it was not escapism. She had not been frustrated in life. Her father, her husband, her sister, brothers and children all loved her. She had numerous friends and had her finger in many a pie where social service was concerned.

How could she turn her back now on all that she held dear to live in an ashram? In the end she decided that the only way to know whether the Call was genuine or not was to go back home again and see. Dada smiled and said: "You have been called, but you have to choose to be chosen."

"What about meditation, Dada?" Indira said. "Everyone talks so much about it here, but I know really nothing about it."

"Sit in a comfortable posture before the picture of the Lord and try to concentrate on a particular point. Thoughts come from outside. Reject the undesirable intruders. Stand back and watch. Don't identify yourself with the restlessness of the mind. If you don't play with the thoughts they will gradually fall off and the mind will become silent. In and through this silence Grace descends."

After a few hours' flight, when she reached her home town and saw the eager faces of her little sons, her heart was filled with joy. Everything was the same. How could it be otherwise in a few weeks' time? And yet everything *had* changed: she was a stranger in her own house; nothing belonged to her anymore; she was enveloped in an unspeakable gloom! What was happening to her?

In this state of desolation, she sat down the next morning to follow Dada's instructions about meditation. It was 8 A.M. and she had to attend a meeting at 9:30 A.M. She locked herself in her room and sat cross-legged on the floor. She remembers praying to her guru for a few minutes, and then, as she closed her eyes, strange things happened: an electric current shot up from the base of her spine in a zigzag movement and, as it rose, peace like a block of ice descended on her head and her body became numb. There was no thought, no prayer, no vivid ecstasy, only a still peace. She was not clear as to what happened thereafter. The next thing she knew was that somebody was shaking her and, when she looked at the clock, it was nearly 2 P.M.

She got up in a daze and attended to her household chores, but everything seemed vague and unimportant. She was gripped by an irresistible urge to just sit silently. It was with the greatest difficulty she could talk or work or even pretend to be interested in anything. For three months this state of intoxication or God-madness overpowered her. A causeless peace settled in her. It would last for days and then, as suddenly as it had come, it would peter out and she would be thrown into a deep well of loneliness and despair. Just as the peace far exceeded any earthly joy she had known, the pain, too, was far more intense than any mental suffering she had undergone so far.

At this time she discovered that she was gradually having

a sort of conscious sleep. She hardly slept for four or five hours and when she did sleep, a part of her remained awake. She could see and feel the slightest movement.

The guru was far away and all that was happening was very novel to her. In her ignorance she did not even know that these things had an explanation, and that is where the guru is so very helpful, for he knows the disciple's state and can give the necessary guidance, protection and guarantee.

If people thought that she had gone mad or astray, they were not far wrong. Only it was a very blessed madness— how blessed, even she did not know at the time.

She followed no given recipe, no set method, no orthodox *asana* (sitting posture). She just gave herself up to Him with all her faults and that was that. During these months of madness, the Lord's and the Guru's Grace steadily grew into a reality and all else became trivial. The question of sin and unworthiness never troubled her. She loved Him and wanted Him *above* all things and not *among* other things and that was enough. He had accepted her in His compassion; Love would change her and make her into what He would want her to be.

This, her love, was something precious and sacred to her. She could not talk about it to others. These experiences were not mere happenings; they were a part of her, a part of the play of love between her frail human heart and the infinite heart of compassion. They were like a series of love letters from the Beloved. Whether they brought blissful tidings or tore her heart apart, they came from the Beloved. Even today, she finds it exceedingly difficult to write about all this. It is not that she is modest, nor that she fears people will disbelieve what she cannot prove. (Is there anything really precious in life that we can prove to others?) It is not of the least importance to her whether anyone believes or not. Truth, unlike democracy, is not sustained by a majority vote or by certificates from all and sundry. Besides, if spiritual experiences are subjective, their expression is nevertheless objective. Their impact on the consciousness and its consequent transformation will be felt by others who are receptive even when they can see only the results.

As far as she was concerned, she had never felt the desire to prove or even discuss her experiences with anyone except her guru. When they came, she accepted them as a sign of Grace, and when they ceased, she knew that they were not necessary for her anymore.

There is only one reason why she talked about them to a few people: her guru wished her to comply. He looked at it from an entirely different and impersonal angle. He said: "Why mustn't I talk about things I believe or know to be true? I know that the majority of people will not understand—even misunderstand and disbelieve. But there will always be a few seekers who will profit by the experiences of a fellow-seeker. It is for those few that we must write and speak."

She did feel that there was a difference between most people around her and herself. The Lord was, more or less, a theory to them: to her He was an intimate reality, her very existence; with Him all was joy and fulfillment. Without Him she could not live. She did not worry about the technique of *sadhana* and meditation. Whatever she did she tried to do for Him alone. Wherever she sat she felt she was at His feet. She was carefree and happy—her guru had taken charge of her and she belonged to the Lord. She knew that she was very imperfect and she stumbled again and again, but she always fell into His lap.

Whoever taught a child the technique of clinging to the mother? *Sadhana* was necessary because just as a noble son brings glory to his earthly parents, a spiritual child, too, must be as worthy as humanly possible of its Heavenly Parents: the Lord and the guru.

But how could one explain these things to people whose

angle of vision was entirely different? How could she lay her heart bare for inquisitive eyes to probe, or alien hands to touch?

After the first few days of her *sadhana*, she started leading a sort of double life: she talked of everything in the world except the one thing that was worth talking about, scrupulously avoiding all discussions about her inner life. She could talk of irrelevant things, but it was not possible for her to think of anything but Him. It was a pull too strong to resist. And she only craved to be alone and pray just as a drunkard craves for the wine he is deprived of. Again and again she would fight this urge, but in vain. She did not have to practice meditation, it was difficult for her not to meditate.

25

THE SECOND VISIT

SINCE THE weather was now warming up, Indira left for Mussoorie soon after her return home. Here the same state of affairs continued. She sat down to meditate at about 10:30 P.M. and when she got up it was dawn. First she thought that she was falling asleep sitting cross-legged, but then one day as she sat down the electric current that shot up from the base of her spine did not stop as it usually did when it reached her head. Instead, as it touched her head, the latter opened, or so it seemed to her, and she found herself outside her body—floating on velvety waves of bliss, expanding and moving about as freely as the air. There was no thought, no desire, no joy, but something that was entirely different. It was another rhythm altogether, another world. There were no barriers of time or space though she retained her separate entity. She could see her body seated on the floor. After a time she felt a heaviness on the head and found herself back in her body. This was her first experience of *savikalpa samadhi.*

At this time Franz was of great help. Indira asked him: "If our subconscious mind can play such havoc with us, why can't all that is happening to me be one of its tricks? How do I know it is not a dream?"

"For that matter," he rejoined, "how do you know that what you are saying to me now is not a dream?"

"That is the difficulty, I am not at all sure which is the dream and which is the reality. Perhaps I will have to wait for the answer till the Final Awakening comes."

Franz smiled and said: "I hope I'll be there when that happens." Unfortunately he did not live long after that. A few months later when Indira was in her meditation, she saw Franz lying in a pool of blood in the snow. Indira was afterward told by his sister that he had died in a skiing accident.

Indira's meditation only deepened with time. Most of the time she lived self-absorbed; the outer world became rather tenuous and hazy as she stood on the threshold of His Castle. Whenever her head opened and she came out of her body there was a great sense of liberation and peace. By peace she did not mean something passive, or a respite from worry. It was a very concrete experience. It sometimes seemed to her that if she could sit still and meditate all the time, nothing more was needed. But this state of world-oblivious ecstasy entailed no end of uncomfortable situations. People around her naturally did not understand and were either thinking that she was "putting it on" or was callous. Things came to a head one day when she remained in meditation in her room for over six hours and an important engagement had to be canceled. After receiving a few frantic phone calls from the people involved, someone became angry and, doubting the authenticity of her meditation, burned her finger with a cigarette. The hand did shake, they said, but the meditation was not broken.

This incident was the last straw and decided her to go again to the ashram. She saw she had been playing for time because she was hesitant to take the plunge. She was sitting on the shore counting the waves; but whoever won the pearl of great price without diving into the ocean?

Indira had to die to her life of pale glimmers to be reborn to the Land of Light.

There comes a time in every aspirant's life when the choice

Indira Devi returned to the ashram to be with her guru. "Indira had to die to her life of pale glimmers to be reborn to the Land of Light."

has to be made. It does not necessarily end in changing the outer environment, but it does mean taking a definite stand and aligning oneself with the Divine Forces.

Men turn to God for various reasons: the poor and frustrated in the hope of a brighter future; the shrewd out of fear, thinking they can fool God as well as man; the rich as a hobby; and the intellectual to know "what on earth it's all about."

Spirituality is not a sentimental and emotional upheaval, neither is it a pursuit for goody-goody weaklings. Such persons are no good to man or God, for true spirituality needs, first and last, sincerity, strength and perseverance.

At this time Indira developed the habit of vigilance. She tried all the time to stand back and watch herself—to note her reactions and thoughts. She noticed that in spite of the resolutions to change herself she kept repeating the same mistakes. Even when she had changed for a while, as soon as she became a little off guard she would again react in a way that needed mending. Vigilance or awareness formed a major part of her self-discipline. No one had asked her to be vigilant or to stand back and watch. It just came to her by itself.

This sense of awareness became a little different with time, for she gradually started feeling His presence around her all the time. When she walked she could almost feel His breath on her cheek and she repeated in deep gratitude: He is here, walking beside me. When she worked she felt Him helping her, guiding her, making her burden lighter. She had not seen His face yet but His shadow had fallen on her. She had heard His footfall in harmony with her heartbeats—His hand had brushed against hers. She thought that He sometimes whispered to her. She encouraged herself to feel His presence all the time—to talk to Him—to try and do her best all the time, for He was present always—within her and outside her, never forsaking, never demanding, never bargaining. He was only a witness who felt a joy when she walked on the right path, helped her up gently when she stumbled and felt pain when she fell.

26

BLACK MAGIC

Aﬀﬆer a three-month stay at home Indira went back to the ashram for a month and a half. Here, too, she meditated during the whole night and spent the days in working, dancing and reading.

It was in the middle of August that she went back home a second time and had one of the most astonishing experiences in her experience-packed life.

After she had been home a couple of days an acquaintance came in a car one morning to say that a very great sadhu, Swami D., wanted to meet her.

"It must be another lady in the house," Indira said. "For I have never known any sadhu except Dadaji."

The friend admonished: "No, it is *you*. Swamiji has mentioned your name, please come. Don't you realize how blessed you are to be called by such a great man?"

Indira went the next morning. She thought that perhaps he knew Dadaji and so wanted to meet her.

The Swami was staying with a Raja. As soon as Indira entered the palace she was told to go to his room but to sit on the left side of the curtain that divided the room, as the Swami did not look upon the face of a woman.

Indira was surprised, she had never heard of such a thing before.

She went and sat on a settee in the ladies' part of the room.

Suddenly the curtain was pulled away and she saw before her an extremely beautiful old man of about seventy. Silver-gray hair fell in profusion on his shoulders, and a beautiful beard adorned his face. "Come and sit beside me, my child!" he said in a low voice. Indira was certainly astonished: how was it that one who was supposed never to look at a woman should be asking her to sit beside him?

She got up and complied.

"Has my Dada asked you to meet me, Swamiji?" she asked.

"No. But I know of Sri Aurobindo and Sri Dilip Kumar Roy. No one has asked me to meet you."

He put his arm around her shoulders. As soon as he touched Indira a shiver of repulsion passed through her body. There was something so repellent in his touch!

She moved away and asked him: "Why did you send for me?"

"Don't you recognize me?" he questioned softly but in an intense voice.

"No, I don't. I am not interested in sadhus, and I have a guru, as you know," Indira said.

"Yes I do, and I also know that you have attained a very high state. We have worked together in past lives and are destined to work together again. Don't you know that in my big spiritual manifestation the woman's help is needed? Shall I tell you what you are thinking? You want someone to enter the room so that you can go away, but you are wrong —you'll never be able to go away from me."

Indira looked up at him and as luck would have it his thoughts came as clearly to her as if she were reading an open book. "You yourself are thinking that since I can't be caught by threats you must be gentle with me," Indira returned.

He burst out laughing. "You see we belong to the same spiritual plane. We are both reading each other's thoughts. Shall I tell you more about yourself?"

"No, thank you," Indira answered. "I don't want to know

anything. I must go away now as there are some people coming to lunch."

"Don't be childish!" he said in an animated tone. "You were not born to be a disciple, a much greater destiny awaits you. We two will bring about a momentous change in the world. I need your help a little to clear up a certain passage after which *samadhi* will be a certainty for me. You will be famous all over the world. So don't waste yourself in Sri Aurobindo Ashram."

"Thank you for your advice, but I must go as I have an important engagement." Indira got up to go.

"Come back in the evening and meditate with me," the Swami called to her.

Indira felt as if she had escaped from a suffocating atmosphere. There was something so uncanny and frightening about the beautiful-looking man! She certainly had no intention of going back to him.

Thereafter he sent many a message, but Indira was adamant.

A week or ten days later Indira got up with a severe pain in her chest. She could hardly breathe. By the evening fever developed. The doctors thought it might be a secondary infection from her asthma, and treated her accordingly. She had a complete loss of appetite and felt very run down.

Then one night, as she was brushing her teeth in the bathroom, she had a bad hemorrhage. She could just reach her dressing room door when she collapsed. Just before losing consciousness Indira thought: "What a prosaic finale to my heavenly romance!" Then as the pain threw her, she cried: "Dada!"

She saw no light, no figure, heard nothing, but just felt someone pick her up from the ground and gently lay her on her bed. Her whole being was replete with peace when she came to. In the morning when the maid knocked on the door with her tea Indira saw that all the doors were still bolted from inside!

A few nights later Indira saw her mother, who had died about twenty years earlier. Looking beautiful in a blue sari, she walked up to Indira and said in a gentle but firm voice: "Don't take anything that is not prepared in your presence."

As Indira could not make head or tail of the message she wrote to Dada, who forwarded her letter to Sri Aurobindo. Sri Aurobindo wrote to him that if Indira did not come away immediately she would die, there was a dark force working on her.

Sri Aurobindo sent Dada to take her to the ashram. When Dada came he took Indira's personal maid aside and asked her if she was putting something in her tea. The maid broke down and said that a member of the household had given her a powder to mix with Indira's morning cup of tea as a cure for asthma. Later on it was found that Swami D. had called an elderly member of the family and told her: "If you want to save your family from disaster, do everything possible to stop Indira from going away as she brings all the luck and prosperity to the household. I am giving you this powder, administer it to her. She may fall a little sick but it will prevent her from going away."

Indira left for Pondicherry on a stretcher. She could hardly walk or eat but she flew in that weak state and reached the ashram.

But Swami D. was not to be so easily circumvented. She had been there only a few days when one night, just as she awakened from her meditation, she saw two bloodshot eyes and then a hand clutched her chest just below the neck. She heard a hoarse voice hissing: "You can't get away. You'll die if you don't come."

In the morning she saw on herself marks of a thumb and three fingers—black painful bruises. She thought they must have been self-inflicted during a nightmare or some form of imagination.

The next night she wore gloves before meditation, but in vain: the same fingermarks appeared. So she decided to go straight back to Swami D. and ask him to let her alone. But Dada demurred and wrote about it all to Sri Aurobindo, who commented in two letters as follows:

11th August, 1949

Dilip,

It is quite evident that all the suggestions that are coming to Indira are part of the pressure that is being put on her from a distance by this evil-minded man: the idea of coming away before the *Darshan* is his idea and so is the thought of going to see him. You must persuade her and tell her that on no account and for no reason should she yield to the pressure. It is clear what he is after and to allow herself to do what he wants in these matters is not to be thought of, the consequences might be very serious. She must on no account see this man or have anything to do with him. Even if she finds it difficult physically or otherwise to bear this kind of pressure she must remain firm; then eventually he will have to desist or he will get his quietus. If you think it necessary for me to write to her directly, let me know and I will do so.

Sri Aurobindo

12th August, 1949

Indira,

I have already written to Dilip my advice and instructions as to what you should do in the matter of this yogi and his pressure upon you. But I am writing to you both to confirm what I have written to him and to add one or two words which are necessary to complete what I have said.

What is especially important for you is to dismiss fear from your mind. In these occult workings fear is a great drawback and handicap; it gives strength to the attack and weakens your resistance. Have faith in the help of the Divine and your ultimate deliverance and throw away fear whenever it tries to come. If you do that you will become stronger and be more able to endure till there is victory.

The physical pain and suffering inflicted by him is hard to bear, but you must try to remain firm in spite of it until his power to touch you diminishes and comes to nothing. Be courageous and push the obsession of him away from you; it is through the nervous being and some pressure of his force upon it which he has been able to establish that he makes you suffer. Try to be calm and steady there; then it will be easier to remain firm.

Be sure that the Mother's help and mine will be always with you. Call for it whenever you need it.

Sri Aurobindo

Indira's chest started bleeding where it was clutched night after night and she was very reluctant to sit alone in the evenings. Things came to a head one day when she was in the bathroom. Suddenly, without warning, the door opened and what appeared to be Dada entered the room. Indira thought to herself: "How strange, Dada would never enter like this without knocking."

"Indira," the form began.

She drew back from it and spontaneously exclaimed: "*Jai Guru Dada, Jai Guru.*"*

At once the spell was broken. The form dislimned and she saw that it was none other than Swami D. Before he vanished, he gave Indira a vicious push so that she fell against the bathtub.

When she next sat down to meditate she was given to know that this evil man's influence on her would cease with the next full moon. And it happened accordingly. A disciple of the Swami wrote to them: "Swami got a paralytic stroke and died in a great agony; he left instructions to cremate Indira's photograph which he had bought in Mussoorie from a photographer."

* *Jai Guru* means "Victory to the Guru." It is a mantra that disciples often use for their protection.

27

IN EARNEST

BEFORE INDIRA had taken the final plunge, she used to think that the day she surrendered all she had would be the day she put an end to her struggles. This naïve idea foundered on the first rock of inner awakening. For no sooner had her lifeboat put out to sea than she realized that the journey had only just begun. How little of the ocean she had seen from the shore of yearning and aspiration! A few breakers of pain and a few undercurrents of earthward pull: what were these compared to the silent storms that rose under the surface and the dark eddies that gripped her? The hidden reefs of self-will that seemed so insignificant all but shattered the boat. No doubt there were islands of exquisite beauty and incredible delight, but the boat merely touched them, as it were. For a while, the heart enjoyed rest and peace and joy, but soon enough the time to move on came and she found herself once again on endless stretches of water. Till one reaches the Final Harbor there is no lasting bliss.

What was it that helped Indira the most during these difficult times? As always, it was Dada's music. More than anything else in the world she profited by his music. Every time Dada sang with his unique voice, her whole being was set vibrating in unison. But it was not the beauty and sweetness alone: *Dada's voice is not of this world.* It comes wafted

Bhajan singing during satsang. "Every time Dada sang with his unique voice, her whole being was set vibrating in unison."

like a haunting call from above. The melodies remind one of Krishna's Flute-notes. It is very powerful and evokes not merely the vital but the psychic emotions of the audience. He sings with his whole soul and helps us share his multi-mooded love for his Lord: yearning, appeal, pain, ecstasy, purity, surrender—all find expression through his songs. Sri Aurobindo wrote to him once that his music has great evocative power. It invokes Light and Grace.

Indira has written at length about Dada's music not to praise him but only to explain how and why it helped her. But though her most beautiful experiences came as a result of his music, the blessing was also a tragedy in that she could never listen to it for very long. After the first few minutes her meditation deepened, the mind became still and she lost waking consciousness.

This experience of *samadhi*, as they call it, was generally of two kinds. Sometimes, during the music, she would feel as if her very soul were being drawn inward. It was an experience of complete absorption, but she did not lose consciousness completely. Only everything outside loomed vague and shadowy and the Lord became the only Reality. There was a great ecstasy or a great yearning, sometimes even a great *viraha*, or pain of separation. In this state she has often danced in rapture. All thoughts, desire, hope and love were centered around the heart, which became His for the time being. Nothing outside was important or clear, but things did exist, as distant shadows. She was told that this was called *bhava samadhi*. Anyway, the name is not important, the experience is the thing—by whatever name you may choose to call it.

The second type of deepening of consciousness would begin with an electric current starting at the base of the spine and crawling or hopping up to the heart, the neck and crown of the head. Then, all at once, the head would open and she would be free: free from the body's bondage, floating on velvet waves of ecstasy and harmony. She would see herself expanding above the body, which remained immobile. There was no thought in this state. Yet the sense of duality persisted. The *I* in her remained—though a very humble and submissive I—now freed from the limitations of time and space. Most of her visions came in this state. After a time, she would feel a heaviness on the head and find herself back on earth.

The cadence of this bliss remained in her normal consciousness—but only the cadence. Sri Aurobindo said that it was *savikalpa samadhi.*

In the beginning Indira found it very difficult to adjust herself to normal consciousness after her return. It was as though she were being tossed between heaven and earth. Having experienced that indescribable bliss, how could one be satisfied with anything else? Dada told her that it could be stabilized only when the outer being was completely transformed. How difficult it is to transform one's nature she knew. Even when the desires fall off to a great extent and the attachments loosen their grip, one goes on indulging in wrong movements from sheer habit. She found that many a time she was doing things that had formerly given her pleasure, but which meant nothing to her any longer. For example, though she had always been a social person, small talk now bored her stiff. Even as it was difficult for most people to concentrate on the Lord and prevent their minds from harking back all the time to worldly things, in her case the opposite was true. Whatever she did, even the most mundane things, her mind returned again and again to the Lord. Yet, often enough, when friends came over she would sit with them and just talk away. The past habit again! Dada never approved of idle talk even when one talked of good things. He said again and again: "Don't fritter away your time and energy in useless things that have nothing to do with your yoga." But this was only a minor difficulty.

Indira came away to the ashram leaving an infant son behind with a nurse to look after him. Her firstborn, who was eight at the time, had already been in a boarding school for three years, so it was the younger one who provided the test. She had often left him at home when she had to fulfill various social and cultural engagements, but somehow this time it was different. She would catch herself thinking of him and the thought that she might not see him again for years was very painful.

After a few months, when she thought she had partially succeeded in getting rid of her attachment for him, the news came, a bolt from the blue, that he was dangerously ill and might not survive. She became quite frantic with grief and anxiety. Indira's attachment and depression created a veil between herself and the guru and barred her from receiving his help. When she showed Dada the telegram he said: "None of us are as indispensable as we think. I would have you have faith in the Lord—but the decision must come from you. *You* must choose." Indira told him he was hard on her as he did not understand a mother's heart, but even when she said it she knew it was not true: Dada *did* understand her more than she understood herself, but he was not being senti-mental about it and it was an ordeal of faith—a dilemma: she had to choose between her child and her Love.

In the evening she almost decided to return on the follow-ing day. Dada said nothing more, but she knew that she had failed him.

At night, when Indira sat down to pray, there was no peace or joy, only unrelieved darkness. The mind pleaded for the child: it was her duty to be with her own helpless child; she would come back after a few days; it was cruel to neglect him in his last hours—and so on. But in spite of all the arguments, she knew she was pleading not for the child but for herself, justifying her attachment. She had been tested and found wanting. All her love, her aspiration—even her spiritual experiences—had failed to give her the faith she so badly needed. She cried at the feet of her Lord. Then a prayer rose up from the depths of her heart. She wanted

Him, she said, above all else and begged for the strength and faith to overcome her attachment. "Do not let me fail my guru and You," she wept.

Suddenly, an incredible peace descended on her head and pervaded her whole being. All her pent gloom was dispelled by the invisible hand of Grace. She knew that she could not go back—no matter what happened. Her place was here—in joy or sorrow, in life or death. She would cling to her Dada alone, who was her father, her friend, her child.

Dada blessed her the next morning and told her he had prayed that she might do the right thing.

Indira mentions this incident for it brought home to her two important revelations. First, she saw that pain was necessary, because it purified and one could never know oneself unless one went through the fire of suffering. She would never have been conscious of her attachment if she had not suffered so much. Secondly, she had a vivid experience of the guru's help and guidance. She would never have known the true attitude if Dada had compromised with her wrong movement. It was *his* strength that made her strong and *his* prayer that made her pray for Light. Yet he had not insisted once on her following him. He explained the spiritual viewpoint and left it at that. The only thing he did say was: "Go if you want to, but fully conscious that you have preferred your worldly duties to your soul's duty. Don't deceive yourself."

He made her see that what was right for most mothers was not right for her. She was called upon to dedicate the whole of herself to Him. She saw that she had not been sincere enough and so fell, but even when she did fall it was only in her Lord's lap. The suffering brought her closer to her guru and the Lord. She realized that spiritual experiences and ecstasies were not enough: a greater vigilance was necessary—and an uncompromising ruthlessness with herself was called for.

Just at this time Indira lost two of her dearest women

friends. She missed them a great deal and the mental suffering was in no way less than the physical. But the pain only deepened her aspiration and purified her love.

Pain was necessary to break down her resistance; since her self-will would not easily bend, the wrath of a storm had to uproot it. Every new disillusionment brought home to her afresh the futility of personal attachments. The breaking of personal bonds only showed the frail plinth all human relationships are based on. Human love, no matter how intense, is limited and thrives on what it receives from another. Even when it is more evolved and there is a mutual give-and-take, the response is indispensable to its flowering. Therefore it must pall after a time. We miss the response when we don't have it, and take it for granted when it is there.

When Indira had first turned to the Light she used to tell her guru: "I hope yoga won't make me dry! How can I live if I don't love? How can I love God without loving His creatures? What is love without attachment?" But as time went on she saw that love does not diminish with the loosening of our bonds of attachment. On the contrary, when love deepens, its expectations are reduced and the strain is diminished. A freedom is felt and love becomes a joy. Love that depends for its sustenance upon the object of affection vacillates, brings sorrow as well as joy, ends in disappointment, or at best becomes a habit and is like a smouldering fire full of smoke. No matter how much you feed it, it increases the uncomfortable smoke and hurts the eyes.

Love that is purged of dross, expectations and reward is its own fulfillment. It is the act of loving and not being loved that fulfills, satisfies and keeps love alive. It is like a raging fire. Whatever you feed it with turns into fire and adds to the luster.

She knew from experience that only those she loved had the power to hurt her sensitive soul, not because she loved them, but because she expected a return or at least a recognition. When expectation ceased, the release came—love was no longer stifled—it breathed the fragrant air freely and opened out in its own light and warmth.

The guru's love comes nearest to the Divine love in this mundane world in that it is absolutely selfless. He does not judge the disciple by his or her shortcomings, nor by what he says or does but by what he aspires to be. With infinite patience and abiding love he tries to mold the very human nature of the disciple into the Divine nature.

Indira saw that in her deepest gloom and suffering the guru was always there watching—patient and compassionate. In her crucial hours of revolt and self-will, even when she did not understand, he never misunderstood or failed her. He never sympathized with her self-will, but always waited for her to come around.

Gradually, as she turned her face toward the sun, the shadows receded. His sunlight of bliss and harmony and gleams of Grace and compassion greeted her and so her life-boat sailed on, with the guru at the helm, to that faraway land of beauty and bliss.

O Krishna's Blessed Maid!
(on Indira's Birthday)

O Krishna's blessed maid! you said to me:
"I saw 'tween your eyebrows a spark that grew
Into a dazzling and unbounded orb.
Then in a moment, before I even knew

"It for a vast, illimitable Sun,
It burst—when, lo! a beneficent blaze
Of beatitude engulfed me and I lost
My world-registering, separate consciousness.

"Thereafter time stood still and space dissolved,
Desire nor motion, name nor form survived,
Abolished was what I had styled my *I*,
How then can I describe what I perceived?

"Only a plenitude of silent bliss,
An absolute light no shadows crossed or marred,

"There was no world nor entity that claimed
A title or status from the One apart.

"No urge of separate self declared itself,
A fadeless and untrammelled ecstasy
Pervaded the unhorizoned void of sky
And reigned in its inviolate majesty!

"Nor was the void a desert vacuum,
But a causeless, self-contained, illumined peace,
The knower at one with knowledge and the known,
Ensconced in nothing, stemming from nought that is!

"Symbols, alas, but whisper—never speak,
And how speak when duality is no more?
When the *I* is quenched in immortality:
An oceaned harmony that knows no shore?"

(*From Indira's description of her indescribable experience*
nirvikalpa samadhi *on her thirty-seventh birthday—March
26, 1957—lasting for six hours from midnight.*)

Dilip Kumar Roy

28

OTHER WORLDS

MUCH HAS been written about the spirit worlds seen by mediums. It was not only these that Indira saw but also many other worlds where Truth or Harmony or Beauty presided.

One night she felt that as soon as her soul left her body it shot up like an arrow passing through different layers of consciousness. She saw that she was rocketing up from the center of a vast cone. When she reached the top her separate entity was lost and there was just one unique blissful consciousness, Peerless and Sole. After this she found herself in a world, or land, of Truth where there was no shadow. They spoke in vibrations, not words. From this world beings could send their emanations down to earth to serve man and God. It was a world beyond time and space.

Then she was in a world where everything was pulsating with life: the trees, the stones, the waterfalls, the flowers and the earth—all were living.

The cone started spreading out and she was in a world where everything dripped harmony and beauty. Nothing was unlovely or disharmonious; even a clod was beautiful.

And then there was the world of sound or, rather, music. Beautiful beings spoke and walked in music. The air was full of music; the birds, the trees, the walls all sang out in different lilts; there was not one discordant note anywhere. All was music, music, music!

Indira felt that these worlds were static and above the wheel of *karma*, though in the world of Truth emanations could be sent down to the human world. After a time she began to feel heavy, and passing through the lowering clouds, she came back to earth where everything seemed mixed up—truth, falsehood, good, evil, hatred, love, nobility, meanness. It was so different from the other worlds but somehow Indira knew that to attain to the highest, one had to touch this rock-bottom land. From here she could shoot up to the apex of the cone. While every other world was a static heaven, this was an evolving world, aspiring for perfection, stretching out its weary arms to heaven. This world was a workshop of the Master—a laboratory where He constantly tried new methods to purify and perfect His models. He chiseled them and cut them with the wrath of heaven, and then leaned down to embrace and caress them, even as a sculptor touches his own handiwork, with tenderness. It is here that the Good Shepherd looks for his lost sheep and rejoices when He finds one of His flock which had, perhaps, strayed away. He brings them home to rest after a long day—to sleep and to *be* till he sends them down to the earthly pastures to graze again.

Oddly enough, one night when Indira left her body she suddenly fell into a dark abyss. Down and down the darkness she dropped till she came to a city. Just like any city on earth, only there were neither doors nor windows. Men and women walked about in and out of the houses. There was a deathly chill in the atmoshphere and she felt as if she were in a cemetery. No raging fires, no punishments meted out, but she saw no light in their eyes—they were living insensitive corpses, incapable of feeling joy or pain. There was no hope, love or hatred. The life-giving Light of the Lord did not accost them—and there were no children. It was a living hell she felt and the next morning when Dada wrote to Sri Aurobindo he replied: "It was indeed hell that Indira visited."

How much talking about spiritual experiences helps, Indira does not know. She persuades herself that it is helpful to others because Dada says so, and Dada certainly knows more than she does. All that has happened to her is only because of his help, love and *gurushakti*. So what is given by or through him is his and she must submit to his will and judgment. She only wants to make it clear that it is very difficult for her to talk of these intimate and personal experiences. And yet, she would like to shout from the housetops that He *is* a living reality and not a myth, that she knows that if we love Him we *can* feel His love.

Indira has already written about the two types of *samadhi* she frequently experiences. On three occasions the Lord's grace descended on this unworthy child to boon her with what they call *nirvikalpa samadhi*. The last occurrence of this was in 1971.

As usual, an electric current rose from the base of her spine. Her head opened and she was free from the bondage of her body. Like a bird let out of a cage, the spirit soared upward, claiming its kinship with the stars. It was as if she were floating through different worlds, following a Flute-Call. Indira remembers seeing Beings of Light and Harmony —and feeling the ecstasy of the earth-free gods and, above all, she remembers the Call of the Flute. It was so near and yet she could not reach it. Higher and higher she rose till there was nothing but the Flute—Call and that sound had become a Form—a Reality that somehow she wanted to touch. Just as Indira touched it, it changed into a dazzling Sun which broke into a million bits and then there was nothing—and yet everything. There was no *I* left, no one to experience—no form, no duality, neither God nor devotee. She had lost all consciousness to *become* consciousness. There was just Bliss and one vast Reality that reigned—beyond all thought, all description, all imagination. Time stopped—or rather there was no time—yet, after a while, she came back to the shadow of that Reality, this world.

They say this is a stage higher than *savikalpa samadhi*. But to Indira the stature of her supernormal consciousness is not important. If she can be in a state where she perceives Dada or the Lord smiling on her, she asks for nothing more. *Nirvikalpa samadhi* is not her goal. All she prays for is to be able to give herself completely, without reserve, in her normal consciousness. It is not her aim to be able to help or better the world. If she can change herself and let the guru mold her, she is fulfilled. It is possible that some people may change through her contact, even as it is possible that she may go away unheeded and unknown. Both are the same to her. If only He recognizes and heeds her, what else can matter? If her surrender at her guru's feet is complete, and he can make a perfect offering of her life to the Perfect, she is fulfilled. Nothing less can satisfy her. Surrender or God-realization, the two are synonymous.

29

KNOWLEDGE BY IDENTITY

I<small>T HAPPENED</small> first in September, 1956. Hari Krishna Mandir had not yet been built and the evenings offered no privacy for Dada in the cottage where he and Indira were staying. So they often went out in a friend's car and Dada drank a cup of coffee at a wayside café. One day, after the coffee, Dada and his friend were walking on the promenade while Indira waited in the car. As she looked out of the window, she saw a half-starved dog go up to the café and look longingly at the bread, only to be driven away by the counter man who brandished a stick. Immediately, Indira experienced the most terrible pain of hunger in her stomach. It was as if this hunger were gnawing at her inside. She had never dreamed that hunger could be so unbearable. Without thinking she quickly got out of the car and bought a couple of buns which she gave to the dog. As soon as it ate the buns she felt her normal self again.

The second time, she was standing near her window watching a man plough his field opposite the ashram. Suddenly he took a thick stick and hit the bullock hard on his back. Indira screamed out in pain as though someone had struck her. When she picked up her sari, Dada and the other inmates of the ashram saw that there was a round, black bruise on her thigh. This bruise caused her severe pain for some days.*

* Sri Aurobindo writes about this type of supernormal experience in his *Synthesis of Yoga* in the chapter entitled "Cosmic Consciousness."

The third time involved a bougainvillea plant. Between two red plants there was an orange flowering bush. The orange color clashed with the red and she asked her brother-disciple who was in charge of the garden to remove the orange plant. That night when she was meditating she saw the trunk of the orange blossoms part in two, revealing a young boy standing within, in orange robes. "Why do you want to destroy me, mother? I am still young."

The next morning Indira told her brother-disciple to let the orange plant stay as it was.

Thereafter Indira forbade anyone to cut any branch from the trees or to uproot any plant without asking her.

One afternoon, while meditating, she saw some little boys and girls in green dancing happily around the mango grove in the ashram. Suddenly, there was blood on the grass and two little boys shouted: "Ma, they are cutting our arms!" Indira jumped up and ran downstairs, but as she was going down she told Dada what she had seen. She felt so deeply moved that she was sobbing, and there she saw the gardener cutting down branches from the mango trees! The brother in charge had forgotten to issue her instructions.

They would forget again and again and she would weep for the mutilated trees and plants. How could they understand with their hearts what they knew with their minds—that Indira was a truthful person and that these flowers and plants spoke to her through their vibrations and felt joy and pain even as we do?

Why did all this happen to her? She only knew that it *did* happen, and she accepted it on bended knees as a sign of His Grace. She realized with every fiber of her being that the credit was not hers, she was only an instrument.

Indira could see that she was in many ways an abnormal person. She felt vibrations of persons, of anger, fear, greed and jealousy. She knew when people were lying in her presence, yet she did not have the power to know what would happen to herself two days hence.

When she first developed the faculty of reading other people's thoughts she was very much troubled by it. She even asked her guru to appeal to Sri Aurobindo to deliver her from this unwelcome gift. Dada wrote to Sri Aurobindo in March, 1949, whereupon the latter replied:

Dilip,

About Indira's faculty of receiving the thoughts of others, if this had been of the nature of thought-reading, that is to say, looking at the minds of others and seeing what is there, the remedy would have been simple: refusal to look would have been enough and even the faculty might disappear by atrophy through long discontinuance. But if the thoughts of others come to her by themselves, it may be the psychic opening in her inner mind which it would be difficult to get rid of. If she could remain indifferent or push away these unwelcome visitors behind her and not think of them again, that would be one remedy; it might even be discouraged from coming after a time by this lack of reception. As for why it comes, it is not something that comes but something that is there, a faculty or psychic habit of the nature; if she practiced yoga and makes some considerable progress, then it would be possible for her to bar the door to these visitors. At the same time I might say that this power need not be a mere source of trouble; it can be helpful even; for it can give one who has acquired mastery over her own nature the knowledge of the thoughts and feelings around her and she can then help, guide, change what has to be changed in their minds so that they can become more effective for the divine work. I shall await what further you have to tell me before saying anything further. . . .

Sri Aurobindo

Indira took Sri Aurobindo's answer as a sign of His Grace. He had said so much in a few sentences. It was a warning—an admonition as well as a blessing. She knew that the thoughts of people came to her by themselves. It was not intended that she should try to read them; indeed, the few times she had made such an effort she had drawn a blank. Whenever it was necessary thoughts were revealed to her, though how this helped her she didn't know. She promised to herself that she would never again make an effort to read anyone's thoughts.

This gift did help her, however, in one way: she saw clearly that it was not right to judge a person by what he was thinking at a particular moment. The best of men sometimes harbored bad thoughts and men who were not so worthy sometimes had noble thoughts. She also realized that many of the thoughts we take to be our own actually float in from the atmosphere and that it is our own free choice whether to accept or reject them.

She had a very vivid experience of this once. She was sitting down to meditate in her guru's temple hall in Poona with a group of friends. She could see very clearly that most of them had an aura of tension around them. They were concentrating so hard to silence their minds that it only heightened their awareness of the thoughts. Not one person in that group was completely relaxed—the first condition necesary for meditation.

Suddenly she *saw* a sex thought floating in from without and touching one person who accepted it. He became restless, but the thought developed in his mind in the form of jealousy, which is one of the concomitants of sex. He played with the thought and was soon carried away on the wave of a grievance and anger against the guru, the world and God.

The thought touched two other people but as they did not give it a fireside seat, it quickly turned away from them. Another friend accepted the thought as his own and felt terribly anxious about his health.

It was fascinating, though the whole thing did not take more than a minute. It was borne home to Indira that she should not judge people by their thoughts. It made her much more tolerant and understanding toward her fellow-beings.

30

THE ADVENT OF MIRA

It was around 1949. Indira was in Mussoorie meditating at least fourteen hours out of twenty-four. One afternoon, when she got up from meditation, she found herself repeating a few lines from a song: *Bari anokhi reet piyaki bari anokhi reet.* . . At first she thought it might be a song from one of the movies she had seen in the past. The song was in simple Hindi, and though Indira's language was Urdu she could follow the meaning. Dada has translated it:

His ways are strange, bewildering!
To fathom Him I fail.
How He fulfils our hearts with His love
O friend, I cannot tell.

I learned to laugh through tears and staked
My all to glimpse His Face:
I won Him by becoming His,
Lost all and gained His Grace.

Relentlessly He weaned me from
My lesser loves, my kin,
Till even the mate I once had hailed
Loomed far and alien.

Now dead I am grown to fear and shame
In my lone quest for Thee:
Strange, none befriends when thou becom'st
One's friend, O Mystery!

Indira did not attach much importance to the song but it kept intruding in her memory and so insistently that at last she sent the song to Dada who was in Assam at the time. As soon as she asked one of her maids to write down the song in Hindi, which script Indira did not know, the song ceased.

After a few days she got up with the words of another song on her lips. In this way about a dozen songs came to her—one after the other. She saw nothing, heard no singing, just remembered the songs.

After that she went to Pondicherry and the incredible drama started. One morning while Dada was singing in his flat, Indira saw (she is not sure whether it was with open eyes or closed) a beautiful lady dressed in a Rajasthani dress. She was slim, extremely graceful and had the most lovely eyes. She sat next to Dada, beating time, and seemed to be lost in the music. Indira wondered why she did not have on the white dress of the ashram ladies. "She must be a visitor or a close friend of Dada's," Indira decided, but when the lady got up to leave with the others, she cast no shadow and her feet did not quite touch the earth.

A few nights later something even stranger happened. While she was meditating, Indira saw the same lady approach. She was singing, and seemed to be totally oblivious of the world. Her voice was lovely and the song ended with the name "Mira" in the last line.

The next morning, Indira told Dada what she had seen. He was equally puzzled. It could not be imagination since it was so vivid, and autosuggestion could be ruled out as Indira had never even thought of Saint Mira. When Dada asked Indira to question the lady as to who she was, Indira replied: "But there is no thought in my meditation, Dada, my mind falls still like a lake on a windless morning. There is not even a ripple." And then she confided: "I have become a split personality. One part of me is always silent, witnessing what the other part does—like the mother watching her child playing pranks. It is to my witness consciousness that this lady comes and it asks no questions, demands nothing, craves nothing. It is just a witness, a friend, a guide who guides in silence or whispers in the heart."

The whole thing was so amazing that most people found it difficult to believe. Indira did not blame them as she herself found it equally inexplicable. Yet it was true and with time became the greatest truth in her life. It became the most precious part of her life. She needed no verification from others, wanted no certificates from anyone. Even if the whole world disbelieved her, even if her own mind started doubting, it did not matter a row of pins. She was like a poor woman who was left an unexpected legacy and so could keep a million rupees in the bank. No one believed her. They said it was all a made-up stunt and insisted that she prove it to them by showing her bank account. The woman laughed. The fact that she had the money was so much more important than the ridicule of the wise skeptics. It is the same in spiritual life. If you are blessed by the Lord nothing else matters, and if you have not received anything from Him what does it matter what people say? For then, even if you announced His advent with fanfare your heart would remain empty.

Whenever they were in some financial difficulty Indira knew that if only they mixed in a little falsehood in order to put no pressure on people's egos, the crowds would flock around them and money would pour in. But there was one great difficulty. After the day's din was over and she had put away the money and gone to meet her Beloved, she would wait and pray in vain as the Lord would never come to one who was false. Not for the wealth of the three worlds would she exchange her meeting with her Lord. Never, never, never!

Mira's advent was incredible, and even after years Indira found it so fantastic that she could hardly credit it herself. The songs were in Hindi and some of the words Indira did not know—she marveled at this till she discovered that Mira spoke in vibrations and not words. If the mind was completely silent all the words came down faultlessly—if there was a ripple in the mind, then when the vibrations passed through the mind, a certain word would be dropped and replaced by a similar word in Urdu.

One day Indira wrote in ecstasy:

From far away beyond thy reach, O mind,
    On wings of love she comes to this dark land.
My heart reveals its petals to her gaze,
    Enfolding all I am she seeks my hand.

Swiftly we cross the pale of your horizon
    On murmuring waves of soft delight we roam
Where silence whispers and where stillness flows
    Where all is love, my soul is there at home.

In the silent cadence of night's moving hour
    When sleep caresses every care-worn brow:
There blossoms a flowerlike dream in my heart's bower,
    A fragrant form takes shape I know not how.

A lovely sadness shimmers in her star-eyes
    Her lips like rosebuds bloom into a smile:
Pure as a lily, a radiant dawn from skies,
    Comes my love to make dreams real for a while.

31

GRACE

INDIRA OFTEN asked herself if the experiences helped her in any way in her upward journey. After all, what was the use of experiences if they did not help you to aspire more?

Why, for example, had Mira come to her? Surely it was not only to demonstrate her miraculous powers? Why did she sing hundreds of songs to Indira, guide her, speak to her, bless her and love her?

Was it not to help Indira? This is certainly what it seemed to be. For after every experience the consciousness changed a little, the heart became a little purer, a little more understanding and tolerant, a little more humble.

Mira's advent deepened the experiences. She had only to relax a little and her soul would shoot up and out through the crown of her head. Even while talking to people she would find a few moments of silence and be out floating about on waves of bliss.

She gradually found that without any effort on her part she was repeating the Lord's name with every breath. Sometimes, though rarely, she had the wonderful experience that every pore of her body had a tongue and was repeating the Name. This Name became a living Presence in her and filled her whole being so that whenever this repetition stopped she felt a great void in the heart.

Once when she met Mira in her meditation she told her

that people found the whole phenomenon of Mira fantastic, and she, Indira, agreed.

Mira smiled and said: "If you tell your friends that you see a ghost who frightens you, disturbs everything in the house and makes frightful noises, very few will disbelieve you. You will hear ten other stories of the ghosts who materialize to destroy. But if you say that a spirit comes to you that builds and does not destroy, who helps but does not frighten you, who sings of the Lord and dances in joy, it is difficult for human beings to believe. There is a perversity in the human mind that cannot receive selfless love or help from the Divine directly or through His agents."

"But," insisted Indira, "It is a miracle. You can't deny it."

"Is it any more miraculous than a rosebud, a golden dawn or a blade of grass? We see miracles all around us. As a matter of fact, this world itself is a miracle which just could not have been and yet *is*. Whatever we see daily our mind accepts after a while and learns to live with, whether a horrible thing like war, or a beautiful thing such as a waterfall or lovely birds or devoted dogs. One has only to see a thing again and again, and then, no matter how miraculous, one takes it for granted. Men shy away from anything new or unknown and dismiss it as impossible. Human beings cannot do much but for God all is possible, as the Christ said ages ago."

To wonder is a blessing, to doubt is a sin for an aspirant. Indira wrote in deep gratitude inspired by a Bengali song.

> What love is this you bear for me, O Friend?
>> What a baffling deal, a heavenly give and take!
> You measure not my sins, my million faults,
>> But only give; for what? For love's own sake.
>
> I reckon not your gifts nor heed your Grace;
>> I smile on my rebellious heart and spurn
> All I receive unmerited, unasked,
>> Still you give on and ask for no return.

I roam around your nectar-spring, athirst;
　My restless heart's unslaked, yet wants for nought;
For all I crave and more—you grant to me;
　But tell me, Friend, from me what have you got?

You lean to hold me, anchored to your love,
　I slip love's bonds, from heaven's own door I flee;
But when I fall, forsaken and forlorn,
　"Look back!" you call. "I still abide with thee!"

The problem of Grace has never troubled Indira as it has so many of her friends. It looks as though they are not satisfied with receiving Grace; their main concern is that its existence should be *proved* to them. Since Indira sees hundreds of proofs of Grace all around her, she has not the slightest doubt about what she cannot see. How have we deserved to be born here as human beings? How do we merit all the priceless gifts of Nature? How can we claim we have *earned* all the love, nobility, gratitude and friendship that we see and receive. Is not all this a sign of Grace?

Can anyone of us be *worthy* of all this? Or is there anyone so unworthy that the Lord denies his choicest gifts to him? Of course, Grace is not a mere meaningless and arbitrary whim of the Lord, but she *is* above human logic and mental comprehension. In other words, Grace has her own laws and ways which are nor ours.

Day after day, at the feet of her guru, Indira realized the miracle of Grace in a vivid way. She saw this silent Friend at her elbow pushing her gently, but firmly, toward the Light. Grace is not a slave ready to do our bidding at every turn, nor a mistress easy to please, who can be propitiated by little gifts, still less a medal that we can earn for good conduct. Grace is the mother's kiss on the infant's brow. The mother's love for her children is spontaneous. She loves them all equally. Only some receive her love gratefully, some reciprocate partially, while others take it for granted or even reject it.

In many instances, we see people who, though utterly unworthy in human eyes, suddenly take a somersault and turn toward the Light. Indira has always felt that when the psychic being is evolved but the mind and vital are equally dominating, the child-soul, unable to cope with the storms raging around her, turns in utter helplessness to Mother Grace. She then descends and takes charge, and the rebels either mend their ways or have to quit. This may be the reason why those who seem so unfit are often found receptive to Grace, while others who are correct and pious can never break the ivory shells of their self-righteousness. In the former case, the psychic being dissociates itself from the vital and the mind and fulfills itself. In the latter, the psychic being is not evolved enough to want anything better. So, it supports the egoistic movements and is content to sit under its own rushlight rather than break out and be flooded with His Sunlight.

Whatever be the explanation, one thing is certain: that the Divine does not judge us by our *human* standards. We have a very limited and superficial vision: He knows our every heartbeat, all that we were, are and can become. To us, aspiration is just one of the hundred traits of a fellow-being and, most of the time, it is hardly noticeable: He overlooks the outer traits, good or bad, and fosters our inmost aspiration so it may flower. How could He who is the essence of love and compassion want anything else from us?

It is not that Grace is not there, but that we do not love Him enough to keep faith with Him. We have faith in our parents, our dear ones, our friends. We expect decent behavior from strangers and even from our enemies, but we want proofs of *His* playing the game. We do not know the rules of the game but are bent on judging the Referee.

This world is sustained by Grace. We could not draw our next breath if He did not breathe His Grace into us. Of course, Grace cannot be always pleasant, because Her business is not to please us or to make us happy, but to help us

Indira Devi worshipping Lord Krishna. "She is *His* child. She knows nothing except that He exists and loves her and that if she wants Him to the exclusion of all else she must attain to Him."

fulfill ourselves. She may come in the form of an opportunity, an admonition, a warning or even a blow. It is not the form but the ultimate purpose or outcome that is important.

Grace involves responsibility. It is difficult to give, but, in spiritual life, it is equally difficult to receive. What we receive we take for granted, and when that which we want is withheld, we resent it as an outrage. Indira came to realize how, year after year, she had enjoyed good health in spite of the fact that she was breaking so many of the body's laws. Her heart was then filled with gratitude. The more she concentrated on all she had received, the more insignificant seemed her ailments. The physical suffering was, indeed, there, but every single breath drawn in pain during an asthmatic attack brought to the fore the blessings of free breathing she enjoyed most of the time. When arthritis troubled her too much, she realized the delight she had had when dancing and moving freely. How many months and years of painlessness has she not had! How many nights of undisturbed sleep! How, then, could she possibly complain, and anyway, why against the Divine? If she puts her hand into the fire it must get burned. If she transgresses certain laws of Nature, consciously or unconsciously, certain consequences must follow. Isn't it a wonder how often and to what extent we still escape these consequences?

The physical has its own laws and following the spiritual life does not mean that the body is thereby divinized straightaway. No doubt, at a certain stage of evolution Light will be able to descend into matter and succeed in transforming the physical. But when this will happen Indira does not know. Anyway, this is His lookout and He will solve the problem in His own time. The great prophets and seers may think or talk about it because of their compassion for suffering humanity; but Indira is neither a missionary nor a saint. She is *His* child. She knows nothing except that He exists and loves her and that if she wants Him to the exclusion of

all else she must attain to Him. She has sold herself to Him and her only prayer is: "Let me think of you all the time. Whatever comes from You or is sanctioned by You is a blessing for me: joy or pain, love or rejection, whatever I receive, let me accept on bended knees. Only reveal to me your will and the way to do your will. Give or take what you will, but let me not take my eyes off the Goal. I do not know what is good for me, nor want to know why or how you are drawing me toward you. That you draw me close to you is all I ask. If this self-will does not bend, break it with the wrath of your Love. Let me learn to give all I have and am—keeping back nothing. All that I give I save, all that I hoard I lose. Let me become what you want me to become. Good or bad, whatever I am, I belong to you. To become yours is my job. The rest is *your* business, not mine."
And I wrote:

> Why should I grieve?
> Yet I shall see another dawn,
> Another golden morning born,
> When Mother Earth a christening robe
> Of roseate hue shall weave?
>
> Sad—why should I be?
> Yet I shall see a rose-bud smile
> And open its dew-kissed eyes awhile
> A blossom-hour, a fragrant life,
> A packed eternity.
>
> Why should I cease to be?
> Yet I shall hear my Master's call
> And know the urge to stake my all,
> The urge to know, the urge to grow,
> Be perfect even as He.

My heart has taken wings:
Far, far above the pull of life,
The day's upheavals, struggle and strife,
Far, far above the mind's domain,
The ken of thought—of joy and pain
Of fortune's smiles and slings.

My heart has taken wings,
Like a ray of sun at the close of day,
A homing bird, it sails away:
Faint grow the flickering lights of earth,
Time's measured steps of death and birth
And maya's smoky rings.

My heart has taken wings
Where silence sings of timeless themes
And music flows in self-lit streams,
Where day and night stand out as guards
And love and light are heavenly bards:
It soars to the stars and sings.

What love is this, o friend, that floods my heart again,
Sweeping all dams of thought and time and space away?
The long-forgotten past comes pouring down in rain
And flows in this life's pool the stream of yesterday.

A dream of ages gone flowers out on life's hard stem,
Defying reason's grasp, untouched by mind's rough hands;
In the grey drab sands of time it glows a flawless gem:
An elusive fragrance comes wafted from far-off lands.

Sometimes, I know not why I hear a flutelet call
In the lonely deep of night, in the madding crowds of day!
It calls: Come home, come home, come home, the shadows fall!
Who calls to me? From where? So near so far away.

32

MEDITATION

Indira is often asked the best way to do meditation. So far as she knows, however, meditation is not *done*, it just *happens*. It is complete relaxation, the act of *being* and not trying to *become* anything.

Meditation is not breathing exercises, rigid postures or attempting to silence the mind and in the process making oneself that much more tense. Neither is it a mathematical process or a scientific achievement that can be won in the laboratories. Meditation is a contact with the Beloved, your real self. It is the completeness of being alone with oneself, a state of Grace in which one spontaneously opens one's heart to the Light. See how the sunflower opens its petals to the sun—effortlessly, yet so definitely.

Human beings are afraid to be alone lest they have to face themselves and see themselves for what they really are. They want shortcuts to peace, to knowledge and nowadays even to Divinity. Yoga is sold to them in packets with labels and formulas; they draw their inspiration from books and lectures by professional sadhus.

It is possible that the Lord's Grace sat easily on Indira because she was totally ignorant of all these manipulative methods to become somebody or something. She had no desire to be a great yogini by silencing the mind to merge into the Formless Brahman. This relaxation or, if you will,

293

surrender of her total being was her door to the Lord's inner castle, the key to His Heart. She started with a clean slate and she would very much like her friends to do likewise; to forget all recipes, forget the mind, forget the world and themselves. Just remember Him, and relax, relax, relax.

If they would give Him even half an hour a day, they would arrive at an inner harmony and strength. But this half-hour must be His exclusively. Go to Him and say: "Lord, I have come. Tired and weary from my self-created worries, I come to you for rest. Accept me with all my faults and flaws or mold me to your will. If my mind is restless, accept this restlessness. If it is impure, accept this impurity. I don't worry about your glories and you forget about my difficulties. I am yours for this half-hour. Even if the three worlds are shaken from their foundations, I will not leave you. Let me rest in you for this half-hour so that I may walk beside you, work for you and live for you."

Did not Christ say: "Those who are heavy-laden, come to me and I'll give you rest." Why not hold Him to that promise-why not give the Lord a trial?

"As soon as I sit down to meditate my mind begins to wander. I can neither relax nor concentrate on the Lord." That is the complaint Indira so often hears from people. How can it be otherwise, she tells them, when they make no attempt to keep up their contact with Him during the rest of the day? One should think of the Lord as often as one can. In this way the mind eventually becomes accustomed to the heights and meditation is made possible. Indira always advises new people, regardless of the work they are engaged in, to think of Him for one minute every half-hour. Even this much will keep up the contact.

What is necessary for each of us is to give what we can. Don't calculate, don't plan. Whatever little you have to give to the Lord—give it today. Some days back Indira overheard one aspirant tell another: "I missed two hours' meditation yesterday. Today I'll make it up." He did not realize

"Like a bird let out of a cage, the spirit soared upward, claiming its kinship with the stars. It was as if she were floating through different worlds, following a Flute-Call."

that those moments he failed to think of Him were gone forever!

People say: "As soon as I get out of my present circumstances, I'll give myself up to the Lord." But this tomorrow never comes, it is eternally before us. Does a mother say, "Tomorrow, after I do this or that thing, I will love my son?" No, that is not the way. The hostile forces will see to it that your circumstances remain always with you.

Does not the Lord know our circumstances? It is He who has made them, for what purpose He alone knows. He does not expect of us more than we can give. Even if it is only five minutes a day, let us give it wholly to Him.

If you cannot give yourself completely to Him today, then pray that you may be able to do so tomorrow. Only give what you can today. If we are sincere there will always be time to remember Him, no matter what we are doing. If we truly want Him, He is *bound* to change our circumstances if they are unfavorable. I defy anyone to disprove this. The crux of the trouble is that we do not really want Him.

33

GURUS AND DISCIPLES

In SPIRITUAL life one meets two types of seekers. When the first wishes to see the master of the house, he goes to the gatekeeper and humbly asks if he will take him to the master. The gatekeeper, of course, complies since that is his business. Now as they go along, the man may stop here and there to admire the gardens and the walks. But whenever he does this the gatekeeper reminds him of his mission, saying: "This way, please, if you wish to see the master. There will be plenty of time to look at the scenery later." And thus he takes the man by the most direct route to the master.

Then there is the way of the thief. This man asks no one, but climbs over a back fence. Since he has no idea where the master is, he must look here and there and spend a great deal of time in the search. He is afraid of the watchman and the master's dogs so he climbs through windows. He darts in and out of back places, hoping no one will notice the few bananas he has filched from the garden. Perhaps he wanders into the women's quarters or falls into a pond! Finally he begins to hide himself even from the master. It is then that he realizes he did not really want to see him after all and goes away with his dishonest day's earnings.

The first, the sincere man, is the devotee who takes to a guru. The guru is the gatekeeper who leads us directly to the Lord. He is the servant of the Lord and therefore acts

"True gurus are very rare in this world, but true disciples are still rarer."

only according to the Lord's will. Being His servant he is familiar not only with how to reach Him, but also with the various pitfalls along the way.

True gurus are very rare in this world, but true disciples are still rarer. It is in the nature of human beings to misunderstand the Divine Light and its workings in the guru. They simply cannot believe that anyone could love them selflessly and act only in their own best interests. And so, as soon as the guru puts the necessary pressure on the disciple's ego, everything he says or does is apt to be misinterpreted. These little misunderstandings provide the fuel that supports the hostile attacks and pave the way for the disciple's fall. The disciple comes to change himself but ends by wanting the guru to change, to come down to the disciples's level. It is the pressure of the Light upon the disciple's vital nature that causes these difficulties. Just as insects, lying still in a dark corner, suddenly come to life under a torchlight, so the hidden imperfections lying latent in human beings become restive when dazzled by the light of Grace. The pressure of this light is very difficult for the disciple to bear, and those who are unwilling to change sooner or later pack up and leave.

Of course, it would be ever so much easier for the guru to simply let them go their own way and say, "Yes, yes, you're wonderful." They would feel much happier and there would be less strain on him. But then they would both go to hell! The ego is so subtle and difficult to eradicate. It is like a sore. You can bandage it up, but eventually all the foreign matter will have to come out. By overlooking a disciple's wrong movement, you may, indeed, obviate some temporary pain, but sooner or later he will have to pay for it.

Indira tells Dada's children: "You have given up your homes, your families and income—everything a man holds dear. You have trusted us to lead you to the Divine. We cannot play with your lives because you are ignorant. We cannot give in to your tantrums because it is easier. A guru who does not fulfill his obligation to the disciple will himself never attain to the Divine.

"Be simple, like children. Have faith that whatever the guru says is right. When you will have achieved this, you will experience a great sense of inner liberation. This patronizing attitude: 'I'll do it even though the guru is wrong' will get you nowhere. If the guru has misunderstood and wronged you, that is his *karma*. But don't *you* worry about it. For you such a thought should never come. You can meditate all day long and be pure as gold, but once you've taken to a guru, unless and until this submission comes, there can be no salvation."

As love grows, these misunderstandings fall off. Then one gives himself gladly to the guru and accepts praise and blame as two sides of the same coin, as twin expressions of the guru's compassion. The will to change is no longer a hardship but a joy. How often, when my guru has rebuked me for an oversight or mistake, have I not been overwhelmed by his compassion: that he who has no attachment to anyone in the world and is occupied with so many important things should yet spend his precious time and energy to correct me!

Even though the disciple tries to efface his self-will and surrender himself to the guru, there is no servility in the accepted sense of the term. For it is not as a slave but as a servant of love that he wants the guru to own him body and soul. He serves from love, not fear, and he serves because he delights in serving, not because he must. He is conquered by the guru's love and wins the guru's heart of blessing by his surrender.

When Indira looks back at the years spent at her guru's feet, she realizes once again how blessed she has been. She has tasted the nectar of love Divine. She has seen the heavenly tenderness in her guru's eyes. She has known the master who forgives not once but a thousand times the disciple's faults.

She has touched his feet whose one touch has brought infinite peace to her restless heart, whose one look has charmed away all pain from her aching soul. She has heard that heavenly voice which came like a flutelet to her way-lost soul to wean her from her lesser loves, her illusions and desires. She has loved that guru whose love is secure like the rock, soothing like the morning breeze, pure like the mountain snow, protective like the mother's arms, selfless like the sun's rays, spontaneous like the brook and eternal like the Divine.

Today Indira needs the guru's protection and help as never before. She feels more helpless and dependent upon him than when she first came to his feet. For today she knows what she did not fully realize then: that it is the most blessed thing in the world to be a helpless child of the guru. The sense of liberation that this dependence brings far exceeds any freedom ever experienced by the self-reliant.

34

ASHRAM LIFE

In MODERN times it is technology that is worshipped as God. All our efforts, our resources and our energies are offered to that one end. But what about man? In all this research has not the poor individual been forgotten? Is there no longer any value to be attached to his inner resources and latent excellence? Has he no further need to transform his own nature? One becomes an excellent doctor, engineer, scientist—but what about the man in him? Has he become a better *person?* He has conquered the outer worlds but has he achieved mastery over himself? He may be the leader of his nation, but can he control his own passions, his desires, his pettiness, his anger, his avarice? Is not the inner research far more important? If we had leaders who were God-fearing, kind, generous and humble, would not our world be a much better place?

It is for this reason that ashrams exist. When everybody is busy going about improving others, the ashram enjoins us to first improve ourselves.

From time immemorial ashrams have existed in India. Krishna Himself spent some time in an ashram serving His guru. But there should be no confusion. An ashram is not a convent or a monastery, still less a spiritual-cum-cultural institution. A guru takes a few disciples in hand and they live with him, serving him, following his directions, loving him

"A guru takes a few disciples in hand and they live with him, serving him, following his directions, loving him and aspiring to the Divine. The relationship between the guru and the disciples is a wonderful thing."

and aspiring to the Divine. The guru accepts responsibility for their physical and spiritual welfare. No private property or relationship is allowed. All belongs to the guru and the ashram. Each member works for a certain number of hours and is given what he or she needs. It is a sort of spiritual socialism in which the guru and the disciples are all dedicated to the Lord.

There is no democracy in spiritual life, for each disciple is at a different stage of evolution and has his own peculiar problems. Thus while the guru has the same love for all he manifests it in different ways. The relationships between the guru and the various disciples are spontaneous and spring from the *samskaras*, or inherited tendencies of past lives. It is like a jigsaw puzzle. Some pieces have a large place, others a smaller one. But all have a place. A disciple only causes himself needless pain by not accepting the role that the Lord has assigned to him.

The relationship between the guru and the disciples is a wonderful thing. An Indian guru is not just the head of the instittituion or monastery, he *is* the institution. In the former case one goes to a certain monastery or an order and *then* loves the head of the place, but in the latter one goes to the guru and resides in the ashram because of *him*. There can be no ashram, properly speaking, after the passing of the guru. The disciples may stay on in the ashram building for the sake of convenience, but that is all.

Ashram life has thus a great advantage. In the ordinary life we are self-centered. The whole world revolves around our own egos. It is indeed difficult to focus all one's thoughts, actions, love on the Unseen. The guru makes this possible, for here everything is centered around *him*. The disciples are bound by a common bond of *gurubhakti* and aspiration. Service and love become possible.

When Indira first came to her guru, she was surprised to see that the aspirants around her suffered from all the petty problems of the world—only in a far more pronounced degree than outside, in the thick of life. The same jealousy, intolerance, bigotry and untruthfulness existed among the aspirants as among the worldly-minded. Then the veil of ignorance was lifted for her by her guru. She had always thought she was an even-tempered person, but after a few months in the ashram she noticed she had become irritable and hypersensitive. With a little dispassionate thinking she realized that, being a very proud woman, she had always suppressed her irritation because she thought it unseemly and undignified to lose one's grip. It was her pride that had prevented her from betraying anger. Now, with the pressure that was put on her ego by the guru's grace, all this came to the surface to be eventually eradicated.

No doubt there are many methods of achieving transformation: but for herself Indira knows only one. It is simple and may even sound childish to the erudite—yet it does work. She means the Way of Love. She loves her guru and a spontaneous movement of love *is* to want to please the beloved. Whatever she does, says, or thinks, the question comes automatically: "What would Dada say to this?"

To destroy refuse one requires a fire. The disciple's fire is love, and when this fire is strong enough it consumes everything. All impurities, all dross burn away and *become* fire. But when the fire is weak, nothing that you put into it is consumed. It will only burn a little and change its shape. It then becomes very ugly and gives off a foul odor, and there is a great deal of smoke and confusion. When lust is thus altered, it becomes jealousy, possessiveness, anger, resentment, greed and so on.

Jealousy and ingratitude are the two traits most ingrained in the human composition. You will find a streak of jealousy in almost every *sadhak*. It is really such a petty movement, we should feel humilitated to see it in ourselves. Indira always tells the aspirants: "It is no use saying that if such and such a person weren't here you would not be jealous. You would then be jealous of X, and after X, of Y, till every living being had been removed from the scene. And then you'd be jealous of the dead! Stand back from it. See it for what it is, and don't ever try to justify it. You must reject it ruthlessly. Root it out in the beginning before it grows into a forest through which you will never reach the Divine. Any wrong movement firmly rejected *must* fall off in time. If it didn't, then none of us could ever succeed."

In yoga the things that hamper us most are these small petty problems. Nothing is too small to prove an obstruction and nothing is so large that it cannot be overcome with sincerity, perseverance and the guru's help. Vigilance, vigilance, vigilance all along the line; at every step it is essential. Whenever anything unseemly happens we must look within. That is the difference between the worldly man and the aspirant. The former always looks without and finds fault with all except himself: the aspirant looks within and tries to find the root of the trouble hidden somewhere under the subtle layers of the ego. What happens outside is just a projection of what is inside us. Nothing can affect us if we have no opening to it within ourselves. Unless there were a point of contact between the two we would not be affected.

Once in San Francisco a friend asked Indira: "Don't you think it is cowardly to run away from the world because one can't face it? She answered: "No it isn't, for it requires far more courage to face oneself sincerely and truthfully than to face a few friends across the table who will not tell us anyway what they think of us. It is not easy to be alone with oneself, to see oneself as one really is and not as one believes oneself to be."

The hunter spreads out his nets and hundreds of birds are caught, but in their ignorance they only chirp in delight at the sight of the food they are decoyed by. They do not realize what they have lost. Only a few, here and there, struggle to free themselves, and still fewer succeed. The chosen few on whom the Lord lays His yoke of compassion, drawing them to Him with the reins of love, are like these few birds. What right have those who are still in bondage to criticize the few who thirst for freedom? They may well be reminded: "You are in bondage—break your shackles and come out. If you do, you are strong and brave, but if you can't be sorry for your own plight and leave us to seek the liberation which is our birthright."

PART THREE

by

Dilip Kumar Roy

"In January, 1953, Indira and I were sent by the Indian government on a cultural mission in which we toured the world for nine months."

35

PAPA RAMDAS

IN JANUARY, 1953, Indira and I were sent by the Indian government on a cultural mission in which we toured the world for nine months. We flew first to Tokyo, thereafter to Honolulu, San Francisco, Los Angeles, Santa Barbara, Carmel, Chicago, New York, Philadelphia, Washington, London, Göttingen, Zurich, Rome and Cairo, whence we returned to Bombay in August, 1953. In all these cities I lectured on the sages and saints of India and sang to the accompaniment of Indira's dances.

As Sri Aurobindo had now passed on to the Beyond, we settled, upon our return, in the hallowed city of Poona. For a time we stayed at Dunlavin Cottage, the annex of an imposing mansion. It was badly in need of repair but we could not afford to rent a house with a hall where we could sing nightly. I wrote a few books there to make ends meet. But on such details I feel no urge to dilate, the less so as I must write at some length about a great saint, Papa Ramdas, who with his equally great disciple, Mother Krishnabai, came to stay with us for three unforgettable days, regaling us with stories of their wonderful spiritual experiences. Years ago, I had visited Ramdas' ashram at Kanangadh, near Mangalore, South India, and been captivated by his radiant personality, flawless sincerity and unutterable purity of character. I propose now to write about what he personally meant to us and how he came in our hour of need to stand by and inspire us once again.

Perhaps of all the great saints that lived in India in our age, Ramdas has revealed most about himself and his yoga. He has written a number of books in simple English, *The Vision of God, In Quest of God, Songs of Ramdas,* etc. So I will not do more than write about how he impressed me and what he told me personally. Those who want to know more about him are referred to his inspiring books, where they may drink straight at the fount, the more so as he was too truthful and childlike a man to want to write to impress. He was, indeed, a child of Ram (by Ram he meant Krishna) and talked and lived like a child, loving children and playing with them as one of them. The first time I saw him he had in his arms a tiny baby whose mother had been deserted by her husband. (I myself had recommended this derelict woman to Sri Ramdas and she had been accepted.) "I was born a baby," he once told me, laughing, "without a single tooth, and look!"—here he laughed in glee, betraying his bare gums with not a tooth in his head—"Ram has so ordained that I simply had to revert to my babyhood again!" But to give his life story in brief.

His father had given him a mantra. He went on repeating it pauselessly, when lo, in a few days he reached an ecstasy which nothing could affect! Then Ram asked him to wander about India depending only on Him for his sustenance. Ramdas obeyed and tramped the length and breadth of India from Kashmir to Cape Comorin—literally a beggar in Ram's name. All his experiences and trials during this period of homeless penury—his novitiate days, as it were—have been chronicled by him with meticulous care. His books testify to the amazing simplicity, purity and sincerity of this child and slave of Ram. I will now write about what he said to me when I went once to obtain his blessing and stayed in his ashram for a week.

My first question to him was: How was one to have the

darshan (vision) of Krishna? He answered at once: "By becoming God-mad, Krishna-intoxicated. Love Him not *among* other things but *above* all things. Let Him be your one goal—first and last—and let everything else be secondary. Let me give you a homely simile: A man wants to catch a train; on the way he meets a dear friend, he excuses himself and says: 'I'm late—must run—see you later.' And he runs. You must run for Krishna in this way, saying: 'To Him, to Him first—everything else must wait till I find Him.' If your *vyakulata* [restless longing] to meet Him takes precedence over all other desires, you can be sure He will be waiting for you there around the corner."

He used to visit me in my small room and sit down on the mat with me like a friend and talk and talk of Krishna's ways with a flushed face. "But," he used to say, "do not want Ram's *darshan* merely, as seeing Him is not enough. Ramdas told Him this when He came to him for the first time and danced all over the place, flute in hand. 'Nay, Lord,' pleaded Ramdas, 'this is all very well but it won't do. For you will vanish presently, leaving Ramdas a legacy of darkness.' It is not implied that seeing Him *in* Him is not great. Why, every touch of His is maddening. What is meant is that you must insist on seeing Him in all and all in Him. For then only will you be delivered permanently from downpulls and sorrows of the ego. And this breathtaking revelation came to Ramdas first in a cave in Arunachala just after he had received the blessing of Bhagavan Ramana Maharshi. It was he, the mighty yogi, the king among men, whose Grace expedited Ramdas' final realization.

"And Grace, Ram's Grace!" he went on in a thick voice. "How can one describe the indescribable? It can only be experienced with one's whole being—never portrayed, even in the loveliest of words. Meet Him face to face, for He *can* be so met if you love Him above everything. Love Him as you love nothing else and He *will* come to you—in any form you want. Do not waste time in discussing Him and His

ways nor strive to understand with the mind His incomprehensible *lila*, cosmic play. That is *not* the way. Appeal to Him
to teach you how to love Him, and all will be revealed to you.
Trust Him absolutely and He will take you in hand and mold
you to His will. He will draw you under the wings of His
love if you seek refuge in Him alone."

His eyes glistened as he went on: "Love . . . love . . . we
talk glibly of Love. But what do we, poor fools, know of
love—His love—just a drop of which makes one at once
immortal and dead to everything else! Can the fly know the
weight of a mountain? A mere pebble is more than it can
bear. No, Ram! I tell you, words can never help you even to
imagine the great mystery of His breathtaking Love. They
can, at the most, put you on the way—set the pace at the
starting point. But the whole way, the long steep ascent, you
have to traverse yourself, every inch of it, with all the power
and tenacity of your own aspiration."

"What about the guru, then?" I asked.

"The guru can stimulate this but the flame of your aspiration has to be fanned sleeplessly by your *own* effort and
vigilance. But the paradox is that however you may try you
cannot make much headway if you believe you will attain
by your own effort. That effort leads duly to helplessness—
the zero hour—when His help comes. But nonetheless the
effort has to be made in order to realize the futility of effort
unblessed by His Grace. And this is a very valuable realization
in that it leads you straight into the heart of humility and
submission without which one can never go far."

"That much, I think, I have come to realize, to my cost,"
I replied ruefully. "Only . . . I want to understand also
if I may—a little, at least. . . ."

"Ramdas understands," he said with a lovely smile. "Only,
Ram, in the domain of the Spirit one must first understand
that one can understand very little with the mind—to start
with." He suddenly chuckled in glee and added: "That

reminds Ramdas of a rather funny incident. Listen." He laughed again and resumed:

"It happened a few years after Ramdas had turned a mendicant in Ram's name. At the time he was living on the top of a hill in a small hut when, one evening, an intellectual friend of his sought him out. He had a great many questions seething in his mind to which, he said, he could find no convincing answers. Ramdas was scared stiff as he did not know how to deal with those who love to summon devotees to the dock deposing for the Divine. So he fobbed off his friend and postponed the discussion somehow. But as the ghost had been only warded off for the moment, and not for good, he had to appeal to his one extricator, Ram. To his amazement, in the dead of night Ram Himself formulated some questions and answered them, point by point. And a strange feature of it was that it seemed as if the questions were being voiced by Ramdas himself as somebody's mouthpiece. Next morning he showed these—the questions and answers of which he had kept a record—to his intellectual friend who exclaimed: "You take my breath away! For these were just the questions I came to put to you myself!"

And he showed me these in his book, *At the Feet of God*, from which I will give here but a few excerpts:

Question: What is the result of self-surrender?
Answer: Everlasting bliss.
Question: How?
Answer: When the human will is given up for the Divine will, all responsibility of the instrument, the devotee, ceases and the consciousness of the individual ego is merged in the Divine Consciousness. Then all his actions, thoughts and words emanate from the Divine Source, leaving him free of all doubt, desire and bondage.
Question: How is it that you allow your child's mind to wander?
Answer: All, all is myself, O child! Wherever your mind

wanders it wanders and rests in me. . . . You cannot reason why
it is so, but it is the one great Truth. You cannot comprehend it
but you can realize it.

Question: Why should Ramdas not comprehend it?

Answer: Because it is beyond the range of the intellect.

Question: Then explain why should there be an intellect at all
and what are its functions.

Answer: The intellect exists to help you know that you do
not *know* anything.

The admonition is not something original except in regard
to the context in which it originated—that is, at a certain
stage of Ramdas' spiritual evolution. But when taken in con-
junction with the fact that Ramdas himself voiced the questions which were answered by Ram, as also the singular
circumstance of the visitor who had gone all the way up the
hill to seek light from Ramdas, the miracle that happened
seems even more significant than miraculous. But to resume
the thread where I left off.

The first thing that struck anybody who met Ramdas was
his utter simplicity and unpretentiousness. During my stay in
his ashram we discussed all sorts of questions and doubts
which were afflicting me at the time and he helped me not a
little by relating to me unreservedly how similar doubts had
arisen in his mind and how they were solved by Ram Himself. He told me also how the Lord came to him like a friend
with whom it was possible to joke and laugh. He told me
about his great disciple Krishna Bai who had also attained
Self-Realization through Ram's Grace. He told me about so
many miracles he had seen, the sadhus he had profited by
and, above all, Ram's deep solicitude for him. He regaled
me with anecdotes; some were amusing, but all had deep
spiritual significance. He spoke also of his disappointments,
especially with regard to the ashram he had come to sponsor.
But I cannot recall a single instance when he asserted anything dogmatically or criticized others who were of a different persuasion or held views other than his own. He even

Papa Ramdas. "Years ago, I had visited Ramdas' ashram and had been captivated by his radiant personality, flawless sincerity and unutterable purity of character."

praised most generously people who calumniated him, though I wondered often enough how anybody could have had the heart to throw mud at such a pure and humble soul whose every gesture exuded spontaneous goodwill and friendliness, who refused to be offended and, to crown all, who hymned his great Caretaker even on those occasions when he might well have complained of having been let down. I feel tempted to give a good many instances of this simple trust that flowered so effortlessly in his reactions to life. But as, obviously, I cannot do that, only two of his experiences which related to me himself must suffice. I will narrate them briefly, as he has recorded them fairly elaborately in his book *In the Vision of God.*

Once he happened to stay in Central India as a Raja's honored guest. The Raja and his Rani were his ardent admirers and gave him a regal reception. The whole town paid homage to the saint who, though living at the time in the royal palace, received everybody—the rich as well as the poor—with the same spontaneous welcome. He was taken in procession through the capital and the poets and pundits came and composed songs and hymns in his honor.

After a few days he wanted to proceed on his journey: he wished to visit the places of pilgrimage, *tirthas.* The Raja offered to reserve a saloon for him on the train. But as Ramdas insisted on a third-class compartment, they had to buy him an ordinary ticket.

It so happened that the train was crowded and the only compartment where there was room was occupied by a number of Muslim roughnecks who did not want a Hindu sadhu among them. But the royal guard forced an entry and Ramdas got in unafraid, relying on his unfailing Protector, Ram. As the train moved on, more and yet more passengers entered the compartment, till Ramdas had to squeeze himself into a corner. But they grudged him even that much space and when a few more stalwarts hustled in, Ramdas had at last to sit on the dusty floor. This amused the rowdies, who, taking him for a beggar and a coward, tittered at him and sometimes even kicked his shins in contempt. Tears fell from Ramdas' eyes and he muttered in ecstasy: "O Ram, your *lila* [play] is indeed inscrutable! Last night Ramdas was fawned upon by royalty and today he is kicked by all and sundry! How you love to play with your devotees!"

"On another occasion," he told me, "Ramdas was singing with some other sadhus in a wayside temple, praising the Grace of Ram who takes care of us all, when a big cobra was seen creeping out from a corner. The sadhus leapt up in dismay, but Ramdas, who was in an ecstatic mood, did not budge. 'Why on earth do you leave your seats helter-skelter?' he asked. 'Don't you see that Ram Himself has put on a snake's disguise and come to accept our homage? Come, let us sing to Him.' But the others protested and shouted out to him: 'Come away, Ramdas—don't be a fool,' and so on. But Ramdas went on singing in rapture till the snake crept up to him and, when offered a sugar candy, was mightily pleased and ate it out of his hand. And Ramdas said, in ecstatic tears: 'How unfathomable are your ways, Ram! Fancy your coming to your own slave—to be fed by him whom you have fed all his life!' "

Such was the saint I had the good fortune to be blessed by. I cannot write about him exhaustively. I will only add that when we do meet a saint, we are changed to some extent and grow, unawares, more receptive to a light that is all around us and yet cannot enter our being because our disbelief shuts it out. The saint comes and helps us see how at home we have grown with darkness.

Not that one willfully doubts or disbelieves. But then, being "sons of an intellectual age"—as Sri Aurobindo put it in his *Synthesis of Yoga*—we have grown somewhat opaque to the lights that hail from regions higher than that of the intellect. So we are anxious that our intellect should at least be partly satisfied before we can bring ourselves to concede that any supra-intellectual light can possibly come down to transform us. But, alas, what one has seen from a distance through clouds of rumor and hearsay hardly affords us that solid basis upon which our feet can confidently rest. That is why, even when we have accepted the fundamental position of faith as against reason, we can only accept it somewhat tentatively, with the result that we stumble off and on, and grievously at that. At such times, the testimony of those who have arrived cannot but prove of inestimable value. For were this unavailable we might, indeed, still bring ourselves to accept faith on faith, but such half-hearted conversion is ill calculated to relieve the gloom, as every honest seeker knows, to his cost.

At all events, that is one of the main reasons why true faith finds such a favorable soil in India, because go where you will, you are sure, if you are a true seeker, to meet God-rapt sages and saints who have achieved holiness through a living faith and years of arduous self-discipline. Papa Ramdas—his devotees call him Papa—came as it were to prove this anew to me in Poona, and though we could allot to them only one small room they stayed at our cottage for three days and nights to sustain us with their lovely love and beautiful blessing. Their smile of Grace served almost as a prop of light in our dark days of penury and struggle.

Were space at my disposal I would have inserted here a twenty-page article I wrote on him, but as that is not possible I will do my best to condense in a few pages an account of the inspiration he gave us during his brief stay as our guest.

When he was with us in Poona devotees asked him questions night and morning and he used tirelessly to give delectable replies. One day a seeker asked him how we could know that the Lord was so near and dear to us and how we could grow to love Him without ever having met Him. Papa smiled and answered: "Once upon a time, there was a mother with a small son. The father had gone abroad to make a living. The little boy had never seen him but had grown to love him having heard from his mother daily how great his father was. One day a playmate of his laughed at him when he said he loved his father very dearly. 'How can you love one you haven't so much as seen?' he challenged. The little boy replied, with a touching simplicity: 'But my mother has seen him.' Comment on such a beautiful parable is superfluous: it convinces by its very simplicity. True faith based on hearsay *can and does* help us to love. There is a Bengali song Sri Ramakrishna was wont to sing: 'Na jene nam shune kane man giye tai lipta holo' ['I knew Him not but heard His Name and so my heart was glued to Him']."

Dawned March 1, 1956. "Papa Ramdas and Mataji Krishnabai will leave us tomorrow" was the one thought that made us all sad as we sang the hymn to them in Hindi composed by Indira. Here is my translation, which we all sang in chorus in the same tune:

> We bow to thee, O Ramdas, O Saint, we bow to thee:
> O Rama's child whose love outflowers in light and harmony!
> Thou com'st to bless our arid earth with His Name's rain of
>   Grace
> And chantest: "Ram! I'll sing and sing of Thee in gratefulness."
>
> Who is a king and who is a bondsman, a lonely alien, say?
> Behold with the eye of love: in friend and foe He comes to play;
> On land and sea 'tis He who reigns: all live by his breath of
>   Grace:
> And so, O Ram, I sing Thy glory in deep gratefulness.
>
> Touching thy feet the earth is blessed, O Ram's darling son!
> Blessed is Krishnabai and those who've seen in you the One,
> And known that through you on our earth comes Ram to rain
>   His Grace:
> So, we will sing thy glory and His in fervent gratefulness.

He left his mortal body in 1965, singing Ram's Name. To me it was more than a bereavement, for I lost a friend who had helped me many a time with the support of his love and blessing. I will relate briefly only one instance when, in 1954, I had through his agency an experience of *samadhi*.

Mother Krishnabai. "He told me about his great disciple Krishnabai who had also attained to Self-Realization through Ram's Grace."

We were at the time staying with our dear friend Dr. B. Malik, the then Chief Justice of the Allahabad High Court. I loved to talk to him now and again about Papa Ramdas and the light on his face. On that memorable night I dropped off to sleep after having discoursed on him. Suddenly my sleep was broken. I heard him say: "Come, come—up here!" —when lo, it happened: the crown of my throbbing head opened and I saw myself rocketing skyward, winging the blue, till I suddenly realized I had come out of my body. It was indeed a *samadhi* ecstasy which thrilled me to the core— a blessed leap of liberation (*mukti*) from the cage of flesh. But how can I describe with words a rapture that had to be experienced to be believed? When I came back into my body, a cadence of the rapture still lingered as I described it to Indira with tears in my eyes. Thereafter, when I told Ramdas that he had come to me as a sign of Krishna's Grace he only smiled and blessed me once again.

To conclude now with what he told us in Poona on March 2, 1956. After we had sung to him I told him how deeply grateful we were that he had spent three days with us and filled our lives with peace and joy from dawn to midnight. He said with a lovely smile: "We came to you because you two have created here a nucleus of love, for I feel the vibration of love at every turn from the devotees you have attracted."

"We have little else to offer Papaji!" I said in a thick voice. "All we have is love. We are but two drops—"

"Not drops," Papa cut in. "You have dug a sweet lake of love's pure cream here which is so inviting and cool that I have grown hoarse, don't you see, dipping into it again and again." And how he laughed! (The context is: Papa had grown hoarse answering our questions morning and evening for hours. So he made light of it by assuring us that it was all because he had been overfed with sweet cream!)

"Papa," I said, "would you mind telling us about your final Realization?"

He readily acquiesced and gave a long description of his burning aspiration and yearning which had led him to Arunachala Hill, hallowed by the *tapasya* of the peerless saint, Bhagavan Ramana Maharshi. I can only give here the gist of his long narration.

Papa said: "There Ramdas was in a cave, living on but one meal a day. He went out in the morning to beg, and came back to boil a little pot of rice—just rice which he shared with the squirrels who were his only companions in the cave. One day, somebody suggested Ramdas pay homage to Ramana Maharshi, the saint of saints. Ramdas instantly agreed and went straight to where the Maharshi was staying. Ramdas prostrated himself before the Maharshi and said that he had come only for the great saint's blessings. The Maharshi looked at Ramdas so compassionately that he felt a thrill of joy and understood that he *had* won the boon he had come for. He said nothing more and went back to his solitary cave where he went on repeating the Name in an ecstasy of longing, when lo, suddenly his Lord Ram, that is, Muralidhar Krishna, appeared before him and danced and danced. It was a maddening dance, accompanied by His flute."

"Did you see Him with closed eyes or open?" I interjected.

"With open eyes, as Ramdas is seeing you," Papa answered. "But it was not this momentary vision that Ramdas' heart had craved. He knew that a vision like this was not going to last and that when the Lord would vanish, Ramdas would have to revert to his native darkness. So he prayed for the great *darshan*, the Vision of visions, which comes to stay forever so there is no more parting. In a word, Ramdas yearned only to see Ram always in everything, nothing less would satisfy Ramdas." He paused and then resumed with a beatific smile: "And it came one morning apocalyptically—when lo, the entire landscape changed: All was Ram, nothing but Ram —wherever Ramdas looked! Everything was ensouled by Ram—vivid, marvelous, rapturous—the trees, the shrubs, the ants, the cows, the cats, the dogs—even inanimate things pulsated with the throbbing Presence of the one Ram! And Ramdas danced in joy, like a boy who when given a lovely present can't help breaking out into a dance. And so it was with Ramdas: he danced for joy and rushed at a tree which he embraced because it was not a tree but Ram Himself! A man was passing by. Ramdas ran toward him and embraced him, calling out: 'Ram, O RAM!' The man got scared and bolted. But Ramdas gave him chase and dragged him back to his cave. The man noted that Ramdas had not a tooth in his head and so felt a little reassured: at least the 'looney' would not be able to bite him!" He laughed and we swelled the chorus.

"And then?" I asked, after the laughter had subsided.

"The bliss and the joy came to be permanent, like a torrent rushing downhill till it finds a placid level of limpid purling stream. In this experience you can never be cut off from the consciousness of being one with the One who has become all, in which you feel you are one with all because you have perceived that all is He, the One-without-a-Second."

The room throbbed with a discarnate Presence. And we loved Papa because he could talk thus to us all so naturally of the only thing that is worth talking about: the Lord and His *lila*, cosmic play. But, alas, we talk on of this and that, jabbering away our precious energy, because we have nothing better to speak (or hear) about. Our hearts' homage to this great child of Ram, who never grew up, thank God, so that we might hear through him the Flute he had heard and see the One he had visioned in all.

And that is why he could captivate our hearts at once, because he could make us feel a fraction of the godly thrills he had felt over and over again.

After his departure I wrote to him a long letter telling him all about our yoga in Poona, and thanking him for the great joy and inspiration he had given us during his stay.

An indefatigable correspondent, he wrote back at once:

"It is not only that you enjoyed our stay with you, but we, too, had an overwhelmingly blissful time in the company of yourself and Indira Devi, bathing in the holy atmosphere of your Hari Krishna Mandir. The days we spent with you are unforgettable."

When he left our ashram I was reminded again of a famous saying of Acharya Shankar: *Asya jivanmuktasya dehadharanam lokasyopakararatham* [The liberated soul lives only to serve others].

36

MIRACLES

ALTHOUGH I have always believed that miracles were performed in all ages and climes by reputed yogis (not to mention Messiahs like Krishna, Buddha, Christ, Sri Aurobindo, Sri Chaitanya and Sri Ramakrishna), I often caught myself yearning to bear witness to a few, if only to be able to attest from personal experience that Divine Power can repeal the so-called laws of nature and decrees of fate. One such experience I will relate here by way of preface as it is both relevant and convincing.

As I was diffident about going to Pondicherry, I persuaded myself—to obviate my malaise—that Sri Aurobindo had categorically declined to give me initiation. So after a time I decided to search for a guru who could give me the needed guidance. At this time, in 1926, I met Swami Abhedananda, the illustrious disciple of Sri Ramakrishna. When I told him all he very kindly agreed to initiate me in yoga—or, to be more precise, the *ashtanga* yoga of Patanjali.

Now it so happened that a dear friend of mine and a disciple of Sri Aurobindo, Nalinikanta Sarcar, suggested that I consult a friend of his, a mighty yogi, Barodakanta Majumdar, who stayed for hours in *samadhi*.

He lived in Lalgola, about a hundred miles from Calcutta. When Nalinikanta wrote to him he cordially invited us both.

So we went by train to Lalgola and stayed with him as his guests.

When I told him about my groping in darkness for a clue to light he asked me to sit down and meditate with him. "I will find out all about it," he said somewhat cryptically.

I was not a little intrigued and tried in vain to meditate with him. What is he going to find out, I kept asking myself as he went off into a *samadhi.*

After about a half-hour he came to and said without ado that I must on no acount accept anybody other than Sri Aurobindo as my guru. On my telling him that Sri Aurobindo had turned me away he shook his head categorically and said: "No, he hasn't."

"How do you mean?" I said, utterly at a loss.

"I mean what I say."

"But Sri Aurobindo told me himself—"

"No, Dilip Kumar," he cut in, "he has accepted you already —he told me this himself just now."

I was nonplussed and started wondering whether it was all a hoax or I was daydreaming.

He looked kindly at me.

"As you disbelieve my assurance," he smiled, "I will give you a proof. Have you got a chronic pain in your right abdomen?"

"I have," I said, startled. "It's hernia."

"I know. Now tell me: didn't Sri Aurobindo tell you to undergo an operation before you entered the path of yoga?"

I was dumbfounded, for Sri Aurobindo *had* written to me in 1924 those identical words.

Then Baroda Babu gave me a long discourse on yoga and yogic powers and enjoined me not to be skeptical. He even told me about a few miracles he himself had performed, mostly to heal people.

His personality was impressive and his exposition all that could be desired—sober, to the point and unmarred by braggadocio. So I came back a wiser, though a trifle sadder, man, turning over in my mind his categoric reassurance: "Sri Aurobindo told me that he would call you to Pondicherry, in due time. So don't you look this way and that nor dream of accepting anybody else as your guru since Sri Aurobindo *is* your guru and no other."

But when will he call me? I kept asking myself again and again and the answer was silence.

I met Baroda Babu by accident twelve years later, in 1937, when I had returned from Pondicherry to Calcutta for a few months after a stay at Sri Aurobindo Ashram for nine years. I thanked him from my heart for his helpful advice and told him how happy and blessed I felt at the guru's feet. He gave me a kind smile but said pointblank: "That's all as it should be, my friend. Only I want to tell you one thing: that you won't realize Krishna in Pondicherry. For that you will have to wait till the advent of a highly evolved lady. When she will come to cooperate with you as your disciple, then only will you get your heart's desire."

Realization or no, I wanted to see a few miracles at the Pondicherry ashram, as I was told that many a miracle had, indeed, happened there. So I waited on, with my heart in my mouth, till Indira dawned on the horizon, when she touched off miracle after miracle.

Indira, herself, has already related how all this came to pass and how she was taken up on the wave-crest of mystic experiences. But she has not sufficiently stressed how diffident I felt to act as a guru to one who had already attained *samadhi* and manifested *yoga-bibhutis** that stupefied us all. So I must supplement her accounts by a brief description of my then state of mind.

In Sri Aurobindo Ashram no aspirant is allowed to have a disciple. So I wrote to Sri Aurobindo that he must ask Indira

---

* Miraculous powers attained through the practice of yoga.

to accept *him* as her guru. He replied that he would be prepared to give her the initiation if she so desired. But here Indira was adamant and said that though she admired and adored Sri Aurobindo she could not possibly accept him as her guru. So if I declined to accept her, she would just go back. When I informed Sri Aurobindo about her stand he wrote back that I might welcome her as my disciple as she was a person of "advanced spiritual consciousness" and as such would be a help rather than a hindrance to my yoga. I was utterly at a loss. What was I to do? How could I presume to guide a proficient who is endowed with *yoga-bibhutis* of a very high order? But since Sri Aurobindo had assured me that she would be able to help me on my path I accepted her as my disciple in August, 1949.

Thereafter, on her return to Jubbulpore, she fell so seriously ill that she was bedridden and the doctors gave her up. Her husband sent me a frantic telegram: "Come immediately, only you can save her."

At this time I had made a serious blunder (ignoring Gurudev's advice) in that I had written to her insisting that she accept *him* as her guru since, obviously, I had no mystic power to heal, a power he had and could wield to save her. This she misinterpreted as my repudiation of her as my disciple and wrote to me that she did not choose to be saved by anybody other than the guru of her heart. "Something has snapped within me," she wrote. "All the warmth is gone; I can't feel anything." Deeply alarmed, I confessed to Gurudev that I had, impulsively, perpetrated just what he had warned me against so categorically. The soul of compassion and understanding, he wrote back at once, advising me to proceed to Jubbulpore, promising to do his best to save her. "I hope," he wrote, "that it is a passing depression created by her misunderstanding of what you wrote to her and that the elasticity of her psychic temperament and aspiration will help her to recover from it rapidly, if not at once. Still, wires and letters may not help her to recover her natural condition

Dilip Kumar Roy, at Indira Devi's insistence that he was her guru: "I was utterly at a loss. But since Sri Aurobindo had assured me that she would be able to help me on my path I accepted her as my disciple in August, 1949."

immediately and your presence there may be necessary and certainly advisable, since it will set things right at once. So you can start tonight as you propose."

So I started the same afternoon by car and was by her bedside the next evening, hoping against hope that Gurudev's yogic force would work the miracle. But when I saw her my heart misgave me, for although I knew for certain (from all that Sri Aurobindo had written about her to me and her) that she had been both called and chosen, I did not see how her terrible convulsions were going to be remedied. So, I took my courage in both hands and risked enjoining her to dismiss all the doctors who were attending on her. She readily agreed and told them that she would leave it all to the Lord who must prescribe for her henceforward. Her people were aghast, but when I wrote to Gurudev about her resolution (I was writing to him daily about her symptoms and experiences), he wrote to me, endorsing my advice and belauding her faith warmly. (Apropos, a few days before I started for Jubbulpore he had written to me explaining much about what had been happening to her "because of her advanced spiritual consciousness" and added that her *samadhi* was of the "*savikalpa* kind.")

Lastly, in a letter which I received in Jubbulpore he wrote: "Of course, I will try to the end; for my experience is that even a hopeless effort in the fields of the working of the spiritual force is often better than none and can bring in the intervention of the miracle."

I shook my head ruefully and wrote back: "But, alas, Guru, I have never had a congenital weakness for what we Indians so wistfully call 'faith in miracles.' So, If you will pardon me, I can only hope against hope that its agency may come to our rescue before it is too late." Then after giving him a long account of her ailments I added: "From the doctors here I have gathered—what has fairly staggered me— that Indira has been suffering from cardiac asthma, coronary thrombosis, dilatation of the heart, osteoarthritis, low blood pressure, utter lack of appetite, anemia and God knows what else, still undiagnosed. So I am afraid you will have to invoke a *major miracle* if you really mean business."

But the major miracle did happen after all: at the eleventh hour, when all seemed lost and people had started crying, she recovered after having obstinately refused all medicines for well over three months.

This made a difference even to my skeptical mind in that I won here a *point d'appui* for my faith in yogic powers achieving results which I can only describe as too incredible to be discredited. But I prefer to close this episode with a relevant letter which Gurudev wrote to me in reply to some questions which I had to discuss with Indira during her illness about the application of spiritual force to preserve health or cure physical ailments. I had asked him in my letter, among other things, how far he endorsed Sri Ramakrishna's condemnation of the utilization of spiritual force to keep the body in health. He wrote:

I might say a word about Sri Ramakrishna's attitude with regard to the body. He seems to have regarded it as a misuse of spiritual force to utilize it for taking care of the body or curing its ailments. Other yogis—I do not speak of those who think it justifiable to develop yogic *siddhis* [powers]—have not had this complete disregard of the body: they have taken care to maintain it in good health and condition as an instrument or a physical basis for their development in Yoga. I have always been in agreement with this view: moreover, I have never had any hesitation in the use of a spiritual force for all legitimate purposes including the maintenance of health and physical life in myself and in others. . . . I put a value on the body first as an instrument of *dharmasadhana*, or, more fully, as a center of manifested personality in action, a basis of spiritual life and activity as of all life and activity upon earth, but also because, for me, the body as well as the mind and life is a part of the Divine Whole, a form of the Spirit and therefore not to be disregarded or despised as something incurable, gross and incapable of spiritual realization or of spiritual use. Matter itself is secretly a form of the Spirit, and has to reveal itself as that, can be made to wake to consciousness and evolve and realize the Spirit, the Divine within it. In my view the body as well as the mind and life has to be spiritualized or, one may say, divinized, so as to be a fit instrument and receptacle for the realization of the Divine. It has its part in the Divine *lila*, even, according to the Vaishnava *sadhana*, in the joy and beauty of Divine Love. That does not mean that the body has to be valued for its own separate sake or that the creation of a divine body in a future evolution of the whole being has to be contemplated as an end and not as a means—that would be a serious error, which would not be admissable.

Sri Aurobindo's salutary approval of the true place of the human body in spiritual life cannot but be acceptable to the modern intellect even as his rational outlook on the place of *yoga-bibhutis* must be to an aspirant. So I quote a letter he wrote apropos in 1934:

Dilip, the idea that true yogis do not or ought not to use such powers I regard as an ascetic superstition. I believe that all yogis who have these powers do use them whenever they find that they are called upon from within to do so. They may refrain if they think the use in a particular case is contrary to the Divine Will or see that preventing one evil may be opening the door to a worse one or for any other valid reason, but not from any general prohibitory rule. What is forbidden to anyone with a strong spiritual sense is to be a miracle-monger, performing extraordinary things for show, gain, or fame, out of vanity or pride. It is forbidden to use powers from mere vital motives, to make an Asuric ostentation of them or to turn them into a support for arrogance, conceit, ambition or any other of the amiable weaknesses to which human nature is prone. It is because half-baked Yogis so often fall into these traps of the hostile forces that the use of the Yogic powers is sometimes discouraged as harmful to the user.

But it is mostly people who live much in the vital that so fall; with a strong and free and calm mind and a psychic awake and alive, such pettinesses are not likely to occur. As for those who can live in the true Divine Consciousness, certain powers are not "powers" at all in that sense, not, that is to say, supernatural or abnormal, but rather their *normal way of seeing and acting, part of the consciousness*—and how can they be forbidden, or refuse to act according to their consciousness and its nature?

I suppose I have had myself an even more completely European education than you, and I have had, too, my period of agnostic denial, but from the moment I looked at these things I could never take the attitude of doubt and disbelief which was for so long fashionable in Europe. Abnormal, otherwise supraphysical experiences, and powers, occult or yogic, have always seemed to me something perfectly natural and credible. Consciousness in its very nature could not be limited by the ordinary physical human-animal consciousness; it must have other ranges. Yogis or occult powers are no more supernatural or incredible than is supernatural or incredible the power to write a great poem or compose great music; few people can do it—as things are, not even one in a million: for poetry and music come from the inner being and to write or to compose true and great things one has to have the passage clear between the outer mind and something in the inner being. *That is why you got the poetic power as soon as you began Yoga—Yogic force made the passage clear. It is the same with the Yogic consciousness and its powers; the thing is to get the passage clear—for they are already there within you.* Of course, the first thing is to believe, aspire and, with the true urge within, make the endeavor.*

I have already mentioned how, following Indira's advent, my prayer to verify the truth of divine miracles was granted with a prodigality I could otherwise never have dreamed possible. As a result, I began to keep a typescript entitled *No Reason Can Explain* in which I recorded, day after marvelous day, the various supernormal experiences and phenomena that passed before my astonished eyes. The reader who has come all this way with us without doubting our sincerity or objectivity will perhaps find a fewer further examples of some benefit, especially as in Indira's case such

---

* The italics are mine. This letter is given in full in my *Sri Aurobindo Came to Me*, Chapter IX.

miracles are seldom without a significance above and beyond their implications as phenomena *per se.*

Sri Aurobindo passed away about one o'clock in the morning, December 5, 1950. I received the news on the radio in Benares about 10 A.M. on the same day. At noon I received a telegram from Indira sent from Bombay at 9:55 P.M. on the previous night which I decided to preserve as a document. It was worded: "Had a terrible vision last night about Gurudev. Completely shaken. Wire blessings."

She started for Pondicherry from Bombay and I from Benares on the afternoon of the 5th. I arrived at the ashram on the evening of the seventh. Indira had arrived on the previous night. She had kept a diary, from which I will quote a few excerpts:

Bombay Dec. 2, '50. I was having a terrible pain in my body, and whenever I sat down to meditate I saw Gurudev Sri Aurobindo lying in bed. A dreadful chill in the atmosphere. Death hovering around. It was such an agony!

Bombay Dec. 4, '50. At about midnight I saw Gurudev again lying stretched on his bed in his room at Pondicherry, when, suddenly, I saw his body rising up. I knew at once that he was leaving his body. I noticed a black mark on the back of his hand. [Later, we inquired and learned that there was, indeed, a black scar just there, the legacy of an injection.]

On August 9, 1951, I received a thick envelope. As Indira gave it to me she said: "Don't open it for a moment, I can see from the address that it is from Lal." (Lal, whose full name is Dewan Surindar Lal, and who is a dear friend of ours, had been our host in Shivpuri, Gwalior, in 1949.) And she showed me what she had recorded in her diary dated August 2, 1951: "Saw Lal writing to Dada when Biji [Lal's mother] requested him to enclose a little garland she had woven for Dada."

Now I opened the letter and was astonished to find enclosed in it a tiny *bakul* garland beautifully woven. In the closing paragraph of the letter, which was dated August 2,

1951, Lal wrote: "Enclosed please find a garland sent by my mother with all her respects and *pranams.*"

This garland I have kept as a souvenir.

On September 21, 1951, Indira saw a vision which she recorded in her diary on the same day.

Saw Dada reading a letter from America (probably from Dr. Frederic Spiegelberg). The letter was dated 21st September. Dada would be ill advised, so he wrote, to try to publish in America his *Sri Aurobindo Came to Me*, as American publishers were not encouraging. Also there was something about its being "wonderful with you and Indira here."

On the 29th of September I duly received a letter from my dear friend Dr. Spiegelberg who wrote (on September 21, 1951) from Stanford University:

Dear Dilip,

Your letter poses a double problem: Your coming here and the publication of your book. I might say that reading your book in all the installments in *Mother India* has fascinated me throughout and makes me regret even more your reluctance to come on a visit here. I do hope you will soon make up your mind realising the importance of your help to our work and join us next year for sure. Without your presence at our India Art Festival this whole enterprise would be condemned to a matter of minor importance. With you and Indira present, it will be something wonderful. As to your book, I feel like advising you to have it published in India where it will surely have a large and enthusiastic audience. To publish a book in America now-a-days is no joy. . . .

In July, 1951, something amusing happened. Indira brought me a long envelope from the ashram and said: "There is something very pure in it, though what it is I cannot say. But it has given me a feeling of an aroma of purity." On opening it I found that it contained a photograph of Indira herself sent to me by a Punjabi friend of mine, R. Kapur. I laughed

"But she had mistaken her customer: to think that I who love laughter could ever agree to keep such an experience to myself."

and Indira implored me not to tell this to anybody! But she had mistaken her customer: to think that I who love laughter could ever agree to keep such an experience to myself!

We had a friend, L., a good man, though, alas, somewhat overattached, even in his ripe old age (when he should have known better), to his little world of family, money and canny prudence. But I was really fond of him, the more so as he used, often enough, to ask me how to achieve liberation from one's worldly attachments with all their attendant worries. I had, in reply, given him the only solution I could (which, I fear, he didn't find altogether palatable), to wit, that if one wanted to achieve true liberation and bliss one must try, not in thought alone but in action also, to live for the Divine and not for one's family and children. But he didn't want to change and thought that a little meditation and "spiritual talk" would do the trick. However, to come to the drama.

In November, 1957, while we were in Calcutta, we heard that he had had a serious heart attack. On our reutrn to Poona we visited him at his house on December 1. He looked all right and hoped that all would be well. But Indira told me—as soon as we came out of the house—that she had seen a deep shadow over him. "He will have a relapse, Dada, I'm afraid," she said darkly. I felt so sorry for him as we both saw that he was still clinging to his little world of attachments.

On December 5, he died suddenly, a little before midnight. We felt sad, the more so as a chance had been given to him by the Lord and he did not want to profit thereby. A couple of days later, while Indira was meditating, he materialized before her. Indira said he looked extremely worried and when she asked him why, he looked peaceless and replied: "I can't enter the new house—I have no key."

"Perhaps you have left it at home," Indira suggested.

"No, no. The old keys—the ones I have left with Ratna—can't help here."

"Then what's to be done?" Indira asked.

"Tell Dadaji—*he* has the new keys." With this he vanished as suddenly as he had appeared.

A few days later his eldest son, who had come from Calcutta to settle his father's affairs, called on us. During the conversation, he told us: "My father had a terrible nightmare after his first attack. It happened in the nursing home. He said: 'I saw that I was dead. I was knocking frantically at a door. The door would not open as I had no key. It was a terrible feeling of fear and loneliness. I woke up in a cold sweat.'"

I asked him who Ratna was. He said she was his wife, who had been entrusted by her father-in-law, L., with the keys just before his death. I have always believed that the keys in question were those which open the gates to the Beyond. Hence I felt enjoined to pray for him, which I sincerely did, and was gratified that he appeared to Indira no more, having evidently found the peace he was seeking.

April 24, 1958. Accompanied by Indira, her eleven-year-old son Premal and Srikanta (Shiv Thadani, a retired brigadier general), I was singing a lovely song Indira had dictated after her *samadhi*. I felt deeply moved, especially while I sang the couplet:

> *Din bhar mai khelke hari ma!*
> *Ab ayee sharana tihari, ma!*

(I have played and played all day, O Mother sweet,
Till, spent, I refuge seek at thy twin Feet.)

When I had finished, Indira, in a half-trance of ecstasy, said: "Dada, shall we have *prasad*?"*

* Food or drink offered to the Lord.

I wondered wistfully as she went down the steps to the garden, accompanied by Premal and then Srikanta. Premal, at Indira's request, put into her palm a handful of black dry mud, whereupon she began swaying in a *bhav-samadhi.* She then put into Srikanta's hand a bit of the mud—or so we thought. "It is sweet *prasad,* Dadaji," Premal cried out. Upon my reaching the scene, Indira poured the rest of the miraculous brown confection into my hands, leaving her own quite empty. Then, as if this weren't already enough, she again folded her hands and, upon reopening them, produced still more *prasad,* this time out of nothing at all!

Curious, I brought down a pair of envelopes, placing in one a little of the dry, black mud, and in the other some of the ex-mud which had been transformed into *prasad.* A few minutes later, Indira said: "Oh Dada, the clay you kept in your other envelope has been partly changed, by Divine Grace, into *prasad.* Go and look!" We all went, agog, to my desk, and there, lo and behold, the dry mud which had not even been touched by Indira was mud no more, but shone, transformed into the same kind of granulated *prasad!*

I should add, by way of a postscript, that three years ago we had a similar experience in the garden of Sir Chunilal Mehta. At the time, five of us, including Sir Chunilal, were meditating, and Mira gave to Indira the following message: "If even mud offered to the Divine could be changed into *prasad* why should not the unregenerate human personality, too, be equally transformed—divinized?"

I have given only the bare lineaments of the event since I want to append a report on it written by Srikanta. As a doughty military man and former dean of the Institute of Armament Technology, his testimony will, I presume, be adjudged objective and unbiased:

It was on the 24th of April, 1958, the second day of Dadaji's stay at the Khandala cottage. Dadaji had just finished his last song on Krishna and Indiraji was found steeped in deep *samadhi.* As soon as she came out of *samadhi,* she dreamily asked Dadaji:

"Shall I get some *prasad?*" We all, that is, Dadaji, Premal and myself, looked at her startled, not knowing what she was driving at. However, she again asked: "Shall I get some *prasad?*" and Dadaji said: "Why not? Where is it?" By then she had come down to her normal consciousness and laughingly said: "There is no *prasad.*" Dadaji, however, insisted: "Let us have the *prasad.* Where is it?" Whereupon Indiraji sprang to her feet and said: "May I get some mud?" and started walking down the steps. The moment she put her feet on the first step, she again went into a deep *samadhi.* We all stood spellbound, looking at her in great reverence, when she came out of *samadhi* and said: "Let us have some mud. Yes, get me some mud." The soil being dry and rocky, one had to scratch the surface with a twig to loosen it before it could be picked up. Premal passed a handful of this sandy earth to Indiraji who had by then come down the steps. Not finding it enough, she asked for more. She then held the earth in her folded hands and went off into a *samadhi* again, swaying as she usually does when she goes into a trance, standing. We all encircled her—watching intently and guarding her against falling. It was hardly a few seconds before she came out of *samadhi* and, unfolding her hands, asked me: "Shall I give you some *prasad?*" I offered my palm and she put a little bit in, saying: "Now eat it up." I hesitated for just a micro-second, when faith prevailed and I immediately flung the contents into my mouth, and lo! the hard rocky soil had turned into sweet, crisp, granulated *prasad!* We all burbled in delight! She then poured all the *prasad* into Dadaji's hands, who gave a little to Premal. While we were still marveling at the great spectacle, she again folded her hands, this time empty, and went off into *samadhi.* In a few seconds she came out and, as she unfolded her hands, we found to our amazement, that there was in her left hand a little more *prasad* which she gave to me. Dadaji then proceeded to stow the *prasad* safely in an envelope and told me to do likewise with mine. Not quite content, he asked for a handful of the soil which was originally handed over to Indiraji, and put it into a separate envelope, saying "For all you know, this might also turn into *prasad.*"

It was now time for dinner and we all proceeded to the dining hall. On our way back Indiraji told Dadaji: "The mud you put in the envelope has also *partially* turned into *prasad.*" On hearing this, Dadaji made a beeline for his room to examine the envelope. He distributed a few grains to each of us to taste and we all found that it had also turned into sweet granules of *prasad!* On further examination, however, we found, as Indiraji had rightly said, that a portion of this mud had *not* been transformed.

On June 6, 1959, we went for two days to Belgaum, which is a night's journey (by train) from Poona. We do not often make such flying visits as we have to perform our daily worship at the temple. But we simply had to make this trip and thereby hangs the tale. Let me start at the beginning.

About a year previous, we had had as our neighbors a Punjabi family, the head of whom was an army officer. His wife and two daughters became our disciples. The younger daughter, C., was then about seventeen and reading for her B.A. degree. Now C.'s parents wanted to get her a good husband. One day her father came to us and asked our advice with respect to a very promising Punjabi youth, A., a bomber pilot whose father, also an officer in the Indian Army, used to come now and then to attend our temple services. I have no doubt that the marriage would have taken place had not Indira been accorded a prophetic vision about A.'s dying in an air crash. Since none of Indira's visions had proved false, the girl's father declined and we all forgot about it.

Now, a year later, on June 1, 1959, to be exact, A.'s father came to us from Belgaum where he was posted and told us that A. had died during the previous month in an air crash in Rajasthan. We were then reminded of Indira's vision. He requested us to visit them at Belgaum where his wife was derelict with grief. We consented and so arrived, as I have said, on the 6th, giving them such solace as we could, explaining what was expected of them: namely, to accept whatever is ordained by the Lord. I told them all that had happened when Indira's life had hung in the balance in Poona.

She had vomited blood and all hope was gone. She could not even sip water although she was dying of thirst. She then dictated a song to me which I sang in tears—*Karne-wale jo hai kiya, bhala kiya bhala kiya*, which means: All, all you have done and ordained is good for my soul, O Friend! Then I sang another of Indira's songs, the theme of which was also gratitude to the Lord. We all shed tears, I as I sang, they in listening, and afterward the bereaved mother said to Indira: "Dadaji's words and songs have lit a lamp in our hearts. I can't tell you, Didi, how he made us conscious of the Lord's Grace!" It was a miracle—the peace that descended and pervaded their bereaved hearts! They cried no more, but spent the whole of the night repeating the Lord's Name. *Jai Guru! Jai Hari!*

But the story did not end there. Let me quote from Indira's letter to the bereaved mother.

My dear sister,

A. came yesterday afternoon in my vision. He kept alternately opening and closing his fists and looked away while talking. When I said "Give yourself to the Lord now, turn to Him," he burst into tears and said: "They (the airdrome people) are not telling the truth, Ma. I did what they said. They were sending just the opposite message (ie., *not* to bail out)." I told him again to forget about this and to turn to the Lord. He said: "I am afraid for my brother." Then after a little talk he seemed at peace and left.

All I can say is: we do not know and He knows. His will be done. He loves A. more than you do and will do what is best for him. We do not understand because we are ignorant. May He give us the love that accepts on bended knees whatever He ordains.

Yours,
Didi [Sister]

Confirmation of Indira's vision came in a most unexpected way. One of A.'s aunts suddenly called on us the morning of June 16 while we were having our tea. She said that a sister of hers, who lived in Delhi, had visited Belgaum and told A.'s mother that the report in the papers about his refusing to bail out was untrue. A.'s radio communication with the airport had been overheard by an independent source who reported that A. had flown around and around, sending frantic messages to the airport authorities who directed him to save the plane and *not* bail out. I was rather glad to come by this confirmation, although I had never entertained any doubt about the authenticity of it all. I mean I was convinced that A.'s spirit had, indeed, materialized before Indira to communicate to her his message. Now for the postscript.

When A. had expressed to Indira his fears for his brother, we assumed it was against a similar mishap since the latter was still an officer in the Indian Air Force. And, in fact, a few months later, the brother's plane crashed in the sea. The co-pilot died on the spot, but A.'s brother was picked up by a fishing boat and he recovered from broken ribs after a three-month convalescence. He came to Indira to seek her blessings in our temple home.

A dear friend of ours, Nilkantha Maitra, a research scholar at the National Chemical Laboratory at Poona, used often to visit us. In October, 1960, while we were at Mussoorie, Indira saw that Nilkantha was depressed because he had just transferred from Poona, probably to Dehradun, she added.

"But how can that be?" I asked. "Surely there is no National Laboratory at Dehradun."

"I don't know," Indira said, "but that is what has happened."

A few days later we received a letter from Nilkantha (it was dated October 28, 1960) in which he wrote: "I have been transferred from Poona. I received an official letter to that effect on October 19. A new Government Laboratory is going to be built at Dehradun, to be named: Indian Institute of Petroleum. . . . When I received the order I could not keep back my tears because *you* wouldn't be there. I could never be too grateful for all that I have received from you and Didiji."

If I take such pains to record these supraphysical phenomena it is only to stress the utter inadequacy of modern materialistic explanations of spiritual and psychic phenomena. To give an instance: A seeker contacts a divine being. The modern psychologist will smile and say: "Oh yes, I have no doubt he saw it. The subconscious is capable of raising all sorts of hallucinations."

Like the obliging deity of medieval polemics, the subconscious mind has become a verbal panacea for those who would substitute convenient labels for empirical experience. Once it was God who could "do anything," and so was summoned to defend whatever seemed otherwise indefensible to theologians. Today, though Science has taken charge, the situation remains very much the same. Physics and chemistry speak of the omnipotence of matter, psychology of a catchall subconscious which pretends to explain whatever eludes the more obvious materialism. And so while consciousness is dismissed on the one hand as a mere illusion of matter, it is conceded on the other hand to be able to influence matter, operate independently of the senses, travel unaided and instantaneously through space and heaven knows what else. Moreover, what is thus credited is not some superconscious faculty operating at a higher level than the intellect and in an occult relationship to it, but an irrational and atavistic animal mind which evolution has already transcended if not transformed.

That such a view is not only self-contradictory but even in its extravagances fails to explain spiritual phenomena is evident on the face of things. For even apart from telepathy and seeing at a distance (which offer superficial analogies to wireless telegraphy and radar), how could the most wide-ranging and energetic subconscious possibly account for the following occurrences, all of which I and a good many others have personally witnessed in the case of Indira, namely: visions of deceased persons who give startling messages that are subsequently verified, prophetic visions that come true, the beautiful Mira *bhajans* (now numbering over eight hundred) which she could not possibly have composed by herself, materializations of a delectably sweet confection (sometimes out of mud, at other times out of nothing at all!), the sudden emission from her hands and feet of a strong sandalwood fragrance?* And there is the testimony, too, of those who have not only borne witness to her miracles, but been the blessed recipients of them.

For example: In September, 1960, Indira's younger sister and disciple Kanta underwent major surgery during the course of which a serious medical blunder occurred. Indeed, it seems unlikely that she would have survived but for a startling intervention by Divine Grace. I will say no more as I want to append a copy of the account which Kanta herself wrote to a brother disciple.

September 7, 1960

Dear Prashantabhai:

Miracles do still happen and sometimes to the least deserving of us. Let me tell you how Ma's and Dadaji's Grace has but recently saved my life. I came to Poona in August for a hysterectomy operation. Ma had asked me to come because she saw a shadow on me. On September 1, they performed the operation and this is how it went.

When they took me to the theatre and I saw all those masked

---

* I had almost forgotten to mention this though it has happened literally dozens of times. It takes place whenever Indira touches the Krishna of her *samadhi* and even occurred once in an automobile while she and a few disciples were threading their way through the traffic of Delhi. As a rule it is only her hands and feet that emit the fragrance, but, on occasion, it has come also from her hair. No less remarkable is the fact that when Indira is in this state whoever is touched by her begins likewise to emit the fragrance. There have been times when, due to her touch, half a dozen or more devotees have found themselves simultaneously affected.

faces surrounding me, I was suddenly gripped by fear. Then they applied the anesthesia and for the moment I lost consciousness. Suddenly, however, I was awake again. I could see all the doctors and nurses and I experienced a severe pain. The fear gripped me again and I screamed for Ma. At once I saw and felt her standing beside me with her hand on my right shoulder. She said: "I'm here, don't worry." Then the anesthetist gave me a second dose and I was out.

While all this was happening, Ma was sitting in the room booked for me which was a block away. She told Mohanbhai: "Kanta is calling me. She needs me—I must go to her." And this, Prashanta, was the exact moment I had cried out for Ma and had her vision.

The moment I came round I complained of a very bad pain which prevented me from moving even my toes. The hospital staff kept assuring me that it was a natural aftereffect of the surgery. Ma came to see me the second evening when the pain was still very intense. At perhaps one o'clock in the morning my whole body started trembling. My friend Dina, who was sleeping next to me in the same room, covered me with four or five blankets, but the shivering persisted. When the resident doctor was called she said it was an attack of rigor, which as you know usually accompanies infection. At about 2 A.M. I asked for the bed pan, which was given to me. The nurse seemed suddenly very distressed and ran out of the room. After five minutes she returned, accompanied by the resident doctor, the sister in charge and two other nurses. They all stood round my bed and said "Yes, yes." I kept asking: "What is it, please?" but they wouldn't tell me. Foolishly, however, they chose to discuss the matter right outside my window. I heard them say: "The gauze is there. How was it left inside? We must inform the doctor immediately." When the nurse reentered, I finally got her to admit that one of the gauze plugs had been inadvertently left inside and about two inches of it could be seen protruding. She added that the surgeon had been informed and had given instructions to prepare me for another operation. My temperature had already risen to 102.8 degrees. All this was recorded by the hospital night nurse in the log-book.

Ma came with Dadaji about 7:30 in the morning. When I saw

her I burst out crying and said: "Ma, they've killed me." Dina related in detail the circumstances which Ma herself confirmed from the log-book.

At nine o'clock the surgeon arrived and examined me, confirming that my stomach would have to be reopened to remove the gauze. Ma asked her to change the operating schedule to the afternoon and to allow her to be alone and undisturbed in the room with me. When we were alone, Ma said: "Forget everybody. Think of the Lord alone and surrender yourself to Him." I said: "Ma, will I be all right?" She replied: "He knows best, His will be done." She caught hold of my hand and said: "Remember Him now." I was still very frightened. As she kept holding my hand, I closed my eyes and vividly felt as though she were conveying something to me by her touch. Gradually as my being relaxed it was permeated with peace. When I opened my eyes it was twelve noon. My body was no longer burning with fever and the pain was much diminished. It was only then that Ma let go of my hand and went out to call the doctor. She duly arrived with her retinue to reexamine me. What was their amazement to find that the gauze had entirely disappeared! They searched everywhere for it but in vain. In the end they agreed that it was, indeed, a miracle.

When Ma came back to the ashram her own temperature had risen to 102.8 and she continued to run a fever for three days. (As I have already mentioned, my own fever, which had been 102.8, had come down, just as Ma's shot up.) She saved my life just as she keeps saving so many others, worthy or otherwise.

Yours affectionately,
Kanta

After my return to India in 1928, I continued to write to Vladia and Marthe regularly, especially after my initiation into yoga at the feet of my guru, Sri Aurobindo.

Then I had news from Vladia at Marthe had become a Communist, and that she had left him and gone to Russia and that he had remarried a delightful Swedish girl, Anna Lisa. Their union was blessed by the birth of a sweet daughter whom they providentially named Mira.

When the Germans invaded Prague, Vladia and Anna Lisa miraculously escaped to Sweden where, however, his anti-Nazi propaganda landed him in jail for two long years. After the war he returned to Prague as a Minister of Rome, but the Russian invasion again forced him to flee, this time to Italy where he rented a little cottage on the bank of Lago Maggiore, eking out a living as a merchant.

It was in Rome, in 1953, that Indira and I visited Vladia, Anna Lisa and little Mira who was then, I believe, fourteen years old. We continued to correspond and, in 1964, I sent him a copy of our *The Flute Calls Still* which describes, among other things, a number of Indira's visions of Mira. Vladia wrote back thanking me enthusiastically: he was thrilled, he said, and could almost see himself praying daily with us in the temple. After this, however, I did not hear from him till suddenly a cable arrived on March 26, 1965, felicitating Indira on her birthday. (Indira was born on March 26, 1920.) I wondered how he had come to know the date of her birth—from what source, inasmuch as I had not written it to him. I felt a little ashamed of my forgetfulness of so dear a friend and was going to write him a long letter when we received the following letters which I have translated from the French:

Dear Indira,
Tonight you came in my dream and said: "It is my birthday. Think of me and you will be thinking of Mira." And I think of you, dear Indira, with a deep intensity and if it is true that today is your birthday, may all our spiritual joy join our hearts in a chorus to sing a hymn of you—to you! May your St. Mira bless us, for our daughter, too, is named Mira and she is our all-in-all. Also we pray to you to take her under your wing in your songs and your dance steps, for she has need of you and your blessing. Protect her, Indira—our prayers go out to you as well as to St. Mira across the distance which separates us even though in our hearts we are close to one another. We greet you, dear Indira.
                    Your devoted Vladia and Anna Lisa

My dear Dilip,

It is truly a miracle that all of a sudden Indira should have appeared to me and that I should find on my table her name written in my book, and that a dream should have inspired me, saying "Write to Indira, it's her birthday." And behold, I feel today as if I were with you both. Dear Dilip, I feel an incredible longing for you two and feel like throwing everything up and going to India to pray with you, to sing with you and finally to live an unqualified spiritual life. Do pray for us, dear beloved friends.

Your Vladia

P.S. I perceive in the air a magnificent fragrance—isn't it the aroma of Indira's hands?

I was astounded since Indira does, sometimes in her *samadhi*, emit a beautiful fragrance of musk or sandalwood, as I have previously described. I might also add that many another aspirant has contacted her at a distance, even as devotees contacted Sri Ramakrishna, Swami Brahmananda, Sri Ramana Maharshi and other sages and saints. I wanted to invite Vladia to our temple home but, alas, it was too late, for he died suddenly. His dear daughter Mira wrote to me that he breathed his last in deep peace. I am sure his lovely loyal soul has found its last refuge at the feet of One whose Grace never once failed him in the darkest crises of his life.

37

REALITY OF MIRA, THE MIRACLE

WHEN SRI Aurobindo first wrote to me that Indira, as a disciple, would be a help not a hindrance to my yoga, I was at once pleased and alarmed: pleased, because I could not have felt otherwise with such a gifted and charming disciple, and alarmed because I had always wanted to travel light. In the end, finding myself caught between their twin urgings, I bolstered up my belief in mutual help and sincerely welcomed her. And the more I came to know her, the more gratified I felt because her spiritual help and personal example proved a corrective to my incurable tendency to vacillate and doubt. Indira had her own difficulties but indecision was not among them. She did need the support of my strength but no other prop. She looked to me somewhat like a helpless daughter who, paradoxically, leaned on her father in order to help him; the lovely songs, *Mirabhajans*, she gave me day after marvelous day she wanted me to set to music and sing—but no more. Whether or not others heard or applauded them she did not care. She even went the length of wanting to veto my eagerness to publish them. "Mira sings them to me, I recite them to you and you sing them back to me—enough is enough—the circuit is complete. Why publish them?" I gave her strong arguments to override her objections but she, alas, turned a deaf ear. In fact, it was against her wish that I published in 1950 her first book of verses which I called *Shrutanjali*, that is, "songs heard," not composed. Over a hundred of these songs I translated into Bengali and sang with great joy. I also translated sixteen into English.

Thereafter Indira went on daily dictating the songs she had heard—till I found, to my thrilled amazement, that she had given altogether more than eight hundred songs which were published serially in six books, an achievement indeed!*

But I hailed these songs not merely as an achievement of this wonder-child of Mira's but also for the filip they gave to my aspiration day after resonant day. It has happened many a time that a song she dictated mirrored my mood at the time. To quote but one song by way of illustration:

> From which shores, traveler, dost thou hail,
>   For which art thou bound still?
> Hast thou forgot in thy blind voyage
>   And missed what thou shouldst will?
>
> This world is but a wayside inn,
>   Thy true home waits thee afar:
> Be not path-lost in thy maze of *karma*,
>   O pilgrim of the star!
>
> Why cull the painted shells, pale baubles,
>   To regret the wasted pains?
> Plunge, dive in the deep, if thou wouldst win
>   The pearl that knows no stains.
>
> No seed is sown in the soil of prayer
>   But flowers in God's own bloom.
> Though steep is the path and unglimpsed the goal,
>   Walk in Faith's light in the gloom.

I loved this song as it reflected in its every line my nostalgic yearning for the Beyond. But there were so many other songs which made me shed tears while singing them.

---

* *Shrutanjali, Premanjali, Sudhanjali, Bhavanjali, Deepanjali* and *Ushanjali.*

Sri Dilip Kumar Roy writing at his desk. "Thereafter Indira went on daily dictating the songs she had heard—till I found, to my thrilled amazement, that she had given altogether more than eight hundred songs which were published serially in six books, an achievement indeed!"

Sri Aurobindo wrote to me that the master urge of my nature was certainly *bhakti* and *karma* (Love and works). But whenever I sang *her* songs and felt *bhakti* outwelling from my heart (for *bhakti* did not always prick my eyes with tears), I longed to turn my back on *karma* determinedly and let myself be swept on the tides of *bhakti* alone to the ocean of His Grace. But, alas, my urge to *karma* would return with redoubled ardency and I would go on writing or composing or reading or teaching music. Our sages said: *Niyatih kena badhyate?*—"How can destiny be circumvented?" But to revert to her songs.

I have seen a great many miracles happen under Indira's beneficent aegis, but to me the greatest miracle has always been her gift of hearing such lovely, inspiring songs and then dictating them year in year out in an endless procession of sparkling, purling waves. I would only add my personal belief that these songs were and are sung to Indira by Mira *in person*. I know my conviction is not likely to be shared by many of my readers, some of whom may call Mira Indira's *alter ego*. But one thing I learned from Indira which has stood me in good stead many a time: that I need not lean at all on outside support or endorsement for my honest convictions stemming from *personal* experience. Which is not to suggest, however, that Indira's contact with Mira is lacking support from those whose opinions are worth hearing in such matters. During the brief period that Sir Aurobindo had to observe the phenomenon, he endorsed it as authentic in three of his letters to me. In the first, on May 7, 1950, he wrote:

There is nothing impossible in Mirabai manifesting in this way through the agency of Indira's trance, provided she (Mira) is still sufficiently in touch with this world to accompany Krishna where He manifests, and in that case there would be no impossibility either in her taking the part she did in Indira's vision of her and her action. If Indira wrote in a Hindi with which she was not ordinarily familiar or in which she was not used to write and it was under the influence of Mirabai, that would be a fairly strong evidence of the reality of Mirabai's presence and influence on her.

To which he added, on June 2:

It is evident that Indira is receiving inspiration for her Hindi songs from the Mira of her vision, that her consciousness and the consciousness of Mira are collaborating on some plane super-conscient to the ordinary human mind: an occult plane; also this influence is not an illusion but a reality, otherwise the thing could not happen as it does in actual fact. Such things do happen on the occult plane, they are not new and unprecedented.

And finally, on June 11:

In any case, the poems Mirabai has written through Indira—for that much seems to be clear—are beautiful and the whole phenomenon of Indira writing in a language she does not know well . . . is truly remarkable and very convincing of the whole thing.

Apropos, I want also to append a pair of memoranda written by Sri Saroj Chaudhuri, secretary of the Calcutta Psychic Research Society, and subsequently sent by him to Sri Birendra K. R. Choudhary who kindly forwarded the same to me:

February 2, 1952

The Psychical Research Society
31/A Brindaban Bysack St.
Calcutta

Sri Birendra Kishore Roy Choudhary showed me the photograph of Srimati Indira Devi now living at Pondicherry. She goes off into a trance when she hears devotional songs. Her spirit-guide is Mirabai. The fact that disembodied souls write through her hand in languages unknown to her indicates that she is a remarkable medium. Generally, automatic writing is produced in a language known to the medium, but when the medium writes in languages unknown to him, there can be no question of the automatic writing being the product of the subconscious self of the medium.

The messages received through Indira Devi are therefore very authentic. Such a medium is rare and materialists who do not believe in the existence of a life after death will have to consider seriously how such phenomena can occur. I have not seen any such medium before.

P.S. My spirit-guide Soham Swami's remarks will be sent later on.

Soham Swami had been a celebrated Vedantist and was the author of *Soham Gita*. The message, communicated by his departed spirit, reads as follows:

Re: Indira Devi (formerly Janak Kumari)

Saroj, I saw in my meditation that this lady is full of *bhakti*. She is an evolved being, thanks to her *sadhana* in her past births. She often has *bhava-samadhi* during which time discarnate spirits from the higher planes write through her hand while ensconced in her. She had a close tie in her previous birth with Mirabai, who is now her guardian-soul and protector.

During her trance she often becomes a medium and does not remember what is expressed through her trance because Mirabai comes then to preside over her entirely—her own soul departing her body for the time being and reaching beyond the astral planes. As Mirabai guards the silver nexus which joins her released soul to her body there can be no danger to its return to the body. Mirabai's messages come to her when she is in such a state of trance.

The Western psychologists, more often than not, place no reliance on the doctrine that there are other worlds besides and beyond our own. That is why they try to explain all phenomena of mediumship by a far-fetched theory of the subconscious mind and double or triple personality. But their findings in such cases are not always valid. Janak Kumari has evolved to the plane of *bhava samadhi* which is described in English terminology by the word "ecstasy." What has been given to her is thus not the common type of trance but the ecstatic state that carries us straight into the inmost sanctuary of mysticism. Her experiences belong to a very high plane. Sri Aurobindo has shed his Grace on her and has been guarding her through Mirabai who is essentially her spirit-guide or guardian-soul.

With respect to Indira's songs, let me add a further remark. On May 13, 1950, Indira heard Mira sing to her a song which I loved to sing off and on because in it *bhakti* and poetry are beautifully blended to form a harmonious whole. Only gradually, however, did it dawn on me that the last line of the song was a remarkable *prophecy*. I give below my translation in English of the entire five stanzas.

> His priestess, I, return to earth
>   His deeds to recall and glory to sing.
> Let me enter the adytum of your heart:
>   I come to worship Him, my King.
>
> Cool I have filched from the moon, from stars
>   The mystic gleam of purity,
> Laughter from flowers, from rivers the ripple
>   From breezes the murmur of melody.
>
> And making a garland of my hands
>   His dawn-rose feet I will now entwine
> And kindle the virgin lamp of my life
>   With the flickerless flame of His love hyaline.
>
> Oh, dateless is my devotion to Him
>   Who still my birth and death commands:
> I am a droplet and He's the Deep
>   He is music and I am a flute in His hands.
>
> To surrender to Him, my All-in-All,
>   My body and soul at His altar I bring.
> Hark back to Mira's lyrics of love
>   Of Him whose Grace she returns to sing.

To me, the last line is not merely significant, but even *startling*, because it does mean that there was definite planning: Mira had resolved to sing to us once again the exquisite tale of her love and yearning, her joy and sorrow, her tears and laughter, her cloud and sunshine.

She has certainly fulfilled her promise: she has sung to Indira more than eight hundred songs and of late Indira has been able to reproduce her tunes as well, which she has taught to me—the teacher has become the disciple!*

I will conclude with two of Indira's letters which will speak for themselves:

Savoy Hotel, Mussoorie
August 8, 1950

Dada,

It is a lovely, peaceful day. Everybody has gone down to Dehradun and I am all alone. I will pray the whole day as there will be no time wasted at the meals with guests.

Last night I saw Mira once again, Dada! I was praying when, suddenly, the whole room was flooded with a blue light! Then, as I raised my head, I saw her. She spoke to me for long. I did not say anything but somehow my heart speaks to her and she knows it. How tender and intimate is her every touch and look! (You know, Dada, she has a black mole right below her thumb-joint—on the palm of her right hand) She said something very beautiful and moving.

"In the soul's journey through millions of years," she said, "You meet someone with whom you stay for a few years and the world says you belong to one another. But then is not such a brief meeting in just one life, among thousands of lives, comparable to meeting someone in one birth for, say, a couple of hours? Such *are* the superficial meetings of this world—brief and casual—whereas true love is everlasting and unshakable and the kinship of souls that love *is* for all times. You may die the water in different colors but it remains water all the time. In the same way, you may change your outer form in your different births but the love that sustains you stays the same and can never really dwindle, nor can there be any real separation between soul-mates since they are all journeying together toward the same Goal Divine. On occasion, it may so happen that one of the two is deflected from the Path—whereupon the other's progress, too, may indeed be temporarily retarded, thanks to the

---

* I have published more than a score of such tunes in notation in my *Suranjali* and *Surbihar*. Someday I may render them in European staff notation—who knows? My own tunes number about a hundred.

backward pull, but for those who ride the crests of the divine
current there can be no question of turning back: the farther
they go, the nearer comes the ocean and the stronger grows the
swirl of the rivers meeting in the ocean. Now you know, Indira,
why you are so dear to me. I told you that I would tell you all.
By and by you will know all."

Love and *pranams*.

Your child,
Indira

Savoy Hotel, Mussoorie
August 19, 1950

Dada,

I am writing this in the small hours of the morning after
having just woken up from my meditation which lasted about
five hours.

Mira came to me again. O Dada, how dear she has grown to
me and how near! How real her love—how close to my heart!
And yet isn't it almost incredible? To think that one so holy,
who comes to me in my dreams and trances, should be growing,
as it were, with my own growth! . . . I am told that people
simply will not believe me. I smile. Does it matter to me one jot
even if the whole world were to laugh at my story now that I
have seen and loved her? A mere dream? But can a mere dream
give one more lasting peace and sustenance of love than all the
realities of the world put together? O Dada, I shall always be
grateful to you: for it is because of *your* blessing, *your* meditation, that she came to me and loved me as she has. And how
precious is her love! . . . I wish you could see her! She is *lovely*
and her beauty grows on one. But I cannot fathom her. I asked
her the other day: "But tell me, are you really real?" She placed
her palm on my head in token of blessing and smiled. "But what
is real?" she asked calmly. I answered: "I mean the real you."
She smiled again and said: "But do you know yourself, the real
you?" . . . I will tell you more about it all when you come here,
to Mussoorie. But one thing I may tell you now as certain: that
she will never forsake me even if the whole world does.

Love and *pranams*.

Indira

A great deal has happened since then till now, 1972: Mira is woven inextricably into our lives. A time was when I hesitated to make her advent public. But now it has become difficult for me *not* to shout it from the housetops—to refrain from letting truth-seekers know this miraculous Truth, that a divine compassion can, indeed, be contacted as concretely through a supraphysical as through a physical form. I know that a day will dawn when such deeper truths about spiritual verities will be accepted universally. But though that day is perhaps far, this much we believe to be certain: that the manifestation through Mira will make itself felt in the present generation when her divine songs and messages will have out-laughed the skeptics' laughter of derision. It is to render this service to her, who has been sent to us by the Lord as His deputy, that I have decided to add an appendix giving a selection of her sayings of which Indira has kept a faithful record in her diary.

38

THE LIGHTS LIT

I HAVE USED the phrase "reality of Mira." But the crux of the difficulty is that such a supraphysical reality cannot be summoned to the dock of the intellect to be appraised by the jury of "common sense." In physical science, certain phenomena occur just as soon as the required conditions are fulfilled. When, however, we look for such empirical precision in supraphysical or psychic phenomena, we look in vain; which is not to say that, in an ultimate sense, it is necessarily wanting, only that to the human mind, ignorant as it is of occult variables, things must perforce appear, if not arbitrary, at least beyond human foresight.

It is true that on the lower rungs of occult experience, where the most exacting procedures are followed and Grace is neither sought nor invoked, a seer may observe something approaching a demonstrable causation. But it is necessary to emphasize "approaching," for even here the results must always remain a matter of probabilities. It is not that cosmic law has been suspended or that the gods have grown careless in its administration, only that the tangled skein of our individual *Swadharma* (aptitude and temperament) and unexhausted *karma* complicate things beyond the possibility of our prescience. If this much is difficult for the rationalist mind to follow, what must be its plight when confronted with the inscrutable workings of Divine Grace? For in the spiritual life, as Indira points out, it is not the performance of any specific thing or things that prove efficacious, but only the placing of oneself in a state of receptivity, after which all that needs to be done *will* be done, but by the Lord and in whatever way *He* deems best.

In my own case, Divine Grace appeared in the form of Mira who came at a crucial stage of my life, just a year before my guru's passing. Had she not come to my aid in my derelict hour, I do not know how on earth I would have picked my way on this hard road full of pitfalls, crisscrossed by ever so many deserts. And I am persuaded that she performed the miracles through Indira, her protégée, to instill hope in my hour of midnight despair. Since, however, all this may sound somewhat cryptic to the general reader I will give one instance of how she helped us, quoting a letter I wrote to an American sister, Natasha Rambobha, an Egyptologist, who loved us and had faith in us as truthful seekers:

December 10, 1960

Dear Sister,

I had wanted to see a sign ever since my initiation, *diksha*. You may solemnly disapprove of such a desire, but I cannot possibly tell you a lie to court your approval. No, I have never once felt any qualms about wanting to see a sign, the more so as I read about so many devotees who had, in the past, prevailed on the Lord to grant them similar prayers. In fact, at one time, I often used to appeal to my Gurudev to manifest to me a sign. On some occasions he did comply as I have recorded in my reminiscences entitled *Sri Aurobindo Came to Me*. But as these may not be adjudged evidential or "convincing enough," I will refrain from repeating them to you. I will give here an instance in which you will have to concede that the evidence is foolproof unless of course you dismiss it all as deliberate concoction on my part. I may add, by way of preface, that I have personally verified many a time what Gurudev so luminously claimed in his *Savitri:*

A prayer, a master act, a king idea
Can link a man's strength to a transcendent Force,
Then miracle is made the common rule.

But let me begin the story. I was then in Pondicherry. Indira
had come and accepted me as her guru in 1949. In a few
months, miracles, did, indeed, become "the common rule."
Nevertheless, I often felt depressed because of the sudden passing
of Sri Aurobindo on December 5, 1950.

It was past midnight, on October 9, 1951. I was praying
alone on the veranda of my flat. Indira was asleep in her own
room. A cousin of mine, his wife and daughter were our guests
and slept downstairs. At the time people were quite jubilant in
our Ashram with sports and drills and bands. They were all
fully persuaded that the Supramental Light must descend and
that soon, as our Gurudev had prophesied. But I saw no signs
anywhere of any descent other than that of prospective atom
bombs. To me the light loomed like night because the only sun
of my humble life—my Gurudev—had set forever. My brother
disciples said that he still presided over the ashram, but to me it
was all words, words, words: I never once felt his beloved presence there. I had staked my all for him, putting all my eggs in
one basket, but although I had quite a number of marvellous
spiritual experiences under his aegis, after his passing I all but
gave myself up for lost as I felt I would not get anywhere now
that he was not there to guide me home. You see, I had come to
my Guru's feet with just one aspiration: that I must meet my
heart's Lord, Krishna, face to face, in the human form as the
Eternal Beloved of man. Nothing less could reconcile me to life.
I lived only to achieve this Goal of goals and no other. I had
had a taste of all the thrills that wealth, fame, travel, books and
romance could bring. But all these joys and raptures had palled
and only deepened the gloom and ennui that followed in their
wake. So, I had set my heart finally on this one Goal—of
Krishna to be realised as Krishna, the God-man. He said in the
Bhagavat that one must follow the Guru as His one Deputy. To
serve the Guru one-pointedly must lead the aspirant to His feet
—so He had told Sridam in the Tenth Book and yet, here was
I who, after having served for years a great Guru, had failed

in the end to attain Krishna! What hope then had I now to arrive? . . . Such thoughts were milling round and round in my brain on that fateful night, nine months after my Gurudev's passing. I felt like a lost soul as I prayed alone at midnight before a picture of the Lord. My eyes were blurred with tears as I appealed to Him:

"If you are, indeed, a Redeemer of the derelict, do not let me peter out like this in deep frustration after more than twenty years of yoga—away from my home, my friends, my relations and everything men cherish. Now that my Gurudev, my best-beloved, is no more, I implore you, Lord, to come in person to my rescue. My Gurudev saved me in some of the darkest crises of my life, assuring me again and again that he would lead me to your feet; but since he cannot guide me anymore, it is up to you now to come and give me a sign that you are still there to care for me . . . " and so on and on I prayed, in tears.

A friend had given me a lovely present, which we have now installed in our temple here: a Figure of Lord Krishna answering Mira singing at His feet; both the Figures are etched beautifully on a thick slab of glass, set in a frame and placed upon a pedestal. Under this is attached a bulb which is connected by a wire with a three-pronged plug. As soon as this plug is inserted in the wall outlet the bulb is lit and the two Figures flash out, beautiful and luminous.

Every night, before going to bed, I took out the plug and allowed nobody else to handle it. On this unforgettable evening, too, I had switched it off, as usual. Now, as I was praying in utter despair, I heard a low but clear voice: "*Go and See: He has lit the bulb.*"

I jumped out of my bed and there, in our prayer room, I was thrilled to see that the Lord's Figure was alive with light as the plug was back in the switch again! It was not easy to insert the plug in the switch—it being a three-pronged plug a little force had to be used and somewhat deftly at that to insert the three prongs into the three holes. I rubbed my eyes in amazement, but there could be no mistake—the plug which I had taken out myself had been put in again, presumably just before I heard the Voice announcing the Lord's intervention!

I called out to Indira and questioned her animatedly about the plug. She said: "You know, I never touch the plug." And she was sure that the plug had been taken out by me before we had retired for the night.

In great joy, I went down and wakened my cousin and his wife. They ran up, thrilled, and we all started singing His Name in ecstasy before His luminous figure, now shining with a new lustre!

But when, after an hour or so, we were about to go to bed again, a fresh doubt crossed my mind. For although all of us were sure that I had taken the plug out, I asked myself if I might not have inadvertently left it there and then forgotten all about it? So what I did was—I now left the plug in, telling myself that if it was the Lord Himself who had put it in, He might as well take it out—if only to convince me.

I was, indeed, not a little ashamed of my doubts, but how to disclaim them when they haunted me like a delirium? So, I prayed to the Lord again, in deep distress. I was repentant, but as I was still unconvinced and could not dismiss my doubts, I asked Him to forgive me. Indira, who was now praying in the next room, had never been one to harbour such doubts: she only prayed now, in tears, thanking the Lord for His mercy. It was only I who still felt unhappy, and that after the rapturous happiness, fancy that! So I started praying once again, when the Voice rebuked me:

"*Doubting still? Go. The plug has been taken out.*"

I touched Indira on the head and told her. She was surprised and said: "But how could you have entertained such a doubt at all?" I gave a wry smile and replied: "I will explain later, but come now."

I made my way again to our prayer room, followed by her, and we attested, in thrilled delight, that the plug had, indeed, been taken out, so the figures were now completely invisible— in the darkness.

Now, dear sister, unless you scotch all this as a deliberate, elaborate concoction—a cock-and-bull story—you must concede that it is not only evidential, but a convincing corroboration of our saints' testimony that the Lord does sometimes answer the prayers of derelict devotees to be given a sign. That is why we are persuaded that Christ must have deprecated the demanding of a sign only when those who clamoured for it were not authentic seekers but "scribes and Pharisees" who heckled from mere curiosity and as such neither needed nor deserved a sign. Anyway, what I have told you now comes from direct experience of a sincere truth-seeker who was at the time in a perfect quandary. So I trust our testimony will weigh with you who are no less sincere in your aspiration for faith and purity, fervor and illumination.

We send you all our love and blessings and pray that you may in future interpret Christ with the light of your spiritual discrimination and self-dedication. For only then can one really profit by His vibrant pronouncements in the Four Gospels which, like all authentic revelations, speak only to hearts which are alight with faith and love and not to loveless minds which can only argue and speculate, but never know.

Yours affectionately,
Dada, Dilip

Samadhi of Sri Dilip Kumar Roy, 1897-1980.

HOMAGE*
to
DADAJI SRI DILIP KUMAR ROY

To you who achieved so much
Yet are greater than all your achievements—
    Our homage.

To you who gave all and did not count the cost,
Who loved all and asked for no return,
    Our eternal gratitude.

To you who judged men not by their faults
But by their aspiration,
    Our salutations.

To you through whose golden voice
The Flutist played His Flute
And enchanted thousands of hearts all over the world,
    Our silent adoration.

To you who had the humility born
From an inner strength
And the strength that comes
From a transparent sincerity and a living truth,
    Our pranams.

To you who were an ocean of bliss,
    Our prayers.

To you who possessed nothing
Yet were a king amongst men,
    Our obeisance.

To you whom Sri Aurobindo called
'A friend and a son
And a part of his existence,'
    Our hearts' devotion.

           INDIRA DEVI

* Engraved on his *Samadhi*

EPILOGUE
MIRA'S MESSAGE

O Endless Cadence, how shall my soul's lyre
Be tuned to thy mystic dominant of flame
Whose mighty overtones awe our timid hearts!
In my cradle I was fed by thy far lore
That set my soul a-heave as, avidly,
I drank in the lone legend of thy love
Cajoling the Formless to wear the mask of Form
And play even as a human mate with thee!
The blue of sky was pent in a mortal plasm:
Incredible, yet how indubitable,
Like sprays of sungold quelling phalanxed night!
What none could even dare conceive came true:
The epiphany of Krishna, the God of gods,
Upon life's dismal plains, and a Queen of queens
Electing at one sweep to abandon all
We cherish here below for what had loomed
At best as a fairy tale, an irised myth!
Oh, that an airy nothing should have come
To companion, woo and wrench thee from the world
To be reclaimed by the Gleam beyond our glooms!
A life lived upon this our peaceless planet
Of flying traces and swift-fading lusts,
A quest mocked of proud Reason which yet proved
An apocalypse of stars—a hymn sung by
Love's aerial voice grown intimate! Hail, O
Thou flickerless beacon in life's waste of eddies,

370

Ensign of sky who cam'st to burn on earth
As an oriflamme of challenge to Destiny,
Staking thy all in a godly enterprise
To wrest deep laurels envied of the angels!
Frail pilgrim, who yet daredst to assault the peak
Which none but the sturdiest mountaineers could climb!
Oh, that such a Rose of fire should have leaned
To a thing of clay and, taking him by the hand,
Guided his aspiration in compassion,
Addressed a human in a human tongue:

"I, Mira, am no modern messenger,
Nor a lover of what is wafted on the surge
Of circumstance: ephemeras of foam
Glittering on the phantom strands of Time
And leaving a legacy of broken bubbles.
I haunt no more life's restless stadium
Where footlights go out swiftly and actors grope,
Where lightning-flares entail but a deeper gloom.
I am inebriate of distilled starshine;
The smokeless miracle Fire lights me home;
The perennial fountain plenished by the Lord,
The source of nectar, I bathe in. The One
Whose absence makes all earth-hues shimmer like mist,
And whose one sun-frank smile makes life a fête
Is my aim of wakefulness and sleep's last dream.
The Eternal Evergreen is my one Swain,
Beyond the clouds and mists my one Polestar.
The truths that, leaping, swoon like wing-clipped moths,
The million-crested waves that hustle along
And break on the shoals of Destiny I pass by.
I stay a denizen of the unfathomed deeps
Even as you, my ward! And so I claim
Your spirit as my kin since you, too, pine
For the One for whom I pined from birth to birth.
It is His gospel I have come to preach.
Enjoined by Him this I enjoin on you:
Live only for Him, speak only of His Grace.

Think, meditate on His unrivalled Beauty.
Nurture the flower of His lavish Bounty
In the garden of your heart. Sing, night and day,
With all the fiery fervour of your Muse,
Of Him, the unseen Beloved, the mystic Minstrel,
Who transforms love's heart by His one miracle touch
Into a Brindaban of bloom and bliss,
A carnival where His Flute calls to all
To swell His dance of Ras. Follow the Flute
Which, once heard, can be unheard nevermore,
Reclaim thy birthright: be a citizen
Of the Kingdom where His Grace is legislator,
Knowledge the dynast and Beauty banner-bearer.
The modern cry of life for drab life's sake,
Of illusive gleams whose aftermath is gloom,
Or the vagrant will-o'-the-wisp of puerile Art.
Or Science that, bewildered, scans in vain
Its island sparks of baffling information,
Presuming to explain the inexplicable
Twinkling feebly in an uncharted sea,
Or fool statecraft that robs more than it gives,
Are not for you. You are not what you seem
To your own eyes: a lonely acolyte
Of groping Reason. And so you turned from these
Half-lights, world-weary, orphaned, disenchanted,
To the one Light no cloud can countervail,
To the Orb beyond the hazes: Radiant Krishna.
The much-vaunted earthly music sated you
Because you hearkened to His magic Flute
Beside whose concord the loveliest strains on earth
Seem dissonance and din. I'll open more
Your ears to His apocalyptic music.
The more you hear its call the less you shall
Cling to your cherished moorings, and the less
You garner your savings, the richer you'll become
Till, chasing the Flute, you meet the hidden Flutist
Whose notes are as soft as their call resistless
Through the aeonic wheel of cosmic Time.

"But be thou warned: the modern seers will laugh

The "pilgrims of the stars" in a joyful moment on the banks of the holy
Ganges.

And challenge: 'How can a rustic Primitive
Keep pace with time? How can a Lotus-eater
Guide us in our sophisticated cravings
Or wean us from our modern pabulum,
So varied, complex, strong, intoxicating?
A picturesque and fabulous figure might
Have served a purpose once but now's outmoded:
The Creator is evolving with His creatures:
What titillated once—His mystic anklets—
Sound now, alas, as toy bells tinkled by children,
Affording at best a pleasant interlude.'

"The Lord outsmiles His scoffing denigrators
And, suffering them to follow the rich illusions
Of their Valley of False Glimmer, He goes on still
Flashing His signals calling, singing, dancing,
Biding His time, attending even upon
The rebels who deny Him in ignorance.
These, too, He will lead back to His everlasting
And evergreen Bower of bliss and beauty,
The one unfailing peak and plinth of all.
Incognito, He pilots even those
Who, mocking Him, vaunt they can steer safe home
Their self-will's cars unheeding His red lights.
He is guiding all—from fools and prodigals
To saints and seers, sages and avatars,
Leading all to the last Haven—His Light
And Love and Grace and all-redeeming Wisdom.
Not one sere autumn leaf falls from the tree
But He, the Sustainer, gives His final sanction.
I have inspired you because He so willed
That I shed some light on your mystic groping
For the all-fulfilling end, His Harbour of Peace,
Where one day must all sailors come to port.
I would deliver you, my pilgrim son,
From thunderstorms to blue repose and, lastly,
From the maze of words to Love's experience,
The one Asylum of all sentient souls.

To dare the viewless heights beyond the reach
Of words however flawless and heart-warming.
Steep is the path that leads to the Pinnacle
Commanding the unwalled vista of His Bliss,
Whence He calls all—the Supreme Tantaliser
Who, beckoning, ever recedes behind the veil!
But whether you will or no, know you are held
By the godly Abductor, resist Him no more
Till, finding Him, the Vast of golden rapture,
You live and move in His all-absolving Will,
Or playing in time, or poised in His Timeless hush."

O Beggar Queen! My heart accepts thy lead.
But can one do aught else who once has heard
With his mortal ears thy everlasting Voice?
Or, having heard, stray back again from thy
Compassion's clasp—or, having answered once,
Decline to seal what the heart has ratified?
Thy words and songs, thy life of fabulous trials,
The world-oblivious Love's one-pointedness
Now hold me in thrall: I can elude no more
Thy ineluctable clutch, to thee my soul
Has capitulated; lead me as thou wilt.
Weaning me from my pride make me His own,
His humble servant: Hearken to my prayer:
May thy Dawn-diapason of delight
Resound in my dark vault! O stainless One!
From Hades' abysm deliver me to His Sun.

                                                    D.K.R.

APPENDIX A
BIOGRAPHICAL NOTES

Q UEEN MIRABAI, of hallowed memory, is acclaimed by all as the greatest among the women saints of India. But had she been no more than a saint, she would not be remembered and adored today by millions all over India. She is cherished as one of the loveliest composers of songs on Krishna, whom she calls in her songs by His various intimate epithets, such as *Ghanshyam* or *Shyam* (the Evergreen), *Chirasathi* (Eternal Comrade), *Gopal* (the Swain), *Chitachor* (the Heart-stealer), *Maharaj* (King of kings) and so on. She addresses Him so familiarly because to her one-pointed Gopi-soul* the Eternal Beloved had responded early, in her childhood. And He had come only to wean her irrevocably from her lesser loves (her palace, retinue, luxury, etc.) in order to turn her into a veritable mendicant in His name. Indeed, she came in the heyday of her youth to be known by and large as a *prem-divani*, that is, God-made. For she *was* intoxicated

* The word *Gopi*—literally, a milkmaid of Brindaban—is equated in Vaishnava mysticism with the eternal bride-soul of the Eternal Bridegroom (*Giridhara nagar*) whose magic Flute symbolizes the imperious call of the Lord to cut away from one's moorings to be anchored finally to His feet. In other words, she is His beloved maid whose heart mirrors His divine beauty and *ananda* (bliss), which pass all understanding. In fact, every Gopi-soul—like Mira's—is, in essence, attuned to the soul of Radha; so in every Gopi, called and claimed by Krishna, presides the unique Radharani, the Queen of the Gopis.

by the love of Krishna the Elusive, "who, beckoning, ever recedes behind the veil." No wonder she sang like a derelict in ever so many of her impassioned songs whose pathos moved people to their depths—the more so as she had grown almost into a legend in her lifetime, a truly spectacular figure haloed by a divine romance!

And it was, indeed, an authentic halo; but what perpetuated the halo for all times was the high poetry and poignancy of her songs. In these her love-inebriate Gopi-soul called passionately to her beloved Swain of Brindaban whose love, manifesting itself through beauty, leads us through unutterable dereliction to the Supreme Bliss of ultimate attainment. And these songs poured out day after heart-churning day, her flaming love moved to tears thousands of devotees in her lifetime and millions after her passing.

The historicity of Krishna or Mira is not questioned in India by anybody except atheists and pedants, who do not count. Besides, for the devotees (who do count) the scholarly problem of historicity hardly exists. Sri Aurobindo presented the point of view of the devotee with his characteristic clarity in one of his letters to me:

There is a cardinal error in the modern insistence on the biographical and historical, that is to say, the external factuality of the Avatar (like Krishna), the incidents of his outward life. What matters is the spiritual Reality, the Power, the Influence that came with him or that he brought down by his action and his existence. First of all, what matters in a spiritual man's life is not what he did or what he was outside to the view of the men of his time (that is what historicity or biography comes to, does it not?) but what he was and did *within*; it is only that that gives any value to his outer life at all. . . . That is why we need not inquire whether the stories about Krishna were transcripts, however loose, of his acts on earth or are symbolic representations of what Krishna was or is for men, of his Divinity expressing itself in the figure of Krishna. . . . What is it that gives Buddha or Christ their enormous place in the spiritual world? It was because something manifested through them that was more than any outward event or any teaching. The verifiable historicity gives us very little of that, yet it is that only that matters.

Likewise, in the luminous example of Mirabai, too, it is the spiritual fact of her utter conversion that really matters, the conversion, that is, which uprooted her utterly from her native soil of royalty to make her flower, in the aura of divinity, into the unforgettable character, the radiant personality of a world-oblivious poet-cum-mystic, utterly surrendered at the feet of her soul's one Lord and Pilot, Guide and Friend.

I could go on dilating on this conversion of the great minstrel-saint whose love, people said, had to be seen to be believed, but due to the exigencies of space I will have to confine myself to giving a brief account of her life based on two sources: first, the salient happenings in her checkered life as recorded by modern scholars,* and secondly, all that Mira's discarnate soul has communicated to Indira day after day all these years.†

From Dr. Goetz's introduction:

Mirabai is one of the most famous figures of early Hindi and Gujarati literature. After half a millennium her songs are still alive among millions over millions of people of all classes in Northern and Western India, whereas most other old works of

---

* See *Mirabai, Her Life and Times* (Bombay: Bharatêya Vidya Bhavan), a recent biography written by an authority on Mira, an eminent orientalist, Dr. Hermann Goetz, who came to India in 1936 and left in 1955, and is now an honorary professor at Heidelberg University and head of the seminar for the Pre-colonial History and Art History of India.

† Many students of history may be inclined to doubt such testimony, based as it is on mystic experience, but there is a wealth of reliable evidence, well authenticated, of such supraphysical phenomena, as is known to all who are conversant with inspiring revelations. For example, in the introduction to his remarkable autobiography *Candle of Vision*, the world-famous poet and mystic A.E. states categorically: "I know by experience that disembodied beings may act upon us profoundly." And he adds in an accent that carries conviction that when a mystic experience enriches one's store of knowledge one ought not to say: "I imagined this," but only testify humbly: "The curtain was a little lifted that I might see."

poetry are forgotten, or known only to pundits and connoisseurs.

And he goes on to emphasize that through her intimate self-revelation

there breaks through with direct intensity a genuine, deeply-felt religious experience, an immersion into a surrender to God beyond all boundaries of creed and sect, pure beyond all human limitations and frailties, and yet immensely human. A great poetess? No, much more: a saint and wonderful human being, living in this world, yet shrouded in the invisible presence of her divine Lord! . . . If poetry is inspired by the Divine, she was the greatest poetess of India during the last millennium, because she was an extraordinary personality, a saint, one of the loftiest and purest of mankind.

She was, indeed, a unique figure in the history of spiritual aspiration, a marvelous poet born with an incandescent personality which dazzled all, cut out to play a great role through the impact of her heart-stirring poetry not only on her contemporaries but on posterity as well. But to tell about her radiant evolution in brief:

She was born in 1498 in a native state of Rajasthan—in a township (now no more on the map) called Kurkhi. Her father, a Raja, adored his gifted and beautiful daughter who became "a cynosure of neighboring eyes" even in her early childhood.

On her seventh birthday fête Sanatan Goswami (the famous disciple of the great Messiah Sri Chaitanya) came to her and made over to her a beautiful image of Balgopal* without telling her that He would be her companion. Little Mira was overjoyed and began worshipping the image with a fervor which amazed all. After a time, the image came to life—or, shall we say, Krishna issued out of the image to play with

---

* This image is still preserved and worshipped in Mira's private temple in Udaipur and was shown to us by the priest when we visited the shrine in 1962 to pay our homage.

Guru Sanatan (D.K. Roy) blesses his disciple Mirabai (Indira Devi) in a performance of *The Beggar Princess*, a play that portrays Mirabai's life.

her day after marvelous day—though none else could see
Him. (This phenomenon is attested to by the evidence of
great mystics in all climes and ages.)

But His ways are not ours, as Mira, too, came to realize, to
her cost. For when she came of age—in 1516—she was forced
by her parents to marry Bhorjraj, the reigning King of Mevar,
the most powerful state of Rajasthan. Mira, who claimed
that she had been chosen as the Lord's bride, appealed to her
husband to let her alone, which he did because he not only
adored her but was overawed by the nameless aura of holiness
around her and entranced by the wonderful songs she went
on composing and singing day after thrilling day.

But her sister-in-law, the termagant Udabai (along with
other conspirators), grew jealous of her fame—for her lovely
songs had begun to be sung by all and sundry, saints and
sinners alike. So they all, in a league, started slandering and
persecuting her in ever so many ways. The noble Bhorjraj
stood by her and shielded her as best he could; but when he
died on the battlefield Mira had none to turn to in her palace,
except her Krishna in her private temple where she spent
most of her time. But He came now only to wrench her from
her moorings, for He commanded her to leave the palace overnight and make for Brindaban where, He said, her guru
awaited her.

Mira did not hesitate once. Depending utterly on the
Grace of her One Beloved, she left Mevar for good. A veritable mendicant in His name, she trekked on, begging her
way to her destination, the Eternal City of her dream, to
meet her predestined guru.

On the way she was tested at every turn and had, sometimes, to undergo dangers and hardships that made her cry
out like a derelict. But she never once looked back, till, at
last, she found her guru in Santan, turning a full circle,
and surrendered herself utterly at his feet to live a dedicated
life. During the few years in which she stayed in his little hut,
she continued to compose her celebrated songs. She became,

indeed, a name to conjure with, a rainbow legend even in her lifetime.

But the deathless cannot die. So, Mirabai lives on and will go on living, to the end of time, inspiring millions of devotees of Krishna. To conclude with Dr. Goetz's closing tribute to her immortal soul:

That Mira has survived all these distortions is the best sign of her greatness. She belongs to the greatest figures of mankind. And I, personally, know only one other similar person, Jesus, the Christ, shrouded in the presence of his Divine Father—as she is in that of her Divine Consort—pure, loving and misunderstood and misinterpreted like her.*

* For a fuller account the reader is referred to our plays *The Beggar Princess* and *Mira in Brindaban*. The life story of Mirabai has been beautifully told by Dr. Ramaswami Aiyar in his warm Introduction to the former. These two plays were printed here in Poona a few years ago and are available at Hari Krishna Mandir, Poona-16.

APPENDIX B

MIRA'S SONG*

by Gopinath Kaviraj

SEVERAL YEARS AGO—in April, 1952, to be precise—Dilip Kumar sent me *Shrutanjali*, a sheaf of sweet and euphonious songs in Hindi. A few of these were composed by his daughter-disciple, Indira Devi. The rest, and the majority, she dictated from memory, transcribing what she had heard in her *samadhi* when Mirabai came to her and sang them. The two types have, indeed, similar traits but are not quite identical in style.

Such living poems permeated with the essence of devotion (*bhaktirasa*) are rarely to be met with, expressing beautifully, in a simple and lucid language, the heart's profound emotion and one-pointed yearning for the Lord. The divine love He manifested through His *Brindaban lila* has outflowed through these in a purling stream conveying a variety of moods vibrant with the ecstasy of mystic love.

As the influence of Mira and the God-love inspired by her came more and more to dominate Indira's life, a second series of remarkable songs, similarly composed, accrued and were duly published a couple of years later. It was my opinion that this new collection, which was entitled *Premanjali*, derived from a still deeper inspiration (*bhava*). In the realm of mystic love lyrics (*bhakti-kavya*), *Shrutanjali* together with *Pre-*

---

* Translated from the original Bengali of the savant Sri Gopinath Kaviraj.

manjali constitutes a veritable gift with a charm all its own.

Now comes her third sheaf of songs, *Sudhanjali*, wherein we find the distinction and sweetness of its predecessors duly maintained, with something superadded: a further enrichment from the point of view of variety of savors and flavors (*rasa*).

Although Indira's songs reflect various moods of God-love, all portrayed luminously, their dominant theme is the anguish of separation from the Beloved, *viraha*, with all its poignant sweetness. This, as everyone knows, is the one refrain of Mira's old songs—the songs that are still extant—as well as of those of other mystic minstrels.

In the domain of the soul's evolution the yearning of *viraha* stands, as it were, at the summit. Love cannot obtain its sustenance, cannot evolve, save through the stimulus of *viraha*. The supreme bliss and glory of union, *milan*, have for their basis the unwept tears of *viraha*. Indeed, *viraha* may well be looked upon as the quintessence of love. Not the mind alone, but the spirit, too, has its Dark Night to be traversed: Radha, the love-mad, is no figment of the poet's fancy.

It is true that there is *milan* after *viraha*, but it is equally true that *milan* cannot put an end, once and for all, to *viraha*, which keeps its vigil in the heart of *milan*. In other words, *viraha* must succeed *milan* every time a new yearning succeeds a phase of fulfillment. Were it not so, the deeper *milan*, with its attendant enrichment, could not trail, as it does, in the wake of *viraha*, thus maintaining the perennial novelty of its savor.

What is *viraha*? A sense of the void stemming from unslaked longing: on one side, we have the void (*abhava*); on the other, a simultaneous sense of fulfillment (*bhava*). The reason is that no sooner does the yearning reach its acme of intensity, than the hiatus that stands between—of space and time and whatnot—is annihilated, leading to attainment (*prapti*). With every attainment the aspirant's receptivity grows, whereafter the soul cries out once again: "I want more, indeed, still more!" As a result, the attainment fails to retain its native status and a new quest begins. How put a term to the Termless? In the infinite *lila* of love one meets with a new attainment with each new approach: one attains and yet feels as though one has failed to attain, one sees and yet feels as though one has not seen enough, and so the pilgrimage to the infinite continues everlastingly. A new savor accrues at every bend: the infinite delight (*rasa*) has infinite lilts, so the journey knows no end.

And yet there *is* an end to everything—everytime and everywhere, for how can motion outpace the Eternal Poise —the imperturbable, the tranquil?

Nonetheless, motion, too, is a reality wherefore the center of every *milan* is ever-resonant with the melody of *viraha*: the *lila* of the Infinite comes floating, unimpeded, into each finite entity. The drop in the Deep and the Deep in the drop are both true—at one and the same time.

Just as the pain of *viraha* lurks at the heart of *milan*, so the anguish of *viraha* outflowers as the eternal bliss of *Mahamilan*, the Last Mergence. At the point of this final dissolution in the Timeless, the drop and the Deep become, indeed, one; but in the *lila* in Time a gulf still persists which, even when bridged, seems unbridgeable. In other words, at every clasp of *milan*, even when a part of the hiatus is spanned, a part still survives which never comes to an end in endless Time. The attainment (*prapti*) does, indeed, come, but only to be overtaken by the void (*abhava*) once more so that the quest can start over again. Fulfillment and frustration (*bhava* and *abhava*) are equally indispensable to the continuance of the Play. This is the glorious glory of *Mahabhava*, the Identity in time: even when one attains, the longing for attainment remains unfulfilled: even when one sees, the thirst for seeing stays unslaked.

For this marvelous yoga to succeed, my will and His must cooperate. When He withdraws His Will, the yoga cannot come about, any more than when I decline to will it, personally. On my part, willing means surrender, and surrender involves not the renunciation of the personal will but only its transformation. My will then becomes one with His—which *is* the yoga. If my will were erased at the outset, this yoga could not be established and there would only be His relationless Poise (*sthiti*). When, however, surrender is achieved, my personal will cannot exist as a separate entity: for then His will becomes mine and I can only want what He wants. Even when suffering pain I must accept it as His Will, nay, rejoice in it as I do in everything else that comes from Him. This is the yoga experienced in *viraha* even as in *milan*: Mira is the yogini of this yoga.

From Mira's own testimony we gather that Indira is her intimate friend and comrade pilgrim on the Eternal Pilgrimage. Indira has yet to realize this but Mira is fully alive to it, being conscious of having attained the Haven. One can get an inkling of this mystic secret from the extraordinary authority she wields over Indira.

Some people may dismiss—as too incredible—the phenomenon of Mira's appearing before Indira to sing to her and lead her "day after marvelous day." But I am persuaded that there is no valid reason for skepticism. Men are acquainted with the sense-world, the perceptible world of fact. But none who *know* will dare deny that this material world is intimately pervaded by and interlocked with a supersensuous and immaculate sphere radiant with the light of a Supernal Consciousness (*atindriya, chidalokojjvala, shuddhasattvamaya rajya*). But till one acquires the inward-gazing vision (*antarmukhi drishti*) one must seek in vain for a clue to this supraphysical world and its rhythms, laws, and data.

One is reminded, incidentally, of Saint Teresa. Once, while she was living cloistered in a Toledo convent, Mother Mary of the Angels called on her to deliver an imporant message. St. Teresa was at the time writing her famous book, *Interior Castle*. Engrossed in her work, she had just started on a fresh page when the visitor called. But no sooner had she taken off her spectacles in order to receive the message than she went off into a *samadhi* and stayed in it, self-absorbed, for several hours. Mother Mary, awed, did not leave the room but waited on, looking at St. Teresa fixedly. When, at last,the latter came to, the blank page was found filled, from top to bottom, with written lines. Realizing that an outsider had come to discover her secret, St. Teresa hastily thrust the sheet away into a box.

It is also reported that a nun, Mother Anne of the Incarnation, was once passing before St. Teresa's cell when she caught a glimpse of her face. She stopped, amazed: St. Teresa's face was irradiant with an intense light as she went on writing rapidly without pausing once to revise or correct what came! After about an hour, at midnight, she finished, when lo, the miraculous light on her face vanished! Thereafter St. Teresa kneeled and prayed for a full three hours before going to bed.*

Such authoritative accounts are on record in the mystic literature of various countries. I myself have had some personal experience of phenomena such as these. So I am persuaded, I repeat, that there is no rational justification for discrediting Mira's coming to Indira in person, singing to her and leading her day by marvelous day.

*Introduction to St. Teresa's *Interior Castle* by Father Benedict Zimmerman, pp. 10-11.

APPENDIX C
MIRA'S DIARY

O_{NLY} A selection is given here of what Mira communicated, in her beautiful, chaste Hindi—translated into English by Indira herself. She endeavored to preserve, as best she could, the forceful simplicity of Mira's Hindi so that something at least of her Old World ambiance might come through. Lately, a rational friend of mine tried hard to dissuade me from publishing such occult truths as these. His contention was that what did not coincide with what is and can be accepted by reason cannot possibly go down with the majority. To that the best answer is one Mira gave to Indira when she had asked wondering how most people would take it were they told that Mirabai actually came to her, large and luminous as life, and talked intimately to her, day after wondrous day. The question arose as most people happened actually to scoff at Mirabai's reality. "But Truth," Mira answered with her characteristic gentle irony, "needs no certificate from 'most people' for the simple reason that it does not draw its sustenance from the votes of the majority." I need only add that Indira had all along been opposed to publishing what is presented here and that her objection was only overborne when I insisted, reminding her that the messages were meant as much for other receptive souls as for herself. Still I hesitated till Mira answered her question trenchantly on September 16, 1951, as reported above. This decided me though I know full well—being, alas, something of a rationalist myself—how difficult it is for the "majority" to accept the objectivity of such outlandish experiences as these. Nevertheless, I decided to risk it because I felt that it would be wrong to claim as personal what rightfully belongs to *all* true seekers of the historicity of one whose fabulous personality and heart-churning love lyrics have converted thousands, throughout the ages, to the gospel of Krishna. And I am fully persuaded that such truths as she has given us the liberty to make public cannot but benefit real seekers provided they approach them with true humility which alone can break down the dungeon walls built by Mental Reason to shut out the beneficent light of the soul.

June 13, 1951—Mira said to me: "I was the only child of my parents. My mother died when I was but six years of age.

"Sri Sanatan, a famous disciple of Sri Chaitanya—who was to become my guru subsequently—had a vision. He used to worship an image of Balgopal (Child Krishna) which came to life and told him to seek 'Mira' out, to whom he was directed to deliver the image. He did not know where I was. So he went about hunting after me till he came to my father's palace where he recognized me at once. Without telling me anything then, he handed over the cherished image to me. I was at the time only seven years old. I took it to bed with me at night and went off to sleep when it came to life and talked to me. This was the beginning of my love for Krishna. Henceforth He became a living personality and comrade. I loved Him and worshipped Him with a child's pure heart. My people thought I had gone crazy. When I was thirteen years old, my father decided to marry me off. I had never given marriage a thought as I felt that my soul had been already married to Krishna, who had become my only Lord, Beloved and Master. I could not dream at the time of belonging to anyone else as I felt that I belonged to Him alone, body and soul. And then He was so real, so true! I had seen Him, experi-

enced His Grace—my body had thrilled to his touch. I protested, but as my father threatened to commit suicide I had
to yield.

"The Maharana, my husband, was a very kind and good
man and loved me passionately. In the beginning he gave me
a very long rope: absolute freedom to worship my Lord as
I would in my little temple, adjoining our palace garden.
But gradually things became very trying for him as I simply
could not stay away from the temple. I used to hear the
Flute calling me in the middle of the night. My first impulse
would be to cling to my husband unheeding its invitation,
but its pull was so imperious that the tie that had held me to
my husband snapped like a worn thread and I was forced to
leave my earthly husband and spend my days and nights
mostly in the temple, worshipping my Eternal Lord and
Master. I could not even bear my husband to touch my body
which, I felt, belonged utterly and irrevocably to Krishna.
The Maharana, though he could not understand it at all, was
very tolerant because his love for me was intense, so much
so that sometimes he would follow me into the temple where
I would pass whole nights in prayer. I would open my eyes
to find his fastened on me. Once I felt sorry for him and
asked why he waited thus on me. 'You are worshipping your
God,' he replied, 'and I am worshipping my Goddess.' But
many people—like his own brother, the Rana, and his sister
—grew jealous of me and tried to persuade the Maharana
that I was play-acting and was, besides, an unchaste woman.
This hurt him and made him suffer but still he never said
one harsh word to me.

"We had been married for thirteen years when he died, and
then his brother, who ascended the throne, did all he could
to persecute me in various ways till, in the end, he brought
me a cup of poison and said: 'For the sake of the royal family and the honor of the Rajput race your life must be
brought to an end, as the whole world has been saying
that you are unchaste.' I was so intoxicated with the love of my

Lord that I drained the cup instantly. Well, it only moistened my throat which had been parched from singing for hours. The Rana was stupefied and decided that I was some sort of a witch. This incident, however, was the turning point of my life. I realized that the royal palace, comforts and worldly relations were not for me and that my place was at the feet of the Lord. It was then that I thought of my guru and this time it was I who set out in search of him, the saint who lived now at Brindaban. I had been told that he had prophesied that I would be a *bhakta*, a devotee of Krishna. I set out now for Brindaban to seek refuge at his feet. The Rana did not try to deter me from my purpose; in fact he felt relieved, if anything, to get rid of a mad person who could not be brought back to her senses. But *now* came my greatest ordeal.

"For two years I suffered excruciating pain. Krishna withdrew his Presence completely and then a big tumor affected a bone on my left thigh. One day, when I was nearly at the end of my tether, a feeling of deep gratitude welled up within me because I suddenly realized that all these years He had kept me in flawless comfort and luxury and that only for two years had I known pain and privation. What Grace He had showered on me! How compassionate He was! Tears rolled down my cheeks. Bending down I picked up a handful of sand and there, in very grain of sand I saw my Lord presiding! At once all pain ceased, there was no sorrow, no questioning, no thought, nothing but Krishna, Krishna, Krishna everywhere! In my ecstasy I pressed my swollen thigh, when lo! all the foreign matter flowed out, giving me instant relief. In sheer exhaustion I lay down. There was no water nearby and I felt very thirsty. Suddenly I saw a shepherd boy pouring water into my mouth. I cried out: 'You may come in any disguise you like, but even if you walked over my grave I would know you by your footfall. *Mira* cannot be mistaken in you.' He smiled and vanished, but from now on there could be no more hiding from Mira.

I had *seen* him in my heart. I had seen that all was Krishna. Every particle of sand, every little cloud, every stray leaf only revealed Him, my Beloved.

"In this state I walked on and on consorting with mendicants and yogis, eating any food, sometimes fasting, sleeping anywhere, sometimes spending the night sleeplessly—but always singing, singing, singing the songs that came to me, but never writing down what I composed, or rather improvised as the mood moved me. My songs have been largely distorted because, unlike the songs of others, they were never written down at the time: the yogis who were with me used to sing my songs with me and then sang them themselves. That is how my songs spread, and many were lost, quite a few were sung with words I had never composed, as it must happen when the songs sung have not been faithfully recorded. To give an instance to explain. Suradas, the great devotee, was the most famous composer of *bhajans* in those days. But his songs were all carefully written down and so escaped the fate which was to overtake mine later—distortion. Now my songs will again be sung and spread all over and Mira's love shall be fecund again everywhere. But to come back.

"I traveled on foot all the way to Brindaban, singing and dancing, and not caring a rush about what was going to happen to me. All that mattered was Krishna first, and then my guru who, I knew, awaited me in the Holy City. I had, indeed, turned full circle—from plenitude to penury—but in my exaltation I never cared. The only thing I lived for now was to meet my guru, whom I had yet to equate with Krishna. That was the call of Brindaban as I had heard it."

June 25, 1951—Mira said: "My Guru, Sanatan, came from the aristocracy. They were three brothers: Rupa, Sanatan and Anupam, who all became disciples of Sri Chaitanya. Sanatan was a Minister of the then Nawab of Bengal, who trusted and depended on him because of his transcendent honesty.

When, therefore, he wanted to resign his post to be able to take refuge at the feet of his guru, Sri Chaitanya, the furious Nawab put him behind prison bars. But he escaped, bribing his jailor, and made straight for his Master at Brindaban. There he became afflicted with severe eczema sores all over his body. Mahaprabhu, who cured him subsequently, used to embrace him daily despite his protests. So, in his extremity, he decided to commit suicide, the more so as he thought himself too impure to be embraced thus, day after day, by his guru whom he had equated with Krishna Himself. Mahaprabhu read his thoughts and rebuked him lovingly. He said: 'How can you think of disposing of your body after surrendering all that you have and are to me? Your body belongs to you no more—but to me, *me alone*. You shall go now, with my blessings, to Brindaban, a beggar in my Lord's name.' But he added that my guru must now become a mendicant, literally, discarding even the last and only blanket he owned. 'You will not only arrive,' he prophesied, 'but live to see something which will make you feel blessed: you will meet someone who is going to come to you as your disciple who yet will teach you what is Radha-Love."*

May 22, 1951—I asked her about how the guru really helped. She said: "A large lock was fixed on the gates of heaven. A man came and started hammering away at it in the firm belief that if he went on hammering persistently, the lock must give way and the gates open. This is the way followed by those who want to take the Kingdom of Heaven by the storm of

---

*After Indira had told me all this about Sanatan I consulted *Chaitanya Charitamrita*, which I had read only cursorily and so missed the name of Anupam as well as the incident about the blanket. I mention this as I had never spoken to her about it and only verified it later on. I had even doubted whether she had heard correctly the name of Anupam, because I had all along been under the impression that Sanatan had only one brother, Rupa. Mira told her a good deal about Sri Advaita Acharya also, which I have omitted for exigencies of space. I add this footnote as I was myself not a little impressed by these details.—D.K.R.

their austerities, that is, by their unaided strength. But then came another who went straight to the gatekeeper and requested him to open the door. The gatekeeper complied and he entered. This is the way of *Guruvad*. The gatekeeper who had the key symbolizes the Guru."

May 24, 1951—"I have such an excruciating pain around my heart," I complained to Mira, "I can hardly breathe."

"Do not think of the pain," she answered. "Seek Him alone. Give all you have to Him: your joy and pain, your tears and laughter, your hopes and fears—in a word, your entire self. Know this that you cannot force Him to heal your pain but if you give your pain to Him *you* shall be healed, that is, if you can take your pain as pain borne for His sake. Believe me, all who suffer *for* Him are dear to Him and He feels their pain much more than they do themselves. This I know from personal experience.

"But pain or no pain, do not seek Him *for* anything, other than Himself: not for any benefit you derive from Him but only for the joy of giving yourself to Him—because without Him life can have little meaning. Why do we not wish to seek Him? Because our souls are like iron covered over with dust and mud. As soon as these are removed, He—the Magnet—will draw us to Himself. So it is for us to play our part: to shake off the impurities, for then we will be automatically attracted by Him till we meet in union."

May 31, 1951—Mira said: "The devotee is the thread and the Divine is the needle, it is with the thread that the needle sews, but the thread is entirely useless without the needle, it is only when it surrenders to the needle and becomes its instrument that it can serve a useful purpose. The needle uses the thread and comes clear out, unattached again, but the thread is nonetheless needed by the needle. Similarly, the *bhakta* is needed by Krishna for His play and manifestation. One depends on the other, or rather, is fulfilled by the other."

June 30, 1951—Mira said: "I reached Brindaban at last on foot. But what was my disappointment when I heard that my guru, Sanatan, for whom I had come all this way, lived in seclusion and had taken a vow never to look at a woman. I sent a messenger to tell him that I had been given to understand that in Brindaban every soul was a Radha soul and so none could lay claim to masculinity except Krishna. He was disconcerted and sent for me. When he saw me he received me with open arms, saying: 'Mira, you are not a woman but a mountain-stream and anybody who comes into contact with you can only emerge clean out of it.'

"Thenceforward I lived with him as his disciple in his hut which was so small that at night I had to sleep *under* his little cot. It was thus I stayed with him for seven and a half years."

INDEX

INDEX

A

Abhedananda, Swami, 327

A. E., quotations from, 58-60, 339*n*

Aiyar, Dr. Ramaswami, 383*n*

Anil, 218

Ashrams, purpose of, 302, 304

Aurobindo, Sri, 1, 7, 13, 18-21, 33, 34, 60-61, 64, 79-81, 90-91, 95, 104, 111, 114-131, 132, 133, 138-39, 142-145, 146-53, 155-166, 169, 179-186, 194, 239, 245, 248, 259, 262-263, 267, 274, 311, 319, 327-334, 352-357, 364
  on avatarhood, 26
  on doubt, 162
  on formal religion vs. spirituality, 147-148
  on the mind's limitations, 163-166
  Paul Richard's view of, 138-139, 143-145
  on Bertrand Russell, 70-71
  On St. Mira's contact with Indira Devi, 355-356
  On spiritual experiences, concreteness of, 162-163
  On supramentalization, 125-131
  on Rabindranath Tagore, 80-81

Rabindranath Tagore's view of, 79-81

B

Basu, Dr. Satyendra, 50

Beethoven, Ludwig van, 63, 66, 71

Bhojraj (king of Mevar), 382

Bliss, experience of, 181-183, 186-187, 190, 253

Bose, Balaram, 52

Bose, Satyen, 73

Bose, Subhash Chandra, 42-44, 57-61, 67-68, 73, 132, 149

Brahmananda, Swami, 51-56, 149, 351

Brunton, Paul, 167, 169

Buddha, Gautama, 131, 327, 378

Burman, Gurudas, 33

C

Calcutta Psychic Research Society, 356-357

Calvé, Madame Emma, 133-135, 146

Chaitanya, Sri, 15, 327, 380, 390, 393-394

Chakravarti, J.N., 96

OTHER TIMELESS TITLES

MANTRAS: WORDS OF POWER
Swami Sivananda Radha

Swami Radha gives answers to some of the most controversial questions of spiritual life: initiation, the Guru/disciple relationship, surrender, and healing. Included are chants with musical notation, and instruction for both the beginner and the advanced seeker.
$7.95 paper, 140 pages, 8 photos

THE DIVINE LIGHT INVOCATION
Swami Sivananda Radha

By invoking Divine Light, you can renew your energy, be a channel for healing others, and experience Higher Consciousness. Detailed instructions are given for this powerful spiritual practice. An excellent introduction to yoga and spiritual life.
$5.00 paper

RADHA: DIARY OF A WOMAN'S SEARCH
Swami Sivananda Radha

Swami Radha is one of the foremost women spiritual teachers in North America today. In *Radha: Diary of a Woman's Search* she shares the story of her pilgrimage to India in 1955-56. A remarkable journal from an extraordinary woman. ". . . a vastly appealing reminder of what the ideal teacher/student bond can be."   *—West Coast Review of Books*
$7.95 paper, 211 pages, 33 photos

KUNDALINI: YOGA FOR THE WEST
Swami Sivananda Radha

Now available in paperback, Swami Radha's classic text is a spiritual road map for the serious aspirant. Kundalini Yoga is a direct path for the evolution of consciousness. Swami Radha combines practical wisdom for everyday living with the inspiration of a true visionary.

"Her insights are profound and lucid, filled with wisdom on life, love, sex, dreams, poetry, dance, aesthetics, and imagination. Recommended."

—Booklist, American Library Association

"An encyclopedic resource." *—Brain/Mind Bulletin*

$10.95 paper, 375 pages, photos
$24.95 cloth, photos, 18 color plates

GODS WHO WALK THE RAINBOW
Swami Sivananda Radha

"Those who have been enchanted by the swami's autobiography, *Radha: Diary of a Woman's Search*, will find this new book equally fascinating and instructive. Written in two parts, this volume is both a thoughtful recollection of some of the personal land-marks in her early spiritual odyssey, and it is a similarly penetrating analysis of the relationship between teacher and disciple."—Georg Feuerstein, Yoga Research Institute

$7.95 paper, 250 pages, 90 photos

SEEDS OF LIGHT
Aphorisms of Swami Sivananda Radha
Swami Sivananda Radha

A beautifully illustrated collection of insights and inspirations, *Seeds of Light* encourages daily reflection and thinking in depth. Special emphasis is given to the spiritual potential of women today.

"Her aphorisms are exceptionally lucid: like a blast of invigorating air, they sweep away the dust and cobwebs of no longer relevant doctrines. Her section entitled 'Especially for Women' contains ideas you're not likely to encounter much in the male-dominated Eastern spiritual tradition."

—*Bookpaper,* Bookpeople

$7.95 paper, 98 pages, illustrated

MANTRAS, BHAJANS, AND SONGS

This charming booklet gives a comprehensive selection of Mantras, bhajans, and songs from Yasodhara Ashram. Musical notation is for all the chants and songs, together with an introduction by Swami Nada-Brahmananda Sarasvati: "It is my hope and wish that through music and chanting you will discover the magic and majesty of the Inner Self . . ."

$5.00 paper

LOOKING DEEPER
A Swan's Questions and Answers
Klong-chen rab-'byams pa
Translated and Annotated by Herbert V. Guenther

Our latest offering is a timely translation of *A Swan's Questions and Answers,* a fourteenth century poem by Klong-chen rab-'byams pa (Longchenpa). Dr. H.V. Guenther's sensitive translation and scholarly commentary allow the poem to speak with a freshness and force that underline its relevance to our times. Dr. Guenther is well known for his many translations and commentaries on Tibetan yoga.

$3.50 paper

A free catalog listing cassette recordings by Swami Radha is also available.

Timeless Books

Box 160 P
Porthill, ID 83853